MULTIMEDIA:
CONTRACTS, RIGHTS AND LICENSING

CONTENTS

11.2	Identification of rights and rights holders	125
11.3	Source materials	126
11.4	Where will the rights come from?	127
12	**Practical Acquisition**	**131**
12.1	Particular acquisition problems	131
12.1.1	Literary works	131
12.1.2	Photographs	132
12.1.3	Works of fine art	133
12.1.4	Performances	134
12.1.5	Film and television broadcasts	136
12.1.6	Graphics and illustrations	137
12.1.7	Clip art and multimedia tools	137
12.1.8	Music and sound recordings	138
12.1.9	Databases	140
12.1.10	Software	140
12.1.11	Other issues	140
12.2	Fees and royalties	141
12.2.1	Key issues	141
12.3	Compulsory licensing	142
12.4	Collecting societies	143
12.5	Copyright Tribunal	144
12.6	Fallbacks	144
12.6.1	Full grant	144
12.6.2	Reservation of rights	144
12.6.3	Right of first refusal over reserved rights	144
12.6.4	Matching right	145
12.6.5	Open rights	146
13	**Acquisition Agreements**	**147**
13.1	Introduction	147
13.2	Strategies for licensing: 'acquire broadly...'	147
13.2.1	Existing rights framework	147
13.2.2	New approaches to rights	148
13.3	Drafting and negotiating	148
13.3.1	Key issues	149
13.4	Contents of the agreement	150
Part 4—Developing and Distributing a Multimedia Work		**153**
14	**Exploitation, Development and Production**	**155**
14.1	Introduction	155
14.2	Exploitation	155
14.2.1	In-house production/direct sale	155
14.2.2	Joint venture or co-production	156
14.2.3	Sub-licensing	157
14.2.4	Factors influencing choice of method	158
14.3	Development	159

14.3.1	Development contract	160
14.4	Production	161
14.4.1	Project management and reporting structures	162
14.4.2	Insurance	163
14.4.3	Source materials	163
14.5	Software	165
15	**Licensing and Distribution**	**169**
15.1	'... and license narrowly'	169
15.1.1	Considerations before entering into negotiations	169
15.1.2	Approach to potential licensees	170
15.1.3	Form of licence	170
15.1.4	Heads of agreement	170
15.1.5	Selecting a distributor	170
15.2	Physical distribution	172
15.2.1	Particular terms in licences	172
15.2.2	Commercial clauses	178
15.2.3	Unfair Terms in Consumer Contracts Regulations	181
15.2.4	Commercial Agents Directive	182
15.3	On-line distribution	184
15.3.1	Introduction	184
15.3.2	Local area networks	184
15.3.3	Commercial on-line services	185
15.3.4	Licensing copyright works for an on-line service	187
15.3.5	Security, encryption and controls	189
15.3.6	Liability	190
15.3.7	Regulation	190
15.3.8	Home shopping and consumer protection	192
15.4	User licence	194
15.4.1	Control of copying	194
15.4.2	Database protection	194
15.4.3	Shrinkwrap licences	195
15.4.4	Limitation of liability	196
15.5	Taxation	197
15.5.1	Withholding tax	197
15.5.2	Payments to performers	198
15.5.3	Value added tax	198
15.5.4	Stamp duty	199
16	**Application of Competition Law to Multimedia Products**	**201**
16.1	Introduction	201
16.2	Applicable law	201
16.3	UK law	201
16.3.1	UK competition authorities	201
16.3.2	The common law restraint of trade doctrine	202
16.3.3	Fair Trading Act 1973	202
16.3.4	Competition Act 1980	203
16.3.5	Restrictive Trade Practices Act 1976	204

16.3.6	Resale Prices Act 1976	204
16.4	EC law	205
16.4.1	EC competition authorities	205
16.4.2	The relevant EC Treaty provisions	205
16.4.3	Article 85	207
16.4.4	Article 86	209

Appendices

1	Collecting Societies	213
2	Copyright Management Initiatives for Electronic Rights	215
3	Charles Clark's Classification of Electronic Rights	217
4	Regulatory Bodies that Exercise Control over Media Content	219
5	Unions	221
6	Performer's Rights	223
7	Moral Rights	225
8	National Copyright Agencies	227
9	UK Organisations Involved in the Administration of Copyright and Rights in Performances	235
10	Signatories to International Copyright Conventions	239
11	European Commission Green Paper on Copyrights and Related Rights in the Information Society	245

Figures

1.1	Advantages of digitisation	6
1.2	Features of convergence through digitisation	9
1.3	Multimedia standards, platforms and formats	10
11.1	The contents of a CD-ROM	127
11.2	The first-tier rights holders of a CD-ROM	128
11.3	The second-tier rights holders of a CD-ROM	129
11.4	The barriers to obtaining rights for a CD-ROM	130

Tables

| 3.1 | Copyright Harmonisation Directives | 30 |
| 3.2 | Copyright in different categories of work | 44 |

Sample clauses

The assignment of copyright in a freelance contract	36
The ownership of copyright in an employment contract	37
Rental rights	54
Diffusion rights	72
Waiver of author's rights	97
Warranty by company where author's rights are waived	97
Grant of performer's rights	106
Grant of multimedia rights	132
Warranty that performer's consents and waivers are granted	134
Performer consents	135
Right of first refusal for further rights	145
Matching right	145

Reversion	148
Confidentiality obligation	160
Acceptance tests	161
Project manager: appointment	162
Source code: supply or security deposit of escrow	163
Grant of rights by producer	175
Exploitation of rights	175
Accounting	178
TV clip licence	179
Governing law and arbitration	181
Shrinkwrap licence wording	195
Terms and conditions of use	196
Index	249

PREFACE

This handbook is aimed at all those who are struggling not just to find, but to find their way along, the superhighway of multimedia rights and licensing; who are struggling past the strange signposts of unusual technical terms, unfamiliar contracts, concepts and strange new deals. During our journey through this project we have discovered an enormous number of by-ways, many of which remain largely unexplored in this edition. Mapping multimedia is an on-going task and so far as the law is concerned, let alone the practice and the technology, we have been aiming at a constantly moving target.

Since we started on this journey, a number of the European Commission's directives should have been implemented into UK law but have not: the Rental and Lending Rights Directive and the Duration of Copyright Directive were due to have been implemented on 1 July 1994 and 1 July 1995 respectively. We still await definitive draft legislation for the former but the Statutory Instrument for the latter was laid before Parliament in November and is anticipated to be effective from 1 January 1996. Although publication of this Statutory Instrument occurred after the copy date, we have managed to incorporate initial comments into Chapter 4, para 4.3. On 12 July 1995, the Council of Ministers approved a revised version of the Database Directive. This remains to be approved by the European Parliament and subject to that is scheduled for implementation in Member States by January 1998; and the Commission has published its long awaited Green Paper on Copyright and Related Rights.

Accordingly, we are not able to claim that the statements of law in these fast changing areas will necessarily be wholly accurate by the time you come to read them. What have we sought to achieve? We have sought to satisfy that particularly difficult market, lawyers *and* laymen and we recognise that we run the risk of satisfying neither. We intend that this book will be understood by the layman; we do not intend that the lawyer should treat it as an authoritative text book. It is far too short for that and there are already a number of excellent text books on copyright, trademarks and passing off, competition and so on; but we do hope that the lawyer will be able to use it as a map providing guidance, and that he or she will recognise the problems we seek to illuminate and will find the text and the checklists helpful.

The examples we have included are intended to illustrate the points being made and the checklists are intended to help you structure your approach to deals and contracts in a logical way. Comments and (hopefully) constructive criticism, both will be welcomed in the hope that if authors, publishers and customers all show willing, an updated version can be made available in due course.

Where we have provided sample clauses we add the warning that they are no more than that: samples, which should be treated with care. There are very few instances where such clauses can simply be 'dropped' into an agreement. All will need thought, and amendment to suit the circumstances.

This book is dedicated to everyone who helped make it possible, including the many

PREFACE

Denton Hall typists (if one calls a wordprocessor that any more) who worked and reworked the texts and to colleagues at Denton Hall, particularly, yes *particularly*, to Nicholas Higham for his learned and thoughtful input; to Jane Douglas, Rebecca Holmes-Siedle, Clive Thorne, Andrew Readman, Tara Donovan and Nicki Parfitt for providing specialist text or checking our work and commenting on it at impossibly short notice; to Jeffrey Boloten for the original idea; to our editorial team at FT Law & Tax without whom this book would never have materialised beyond the draft manuscript stage; and finally, with special thanks to Alison MacDougall of Pearson Professional whose comments and suggestions at an early stage helped us to achieve our goal.

However it is important to make it clear that the responsibility for all statements, propositions (and errors) are ours and ours alone. The law is correct as at 1 October 1995.

November 1995

Alan Williams
Duncan Calow
Andrew Lee

Denton Hall
Five Chancery Lane
Clifford's Inn
London EC4A 1BU

TABLE OF CASES

Bad Boys Megamix, George Michael's Case *see* Morrison Leahy Music Ltd v Lightbond Ltd
Beta Computers (Europe) Ltd v Adobe Systems (Europe) Ltd 15.5.4
British Amusement Catering Trades Association v Westminster Borough Council [1989] AC 147, HL 6.3.1
British Broadcasting Corporation v British Satellite Broadcasting Ltd [1992] Ch 141; [1991] 3 WLR 174;
    [1991] E All ER 833 .... 3.9.1
Centrafarm BV and Adriann De Pejper v Winthrop BV (Case 16/74) [1974] ECR 1147; [1974] 2 CMLR 480;
    [1975] FSR 161, European Ct 16.4.2
SA Compagnie Generale pour la Diffusion de la Télévision Coditel v Ciné Vog Films SA (No 1)
    (Case 62/79) [1980] ECR 881; [1981] 2 CMLR 362 .... 16.4.2
CompuServe v Cubby 776F, Supp 135 (1991) 10.2.2
Computer Aided Systems (UK) Ltd v Bolwell [1990] IPD 13051 .... 6.1.2
Computer Associates International Inc v Altai Inc (1992) 23 IPR 385 .... 6.1.2
Deutsche Grammophon Gesellschaft mbH v Metro-ZB-Großmärkte GmbH & Co KG (Case 78/70)
    [1971] ECR 487; [1971] CMLR 631 .... 16.4.2
Emmens v Pottle (1885) 16 QBD 354, CA 10.2.1
Feist 111s c1282, 20 IPR 121 (1991) 3.2.6, 3.3, 4.5, 6.2
Gale's Patent Application, *Re* [1991] RPC 305; (1990) *Financial Times*, 18 December, CA 7.3.1
Geographica Ltd v Penguin Books Ltd [1985] FSR 208 .... 6.2
Goldsmith v Sperrings [1977] 1 WLR 478; (1977) 121 SJ 304; [1977] 2 All ER 566, CA 10.2.1
Hospital for Sick Children v Walt Disney Productions [1968] Ch 52; [1967] 2 WLR 1250; [1967] 1 All ER
    1005, CA 6.3.1
Hubbard v Vosper [1972] 2 QB 84; [1972] 2 WLR 389; [1972] 1 All ER 1023, CA 3.9.1
Ibcos Computers Ltd v Barclay Mercantile Highland Finance Ltd [1994] FSR 275 .... 6.1.2
John Richardson Computers Ltd v Flanders [1993] FSR 497 .... 6.1.2
Kent County Council v Multi Media Marketing (Canterbury) Ltd (1995) *The Times*, 9 May 6.3.1, 10.3.4
La Cinq SA v EC Commission (Case T–44/90) [1992] II ECR 1; [1992] 4 CMLR 449 .... 8.10
Lee v Walt Disney Co Cal 1d BO 58897 (Sup Ct No C705414) 6.3.1, 11.4
Magill *see* Radio Telefis Eireann v Commission
Maple & Co v Junior Army and Navy Stores (1882) 21 ChD 369 .... 6.2
Merill Lynch's Application, *Re* [1989] RPC 561 .... 7.3.1
Monotti [1993] 5 EIPR 156 .... 6.2
Morrison Leahy Music Ltd v Lightbond Ltd [(992) EMLR 144 .... 8.2, 12.1.3
Nintendo Co Ltd v Golden China TV Game Centre [1994] 1 ELR E-8 .... 6.3.1
Collins (Phil) v Imrat Handelsgesellschaft GmbH (Joined Cases C–92/92 and C–326/92) [1993]
    3 CMLR 773 .... 4.3.2, 7.2.2
Playboy Enterprises v Frena 839 F Sup 1552 (MD Fla 1993) 10.2.4
Prodigy v Stratton Oakmount 23 Media L Rep 1794 (24.5.95) 10.2.2
Radio Telefis Eireann v Commission (Case T–69/89) [1991] II ECR 485; [1991] 4 CMLR 586 .... 16.4.2
Radio Telefis Eireann v Commission (Joined Cases C–241/91P and 242/91P) ECJ Judgment,
    6 April 1995 .... 4.5.2, 4.7, 16.4.4
Rindos v Hardwick (1994 of 1993) 10.2.3
Sega Enterprises Ltd v Accolade Inc 997 F 2d 1510 (1992) 6.1.2
Stewart (James) *et al* v Sheldon Abend 495 US, 109 L Ed 2d 184 (1990) 12.1.5
Sun Life Assurance Co of Canada v W H Smith & Co Ltd (1933) 150 LY 211 .... 10.2.1
Telmak Teleproducts Australia Pty Ltd v Bond International Pty Ltd (1985) 66 ALR 118 .... 6.3.1
Tetra Pak Rausing SA v Commission (Case T–51/89) [1990] 11 ECR 309; [1991] 4 CMLR 334 .... 16.4.4
Time Warner Entertainment Co Ltd v Channel 4 [1994] EMLR (1)1 .... 3.9.1.
Vizetelly v Mudie's Select Library [1900] 2 QB 170 .... 10.2.1
Waterlow Directories Ltd v Reed Information Services Ltd (1992) FSR 409; (1990) *The Times*, 11 October 4.5
Whelan Associates Inc v Jaslon Dental Laboratory Inc [1987] FSR 1, US Ct of Appeals 6.1.2
ZS Associates Inc v Nazis Ltd (1994), unreported, 17 March 6.1.2

TABLE OF STATUTES

Arbitration Act 1979—
  s 1 ....15.2.2
  s 2(1)(*a*) 15.2.2
  s 3 ....15.2.2
Broadcasting Act 1990 ....2.1.1, 10.1.2, 10.1.3, 15.3.7
  s 46(3) 15.3.7
Cable and Broadcasting Act 1984 ....15.3.7
  Pt II 15.3.7
Cinamatograph Act 1909 ....6.3.1
Company Securities (Insider Dealing) Act 1985 .....7.3.5
Competition Act 1980 ....16.2, 16.3.4
Consumer Credit Act 1974 ....15.3.8
Consumer Protection Act 1985 ....15.2.2, 15.3.8
Copyright Act (South Africa) 6.3.1
Copyright Act 1911 ....6.3.1, 12.1.5
Copyright Act 1956 .....6.3.1, 8, 8.10, 12.1.2, 12.1.5, 12.1.8
Copyright, Designs and Patents Act 1988 ....3.1, 3.2,
              3.2.2, 3.2.6, 3.2.7, 3.3, 3.4, 3.4.1, 3.6,
              3.8.1, 4.5, 6.1.1, 6.2, 6.3, 6.3.1, 7.1.2,
            7.2.1, 7.3.6, 7.4.5, 8, 8.7, 8.8, 8.10, 9.2, 9.6,
            9.7, 12.1.2, 12.1.3, 12.1.4, 12.5, 13.3, App 3
  s 3 ....6.2
    (1) ....Tabel 3.2
  s 4 ....Table 3.2
    (2) 6.3.1
  s 5(1) ....3.2.2, 6.3.1, Table 3.2
  ss 6–8 ....Table 3.2
  s 9(1) ....Table 3.2
    (2)(*a*)–(*d*) ....Table 3.2
    (3) ....Table 3.2
  s 12(2) ....Table 3.2
  s 13(1) ....Table 3.2
  s 14(1) ....Table 3.2
  s 16 ....3.8.1
    (3)(*b*) 6.3.1
  s 17 ....3.1.1, 3.8.1, 6.1.1
    (6) ....App 3
  s 18 ....3.8.1
  s 19 ....3.8.1, 4.2.2
  s 20 ....3.8.1
  s 21 ....3.8.1
    (3), (4) 6.1.1
  ss 22–27 ....3.8.2
  s 28 ....3.6
  s 29 ....3.9, 3.9.1
  s 30 ....3.9, 3.9.1
    (1), (2) 3.9.1
  ss 31–44 ....3.9, 3.9.1

Copyright, Designs and Patents Act 1988—*contd*.
  ss 45–50 ....3.9
  ss 50A, 50B 3.9, 3.9.1, 6.1.1
  s 50C 3.9, 6.1.1
  ss 51–55 ....3.9
  s 56 ....3.9, 3.9.1
  ss 57–65 ....3.9
  s 66 ....3.9, 3.9.1
  ss 67–76 ....3.9
  Pt I, Chap IV (ss 77–89) 8, 8.6.1
  s 78 ....8.1
  s 87 ....8.6.1
  ss 107–110 ....7.2.2
  s 136 ....12.4
  s 143 ....3.9.1
  ss 163–167 ....3.5.1
  s 175(1) 3.8.1
  s 178 ....6.1.1, 8.7, Table 3.2
  Pt II (ss 180–212) ....9.1, 9.3, 9.10, 12.1.4, App 6
  s 180 ....Table 3.2
  ss 198–205 ....9.10
Criminal Justice and Public Order Act 1994 ....10.3.3
Data Protection Act 1984 ....7.3.5, 10.1.8, 10.6.1, 10.6.2
Fair Trading Act 1973 ....16.2, 16.3.3
Obscene Publications Act 1959 ....10.3.1
Obscene Publications Act 1964 ....10.3.1
Official Secrets Act 1911–1922 ....7.3.5
Patents Act 1977 ....7.3.1
  s 1(1), (2) 7.3.1
Performers Protection Acts 9.1
Protection of Children Act 1978 ....10.3.3
Registered Designs Act 1949 ....7.3.6
Resale Prices Act 1976 ....16.2, 16.3.6
Restrictive Trade Practices Act 1976................16.2, 16.3.5
  Sched 3 ....16.3.5
Sale of Goods Act 1979 ....15.3.8
Supply of Goods and Services Act 1982 ....15.3.8
Telecommunications Act 1984 ....2.1.1, 10.1.1,
                                        10.3.2, 15.3.7
  ss 5, 7 ....15.3.7
  ss 56, 58 ....2.1.1
Trade Descriptions Act 1968 ....15.3.8
Trade Marks Act 1938 ....15.2.1
Trade Marks Act 1994 ....7.3.2, 15.2.1
Unfair Contract Terms Act 1977 ....15.2.2, 15.3.8
Video Recordings Act 1984 ....3.2.2, 7.4.5, 10.1.5, 10.3.4
  s 1(2) 6.3.1
Video Recordings Act 1993 ....10.3.4

TABLE OF STATUTORY INSTRUMENTS

Copyright (Computer Programs) Regulations 1992 (SI No 3233) 4.2, 4.2.1, 4.2.2, 4.3.2
Design Right (Semiconductor Topographies) Regulations 1989 (SI No 1100) 7.3.6
Duration of Copyright and Rights in Performances Regulations 1995 (SI No 3297) 4.3
Patents Rules 1990 (SI No 2384)................................7.3.1

Performances (Reciprocal Protection) (Convention Countries) Order 1994 (SI No 264) ....App 6
Unfair Terms in Consumer Contracts Regulations (SI No 3159) 14.4.3, 15.2.2, 15.2.3, 15.3.8
Video Recordings (Labelling) Regulations 1985 (SI No 911) 10.3.4

TABLE OF EC LEGISLATION

Treaties
Treaty of Rome (EC Treaty) 16.4
    art 22 ....16.2, 16.4.2
    arts 30–35 ....16.2, 16.4.2
    art 36 ....4.7, 16.2, 16.4.2
    art 59–66 ....16.2, 16.4.2
    art 85 ....4.7, 15.2.1, 16.2, 16.4.1, 16.4.2, 16.4.3, 16.4.4
        (1) 16.4.3, 16.4.4
        (2), (3) 16.4.3
    art 86 ....16.2, 16.4.1, 16.4.2, 16.4.4
    art 90 ....2.2.1
    art 222 ....16.4.2

Directives
Commercial Agents Directive (68/151/EEC) 15.2.2, 15.2.4
Database Directive (96/9/EEC) ....3.3, 4.1, 4.5, 4.5.1, 4.5.2, 6.2, 6.3, 15.1.5, 15.4.2, Table 3.1
    art 3(4) 4.5.1
    art 5 ....4.5
    art 7.2(*b*) 15.4.2
Distance Selling Directive (95/19/EEC) 15.3.8
Duration of Copyright Directive (93/89/EEC).........3.2, 3.4.1, 3.6, 4.3, 4.3.1, 4.3.2, 6.3.1, 9.7, Table 3.1
Harmonisation Directive (89/104/EEC)...........3.1.1, 8.1
Protection of Personal Data Directive
    (95/46/EEC) 10.6.2
Rental and Lending Rights Directive
    (92/100/EEC) ....3.4.1, 3.6, 3.9.1, 4.2.2, 4.4, 5.2, 6.3.1, App 11, Table 3.1
Services Directive (90/388/EEC) 2.2.1
Software Directive (91/250/EEC) ....3.9.1, 4.1, 4.2, 6.1, 6.1.1, 6.3, 15.4.4, App 11, Table 3.1
    art 1(2) 6.1.1
Trade Mark Directive 1988 (89/104/EEC) 7.3.2
Unfair Contract Terms Directive (93/13/EEC) 15.2.3, 15.3.8, 15.4.4
Cable and Satellite Directive (93/83/EEC) ....App 11, Table 3.1

Regulations
Regulation 1983/83 on exclusive distribution
    agreements 16.4.3
Regulation 1984/83 on exclusive purchasing
    agreements 16.4.3
Regulation 2349/84 on patent licensing
    agreements 16.4.3
Regulation 417/85 on specialisation agreements .16.4.3
Regulation 418/85 on research and development
    agreements 16.4.3
Regulation 556/89 on know-how licensing
    agreements 16.4.3
Regulation 40/94 on the Community Trade
    Mark 7.3.2

TABLE OF CONVENTIONS AND AGREEMENTS

Berne Convention for the Protection of Literary
and Artistic Works 3.1.1, 3.2.6, 3.2.7, 4.3.2, 4.5,
5.3, 5.3.1, 5.4, 8, 8.7, 8.8, 8.9,
12.1.11, App 10, App 11
   arts 1, 2 .... 5.3.1
   arts 6 *bis* 8.8
   arts 14, 14 *bis* 5.3.1
   Paris Act 1971 .... App 7
Community Patent Convention 1975 .... 7.3.1
EEA Agreement 16.4
European Patent Convention 7.3.1
   art 53(2) 7.3.1
GATT (General Agreement on Tariffs and Trade) 5.4,
5.4.1, 6.1, 12.1.11
TRIPS (Trade Related Aspects of Intellectual
   Property Rights) 3.2.6, 5.4, 5.4.1, 6.1, 12.1.11
Madrid Protocol Relating to International
   Registration Marks (Cm 1601) 7.3.2
Paris Convention on the International Protection
   of Industrial Property 7.3.1
Patent Co-operation Treaty 7.3.1
Rome Convention 1961 (International Convention
   for the Protection of Performers, Producers
   of Phonograms and Broadcasting
   Organisations) .... 3.1.1, 5.3, 5.3.3, 5.4, App 10
Universal Copyright Convention 1952 .... 3.1.1, 5.3,
5.3.2, 5.4, App 10

ABBREVIATIONS

ACTS	Advanced Communications Technologies and Service Programme
ADSL	Asymmetric Digital Subscriber Loop
AM	Amplitude
ASA	Advertising Standards Authority
ASCII	American Standard Code for Information Exchange
ATM	Asynchronous Transfer Mode
BBFC	British Board of Film Classification
BBS	Bulletin Boards
BCC	Broadcasting Complaints Commission
BIMA	British Interactive Multimedia Association
BPI	British Phonographic Industry
BSA	Business Software Alliance
BSC	Broadcasting Standards Council
BSI	British Standards Institute
BT	British Telecommunications plc
B–ISDN	Broadband Integrated Services Digital Network
CCTA	Government Centre for Information Systems
CD	Compact Disc
CDTV	Compact Disc Television
CD–DA	Compact Disc–Digital Audio
CD–I	Compact Disc–Interactive
CD–ROM	Compact Disc–Read Only Memory
CD–ROM XA	Compact Disc–Read Only Memory Extended Architecture
CISAC	Confederation Internationale des Sociétés d'Auteurs et Compositeurs
CITED	Copyright in Transmitted Electronic Documents
CFI	Court of First Instance
CIX	Compulink Information Exchange
CORDS	Copyright Office Registration and Deposit System
DAT	Digital Audio Tape
DBS	Direct Broadcasting From Satellite (to individual homes)
DGF	Director General of Fair Trading
DTI	Department of Trade and Industry
DVD	Digital Versatile Disks
E&O	Errors & Omissions
EC	European Commission
ECMS	Electronic Copyright Management Systems
EEA	European Economic Area
EFTA	European Free Trade Area
ELSPA	European Leisure Software Publishers

ABBREVIATIONS

EPO	European Patent Office
EU	European Union
FACT	Federation Against Copyright Theft
FAST	Federation Against Software Theft
FCC	Federal Communications Commission
FM	Frequency
FMV	Full Motion Video
FTA	Fair Trading Act
GIF	Graphics Interchange Act
GII	Global Information Infrastructure
GSM	Groupe Special Mobile/Global System for Mobiles
HDCD	High Density Compact Disk
IACC	International Anti-Counterfeiting Coalition
IBCN	Integrated Broadband Communication Network
IBM	International Business Machines
ICCCIB	International Chamber of Commerce Counterfeiting Intelligence Bureau
ICSTIS	Independent Committee for the Supervision of Standards for Telephone Information Services
IFP	International Federation of the Phonographic Industry
IMA	International Multimedia Association
IMPRIMATUR	Intellectual Multimedia Property Rights Model and Terminology for Universal References
IP	Intellectual Property
IPR	Intellectual Property Rights
ISDN	Integrated Services Digital Network
ISO	International Standards Organisation
ITC	Independent Television Commission
ITU	International Telecommunications Union
JPEG	Joint Picture Encoding Group
LDO	Local Delivery Operator
LPS	Licensable Programme Service
MARS	Music Archiving and Recall Services
MB	Megabyte
MCPS	Mechanical Copyright Performance Society
MIDI	Musical Instrument Digital Interface
MMC	Monopolies and Mergers Commission
MPC	Multimedia Personal Computer
MPEG	Moving Pictures Experts Group
MS-DOS	Microsoft-Disk Operating System
NES	Nintendo Entertainment System
NII	National Information Infrastructure
NTSC	National Television Systems Committee
OECD	Organisation for Economic and Commercial Development
OFT	Office of Fair Trading
PAL	Phase Alternate by Line
PC	Personal Computer
PC-LAN	Personal Computer-Local Area Network
PDS	Prescribed Diffusion Services

PPL	Phonographic Performance Ltd
PRS	Performing Rights Society Ltd
PTO	Public Telecommunications Operator
R&D	Research and Development
REAL	Realistic Entertainment Active Learning
RISC	Reduced Instruction Set Computer
RTE	Radio Telefis Eireann
RTPA	Restrictive Trade Practices Act
SME	Small/Medium Enterprise
TEN	Trans-European Network
TRIPS	Trade Related aspects of Intellectual Property Rights
UCC	Universal Copyright Convention
VCR	Video Cassette Recorder
VDU	Visual Display Unit
VHS	Video Home System
VIS	Video Interactive System
VPL	Video Performance Ltd
VRA	Video Recordings Act
VSC	Video Standards Council
WIPO	World Intellectual Property Organisation
WTO	World Trade Organisation

PART 1

A DESCRIPTION OF MULTIMEDIA

INTRODUCTION

First, let us define our terms. 'Multimedia' has been defined in many ways, but for our purposes the most useful definition is: a product which combines text, graphics, audio, images and/or moving pictures in digitised form.

> - Text can include any written material: books, magazines, newspapers, directories and specially written material for the product such as instructions and help screens.
> - Graphics can include all the traditional forms of artwork: graphs, charts, etc, either in still or in animated form.
> - Audio includes recorded music and speech, sounds and electronically generated material.
> - Images can include photographs, film and video stills and PC-generated images.
> - Moving pictures can include film and video, although as explained in 1.2 *below* these have not until recently been high-quality, full-screen images.

Interactivity is a key value of multimedia. Traditional media give the user a passive role, watching or listening to a work linearly as it unfolds. The benefit of digitisation is that it allows users to select precisely the information or experience they want.

> In an interactive game there can be hundreds of alternative narrative paths, depending on the choice of the user. In an interactive encyclopaedia, the user can go to an entry on, say, man landing on the moon and choose between a written description, photographs, a sound recording or a video clip of the event, and can then jump to an entry on cheese.

One of the fundamental changes that the technology will bring is the ability of users to select, from a vast array of information and entertainment, their own personal selection of material, packaged and presented in the way they want and for viewing or listening to order.

The importance of multimedia derives from the underlying technology of digitisation.

INTRODUCTION

— • 1 • —
DIGITISATION AND MULTIMEDIA PLATFORMS

1.1 DIGITISATION

Digitisation (more accurately, digitalisation, but this term is not in widespread use) is an enabling technology, ie, a technology which has generic application.

Digitisation is not a new concept; it can be traced back to the early days of PCs. In essence, digitisation is the breaking down of complex information into a series of simple instructions which a microprocessor can understand and to which it can respond.

In order to understand the implications of this more fully, we need to describe briefly the traditional methods of recording and storing information. (In this context, we use the term 'information' in its widest sense, to include text, graphics, speech, music, films and television programmes.)

Most audio-visual technologies used today, such as broadcast television, video, radio, vinyl records and audio cassettes are analogue systems. The technologies which are used to support these systems are well developed and widely accepted. The characteristic feature of analogue representations is that the information stored is in the form of a continuous signal, which recognises changes in the information by moderating the amplitude (AM) or frequency (FM) of the signal. These signals can be reproduced and broadcast.

> **Example**
> - Video cassettes and audio cassettes employ a stream of continuously changing data stored on magnetic tape to record music and video.
> - A traditional watch or clock with a second hand is analogue because the hands move around the clock face continuously. As the second hand goes around the clock face, it touches not only the numbers represented on the face but also all the points that lie in between.

Digitisation is a totally different system of recording and reproducing information. The work is 'sampled' by conversion into a series of binary notations. Digitisation is therefore the translation of information (including text, speech, paintings and photographs, animations and graphics, film, video and music and other sounds) into a common 'language' consisting of simple binary codes which can be recorded, stored and manipulated by PCs. The combination of these various elements is the very essence of multimedia.

1.1.1 ADVANTAGES

Once a work has been recorded in digital form it has many advantages over traditional analogue systems (*see* Figure 1.1). The main ones are:

(1) It is very accurately recorded and the recording is stable. Analogue recordings are usually less accurate to start with and the storage media, such as tape and film stock, tend to deteriorate over time. Digital signals are less prone to error because there is only one of two possible values for each signal. Most digital equipment also contains built-in features to detect and correct errors as the work is being accessed.

(2) Because digital information can be accessed and manipulated by PCs, access is instantaneous and vast amounts of data can be stored and searched easily. Optical storage media, such as CD-ROM, can store all the UK telephone directories or many of the Ordnance Survey maps for the UK on one disk. Desktop personal PCs are now powerful enough to carry out searches of these databases in seconds. This allows the development of non-linear products which need no longer run with a single predetermined order, which in turn allows increased interactivity between the user and the product content.

(3) The reproduction and transmission of works is quick and easy. Perfect copies of a digital work can be made indefinitely without any loss of quality in either the copy or the original.

(4) The means of distribution of digitised products now include CD-ROM, floppy disk, fibre-optic cable, telephone wires and, recently, wireless personal communications systems. If the carrying capacity of the network is sufficient, on-line systems can be used to distribute information independently of any physical storage medium—dematerialisation! The increasing emphasis on national and international information networks has been driven by the growth in the use of fibre-optic cable as a

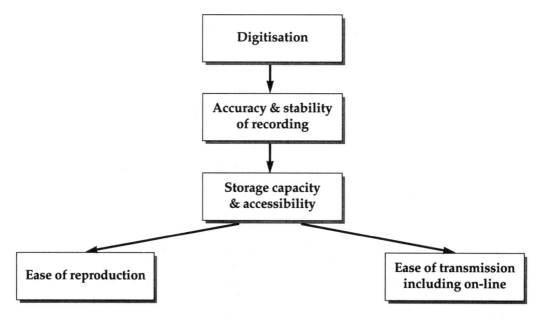

Figure 1.1 Advantages of digitisation

DIGITISATION

means of transmitting electronic signals at the speed of light through telephone lines, cable television networks, integrated service digital networks (ISDN) and so on, creating an 'Information Superhighway'. This is discussed in greater detail below.

1.1.2 LIMITATIONS

Digitisation does however have disadvantages:

(1) Storage space is needed to record complex information. Text on its own presents no problem, but all the other elements of a multimedia work, particular moving images from film or television, require large amounts of storage space. This problem has been largely resolved in two ways:
   (a) by developing storage media, such as optical disks, which have large storage capacity but can be accessed quickly;
   (b) storage of information in digital format has been facilitated by the use of data-compression techniques. Compression is a kind of shorthand for data which can be interpreted and returned to its original form by a microprocessor. Compression has made it possible, especially with the power improvements in processor chips, to store vast amounts of information by passing on the minimum amount of data necessary to reconstruct the information.
(2) Advances in storage and retrieval techniques have not solved all the problems in the area, particularly for film and video. Until recently, incorporating film and video into multimedia works inevitably involved some loss of quality, resulting in grainy or jerky images in small windows on the screen but new techniques and standards for compression of film and video, which will result in large scale commercial availability of full-screen, full motion film and video, are beginning to reach the marketplace (*see* 1.2 *below*).

1.1.3 STANDARDS

Standards exist primarily to ensure quality and compatibility, both of which are of crucial importance to multimedia because of the complex technology involved in creating and distributing multimedia products. At the basic level, the hardware ('platform') and software ('format') for a multimedia product must be standardised, as must the method of distribution, either by physical carriers, such as CD-ROM, or on-line by cable or telephone networks. Standards are necessary to enable interoperability between formats, platforms and on-line systems networks. There are traditionally three ways in which standards evolve.

(1) Proprietary technologies set *de facto* standards by winning such a large share of the market, or such widespread support from industry, that multiple vendors are encouraged to develop complementary products and services.
(2) Industry consortia or partnerships define non-proprietary standards that gain support from a critical mass of manufacturers.
(3) Accredited international standard-setting bodies (in particular the ISO) may define open standards through technological committees.

However, multimedia remains beset by incompatible standards at present. We describe at 1.2 some of the different platforms now in the market, each of which has its own technical standards. The incompatibility is partly due to convergence, the coming together of the telecommunications, television and information technology industries, each with their own standards and seeking to impose their own standards on multimedia. The damaging commercial effects of competing and incompatible standards, particularly in the consumer market, have been clearly demonstrated by previous battles such as that between VHS and Betamax in the field of video and that between minidisc and digital compact cassette in the field of audio. A solution to the problem is the world wide establishment and recognition of conforming and consistent standards; the European Commission has been striving for these goals across the European Union.

1.1.4 CONVERGENCE

Digitisation is leading to the convergence of the information technology, telecommunications and entertainment industries, with increasing interest from other sectors such as banking and retail. Some of the key features of this trend are as follows.

Key features
- Traditional distinctions between literary and audio-visual material, and data, are becoming increasingly outmoded; once digitised they are all forms of information.
- Information may soon be distributed, not only in physical form like CD-ROM, but also on-line over many types of infrastructure, including fixed and mobile telecommunications networks, terrestrial broadcast, satellite and cable television networks.
- Information may be accessed and shared widely throughout the world.

These features are represented diagrammatically in Figure 1.2.

The potential scale of these changes and their consequences give the multimedia revolution profound social and political implications. Governments in many countries, led by the United States and the EU, are becoming increasingly interested in the opportunities and the challenges that will result from the changes taking place and the policies being formulated at national and international level which will shape the development of multimedia markets and the creation of the much vaunted Information Superhighway.

Barriers
Enormous barriers to convergence remain at the level of the marketplace. All the platforms described in 1.2 *below* require very large investments and the markets are in many cases unproven. The immaturity of much of the technology has contributed to this uncertainty; a multimedia PC equipped with a CD-ROM drive currently appears to be the dominant platform for multimedia distributed on a physical storage medium, but other platforms may gain significant market shares. In the on-line market, predictions are harder to make, because both the potential shape and the size of this market remain unclear.

What is clear is that success in these new markets will require substantial financial, marketing and distribution resources, together with personal skills and adequate product content, contributed from many sources. In particular, the acquisition of intellectual property rights in content, ie, audio-visual programming, music, literary texts, photographs, images, artwork and video games, is seen as a key factor; whatever the dominant technology, content will be needed more than ever.

MULTIMEDIA PLATFORMS   1.2

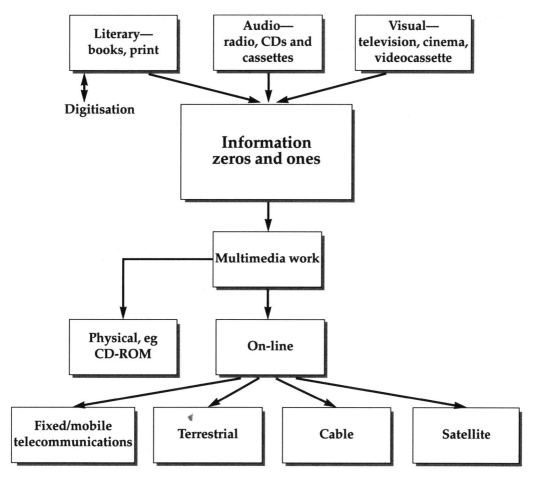

Figure 1.2 Features of convergence through digitisation

1.2 MULTIMEDIA PLATFORMS

The digitised product has reached the marketplace in a variety of forms. There is not space in this book to deal with all the application of digital technology and multimedia products but in this section we list some of the platforms that have developed for multimedia products, concentrating on those aimed at the key home and consumer market. Several platforms have already come and gone as demand has met or failed to live up to expectations, and many of the current platforms may be destined for niche markets at best. We have not dealt with all the possible systems, or provided full technical details, but have listed those platforms—successful or otherwise—that lawyers are likely to come across in multimedia agreements. There is a confusingly large number of competing platforms currently available which of itself highlights the following key commercial issues of which lawyers should be aware:

- The pace of technological change leads to a continual development of new platforms.
- Platforms and formats may be incompatible.

- The availability of quality software is vital to the success of any hardware system.
- There is a risk of being tied to obsolete platforms.
- Whether consumers will view multimedia via a PC or a TV remains an open issue.

We return to these issues in Chapter 15 below.

We have classified the multimedia platforms into two main categories (*see* Figure 1.3):

- Physical distribution systems
- On-line systems

Figure 1.3 Multimedia standards, platforms and formats

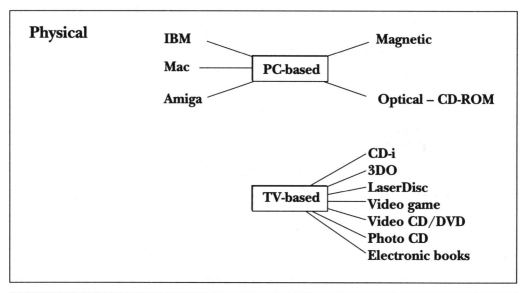

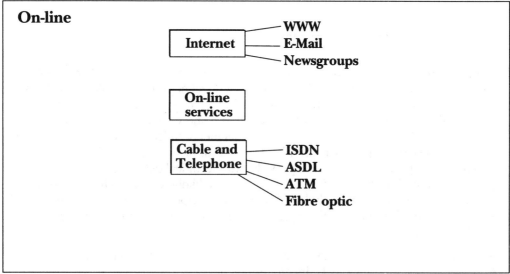

MULTIMEDIA PLATFORMS 1.2.1

1.2.1 PHYSICAL DISTRIBUTION SYSTEMS—CD-ROM

Physical distribution systems allow the multimedia product to be stored and distributed on a physical medium, such as a CD-ROM. The consumer requires equipment to access and manipulate the information contained on the storage medium.

PC-based systems

Information can be stored for retrieval by a computer on magnetic or optical media.

> **Note**
>
> Some people differentiate between IBM-compatible computers and other computers (such as Macintosh or Amiga) by referring to the former only as PCs. In this book we use PC to refer to all types of personal computer.

Magnetic storage media On most computers, information is stored on and retrieved from either the computer's own internal hard disk or floppy disks. Both of these are magnetic storage media. Diskettes offer high processing speeds and the capability to record, erase, edit or overwrite data of all kinds. However, their capacity for holding graphics and moving images is limited and diskettes are therefore becoming less popular than optical storage media for multimedia.

Optical storage media The compact disk is an optical storage medium. It is a wholly digital medium which can be encoded in a range of distinct (and usually incompatible) formats. The first compact disc standard was for recorded music, the CD-Digital Audio (CD-DA), developed by Philips and Sony in 1983 in a set of specifications known as the Red Book. CD-ROM (Compact Disc Read-Only Memory) evolved from CD-DA two years later and is able to store digitised text, graphics and audio-visual material as well as audio. The non-proprietary standard for CD-ROM was set out by Philips and Sony in the Yellow Book. Somewhat confusingly, incompatible proprietary CD multimedia systems are also sometimes referred to generally as CD-ROM.

To ensure compatibility between PCs, data can be laid out in a format known as ISO 9660, otherwise known as High Sierra. Any CD-ROM drive can read a disk in High Sierra, provided that the data is also in a universal form, such as ASCII (American Standard Code for Information Interchange). Single-speed drives are perfectly adequate for text and data, but double-, triple- and quad-speed drives are more suitable for audio-visual material.

Optical media are, however, far slower in supplying data to the PC than floppy disks, and are designed primarily for reading data only, rather than erasing and re-recording. To meet the first of these problems, faster CD-ROM drives are being developed to process more data more quickly and the CD-ROM standard has been extended to combine different data types more efficiently (CD-ROM XA). Erasable CD-ROMs are also being developed to meet the second concern.

TV-based Systems

Magnetic storage media Magnetic videotape such as VHS is an analogue technology; no digital audio-visual equivalent is in commercial use at present.

Optical storage media (LaserDisc) Building on the earlier platforms developed by Philips and others in the 1970s and 1980s, Pioneer produced the LaserDisc specification and licensed it generally in 1989. The standard disk holds up to 55,000 frames on each side, and combines analogue or digital audio with analogue video. This is, as yet, an unbeaten combination for full-screen, full-motion video (FMV) and it has better analogue image quality than VHS video recordings. Like videotapes, however, LaserDisc is tied to national television broadcast standards. An American NTSC disc, for example, is incompatible with a European PAL player, although dual standard players are now widely available. An interactive video system typically combines analogue signals from LaserDisc with digital PC data and this requires a specially equipped PC. Development for the consumer market has slowed with the success of CD-ROM.

Compact Disc-Interactive Compact Disc-Interactive (CD-I) was developed by Philips (together with some support from other major manufacturers, including Sony and Matsushita), and specified by the Green Book standards. It is a purpose-built multimedia system using a proprietary version of CD-ROM. In defining not only the disk structure but also the specifications for the hardware on which it is played, CD-I attempts to circumvent conflicting television standards to provide a platform which may be used with any television set around the world. CD-I add-on boards for use with PCs have also been produced.

CD TV and Tandy VIS In 1991 Commodore launched the CD TV system, a CD multimedia player based on the proprietary technology of Commodore's best selling Amiga home computer. However, large sales never materialised, largely as a result of the shortage of quality software titles to play on it, and in 1993 CD TV was discontinued. Tandy's Video Interactive System (VIS) was launched in 1992. Using a specially modified operating system this television-based multimedia player was designed to be able to use PC CD-ROM titles with only a little modification. Sales were disappointing and VIS was discontinued in 1993.

3DO 3DO (backed by major groups such as Matsushita, AT&T, Time Warner and MCA) has developed a proprietary multimedia entertainment platform which it licenses to other companies to manufacture. The first 3DO Multiplayer—REAL—was released at the end of 1993 by Panasonic. Sanyo released a player in 1994 and Goldstar one in 1995 with other manufacturers set to follow. 3DO is currently developing a new generation player, the M2. Like CD-I, add-on boards for PCs were produced.

Video games Video games have effectively used low-quality digital multimedia since the early 1980s and moving images, music, synthesised speech, text and sampled sound are standard features of most games. The early market leaders, Sega and Nintendo, developed their own hardware and their own cartridge software, creating self-contained and incompatible markets. With the storage capacity of the CD, video images and games can now be stored, played back and processed in an increasingly efficient manner. There are now a number of proprietary CD-based systems in this highly competitive market and as their technical specifications continue to improve they may become closer to the 'educational' multimedia platforms listed above. Listed below are the most advanced systems so far, or soon to be, available:

MULTIMEDIA PLATFORMS

- Atari: Jaguar;
- Bandai: Pippin;
- Commodore (Escom): Amiga CD32;
- Nintendo: Virtual Boy, Ultra 64;
- Sega: Mega CD, 32X, Saturn;
- Sony: PlayStation;
- SNK: Neo Geo CD;
- Apple: Power Play.

Video CD The CD-ROM has demonstrated the possibilities for storing sound, pictures, text, data, graphics and animation on a CD and companies have, therefore, raced to develop CDs which also offer full-motion video (FMV). The Video CD was developed by Philips, Sony, JVC and Matsushita, among others, and announced in 1993. The coding of the video uses a standard known as the White Book, which specifies the use of a digital compression system agreed by the Moving Pictures Expert Group of the International Standards Organisation, known as MPEG-1. There is dissatisfaction with this standard, primarily because it can only accommodate 75 minutes of video, so a feature film has to be split up on to two or more CDs. Secondly, a CD player reads a disk at a speed that is appropriate for sound but produces low moving picture quality.

To tackle these problems compression techniques for video are being improved and a new standard has been developed to succeed MPEG-1, known as MPEG-2. This codes every line of a picture and therefore will improve quality but also requires a disk with at least twice the storage capacity. It is therefore necessary to pack more information on a CD and the result is a number of proposed high density CD standards such as Super Density CD (SD) or Higher Density CD (HDCD) leading to the recently announced Digital Video Disk (DVD).

The versatile Digital Video Disk is an emerging technology that could eventually supplant the well-established VCR. DVD technology allows a full-length feature film to be stored on a single, one-sided, high-density disk. In 1994, two rival groups were promoting their own standards for the high-density compact disk; Sony and Philips proposed one DVD standard, and Toshiba and Time Warner proposed another. However, recent agreement looks like averting the commercial worst-case scenario of two incompatible standards.

Photo CD This is a proprietary photographic storage medium developed by Kodak. One Photo CD is able to store up to 100 digitally encoded images from 35mm film at a choice of quality levels. The disk is recordable and consumers can have a single disk processed along with prints. Professional developers can use the format as a publishing platform, for example, for electronic brochures. Although other platforms can read Photo CDs, standalone devices are produced.

Non-standard CDs/Electronic books Personal organisers and electronic books provide a slowly expanding catalogue of dictionaries, directories, tourist guides and other databases. Sony is the main enthusiast for the electronic book, but it has had very limited success outside Japan.

1.2.2 ON-LINE PLATFORMS

The on-line platform is where multimedia joins the Information Superhighway. At the moment products are transferred primarily by cable—coaxial (older cable systems and consumer tails on newer systems), fibre optic (modern telephone or cable TV) or traditional copper wire (conventional telephone)—to produce an on-line service. In this market, cable TV companies and telecommunications companies are active, but there are also specialised on-line service providers. On-line systems allow users to communicate with each other through interconnected networks of computers and offer huge potential for the exchange and use of information as more people plug in at home and at work. In addition, audiotex systems combining software-controlled voicemail, fax-on-demand and bulletin boards (BBS) accessed via telephone are already widely used.

Developments are taking place now which will facilitate the use of platforms linked by wireless transmission. This can already be done using mobile telephone and a portable PC; but the new 'personal digital assistants' promise more user-friendly technology. At the time of writing, they are playing a very limited role in multimedia because they do not have the capacity to transmit and store large amounts of data. The capacity constraints apply both to the equipment and to the amount of transmission spectrum (bandwidth) needed to transmit multimedia works.

Traditional 'one to many' broadcasting technology is ill-suited to multimedia, because of the lack of the reverse path essential to interactivity. There are many technical problems in using traditional broadcasting networks to send the user's choices back to the broadcaster and then tailoring the transmission to the user. Experimental technologies are on trial to overcome these difficulties, some using telephone links as the reverse path.

Internet

Today's template for on-line multimedia and the 'information superhighway' is the Internet. The Internet is not owned, operated or regulated by any one organisation or authority but is a world-wide, decentralised series of computer networks, linked by common communication protocols. It has free access and usage, except for telephone connect times. Today, the Internet is made up of more than five million computers with an estimated thirty million users in 125 different countries. End users take Internet connection directly from service providers or via other on-line service providers, each of which has entered interconnection agreements with each other. Previously used primarily by the academic community, in recent years it has grown dramatically with the spread of PCs and increasing ease of use. It is made up of many elements which include:

(1) *World Wide Web:* the Web consists of pages of information displayed on a PC screen using a special software package, known as a 'browser' to allow easy navigation from one computer to another, using hypertext links. By clicking on a highlighted word the user can jump from page to page and it is possible to download graphics, photographs, music and audio-visual clips, as well as simple text, over a standard telephone line. Consequently the Web offers a new means of advertising and distribution for products or services. Denton Hall's site is at http://www.gold.net/denton/.

(2) *Electronic mail:* e-mail is a key element of the Internet's appeal. It allows users to send a message to anyone else on the Internet by typing the message into a PC. Text, images, sounds and executable programs can be transmitted by attaching a file to the message. The advantages of e-mail are speed and cost but currently there is a lack of security and service guarantees, as a message may pass around the Internet by any route, direct or wildly indirect.

(3) *Usenet:* similar to e-mail, Usenet allows the exchange of information from person to person through the Internet. Messages are placed in public areas called newsgroups

and can be read by anyone who chooses to look in that area. Newsgroups have descriptive names and exist on virtually any subject ranging from Dr Who to legal reform.
(4) *File transfer protocol:* FTP enables a PC to retrieve information from another PC connected to the Internet, regardless of where in the world it is located, as if copying files over an office network.

On-line services

Many on-line services provide Internet access and proprietary services, and most are operated and monitored by companies on a commercial basis, that is service provision for a subscription fee. The best-known commercial networks in the UK are CompuServe and Compulink Information Exchange (CIX). The biggest market for on-line services is the USA and the three largest service providers there are America On-line, CompuServe and Prodigy, with an estimated six million subscribers in total. Microsoft, AT&T and Bertelsmann have all announced new on-line services.

Most on-line services offer commercial and news information services, together with communications with other users. A user can browse through files containing all kinds of information, download pictures, documents or software or join a conference or discussion group. Specialised services exist for, for instance, playing multimedia games on line and for particular interest groups.

Other on-line systems alternative to the Internet are being developed specifically for transactional and business purposes. Doing business on the Internet is complicated by its anarchic 'information wants to be free' *zeitgeist*. By contrast, the business networks, variously being planned or trialed by, among others, AT&T, Lotus, MCI and BT, will be more focused and, presumably, easier to navigate than the Internet and are likely to include videoconferencing and secure avenues of data and payment exchange.

Cable and telephony companies

The Internet is not the much hyped Information Superhighway offering full multimedia services. The Internet uses ordinary telephone lines, and is limited in the amount of information it can carry. This is a question of bandwidth: the more complex the application, the more bandwidth it will require. In addition, interactivity requires switching of the signal to a predesignated terminating point (the one-to-many broadcast mode being inappropriate to on-line multimedia) and a return path, in order, for example, to request a film or order a pizza.

The advantage that cable television companies can claim over telephony operators in supplying on-line multimedia services, is that their networks are already able to handle the typical volume of traffic generated by a compressed video stream. However, the design of such networks means that delay and interference is possible if the network is heavily loaded; and more seriously, their networks permit only a limited level of interactivity. Telephone networks, by contrast, are designed from the start to handle interactive traffic but have more severe bandwidth constraints due to the use of copper wire in their networks. The cost of replacing this with fibre-optic cable is enormous. Telecommunications companies are overcoming this disadvantage by a variety of means, not just by laying new fibre-optic networks to the door but by developing more advanced compression techniques and running fibre only to the kerb. Public Telecommunications Operators (PTOs) may also be subject to line-of-business restrictions which prevent them from carrying entertainment services. This currently applies in the case of BT in the UK (*see* 2.1.1).

Intelligence must be added to the network. The standards used in the 'set top box', the intelligent network terminal which will connect the television to the network in the home, decompress the signal, allow navigation of the interactive services and provide the return path for user interactivity are all key factors. There are a number of competing prototypes under development, and no single common standard has yet been agreed.

Technology and trials

Integrated Services Digital Network Most conventional telecom networks consist of narrowband twisted copper wire which, as currently configured, can carry speech and simple electronic signals such as those created by modems but, subject to what is said below, not much more, at least without degradation to quality. Integrated Services Digital Network (ISDN), an international communications standard for sending digital voice and data over narrowband telephone lines, provides users with end-to-end digital connections and guarantees high-quality lines. It can be used for desktop videoconferencing and other services requiring greater bandwidth, but it has had limited success in the UK because of the cost of installation, line rental and terminal equipment. Existing copper wire network can be used for ISDN in combination with digital switching systems. While it is still too slow for full-motion video, ISDN is suitable for some video conferencing and multimedia applications, and is seen as the next step for accessing on-line services like the Internet. The European Commission (EC) has been a strong advocate for the introduction of ISDN (*see* 2.2.1). There are proposals for an upgraded version: broadband ISDN (B-ISDN), for use with fibre-optic cable (*see* below).

Asymmetric digital subscriber loop Compression technology has made enormous strides already in recent years and development continues. A number of telecoms companies claim to be able to download video at acceptable (ie, VCR level) quality over twisted copper cables, but most are concentrating on developing the provision of broadband services over fibre or hybrid networks. BT, for example, is running trials of an interactive television system involving 2,500 homes in Colchester and Ipswich which will utilise the existing copper wire network in the 'local loop', the telephone network connecting each subscriber's home to the local exchange. This will offer a range of interactive services such as video on demand. Telephone companies continue to look for technological solutions to the problem of passing video down their existing copper networks. One such, known as asymmetric digital subscriber loop (ADSL), is being trialed by BT. ADSL is considered by some, for technical reasons, to be of limited value, in that the further the signal travels over the network the more likely it is to degrade, but BT's early tests have indicated that this technology could be used up to six kilometres from the exchange, which would cover over 90 per cent of BT's existing network.

Asynchronous transfer mode As mentioned above, cable television networks also have capacity problems, as many were built from coaxial cable and signals are transmitted in analogue form. Through compression technology (the removal of information that is not essential to the signal) the capacity of the existing infrastructure can be expanded, but this is not an ideal solution. In the UK, a trial has commenced of an interactive television system in Cambridge, involving Cambridge Cable, and a subsidiary of Olivetti, Online Media, among others. This will involve 250 homes and use an optical fibre network to the kerb, with coaxial cable for the last few feet to each house. Asynchronous transfer mode

(ATM), will allow fast transfer of compressed digital information in 'packets'. This is a very flexible and efficient way of transmitting data, permitting VHS-quality video to be sent across the network to the home and also allowing the user to send signals back across the network, enabling interactivity. It is a very efficient system for carrying other types of data and can be used for all types of information traffic. Many believe that ATM, with its potential power to integrate all forms of multimedia, will become the main carrier technology for the Information Superhighway, although full implementation will be delayed until common standards are agreed for the network configuration and the economic case for the massive investment needed to create a new network is proven.

Fibre optics Fibre optic technology involves the use of tiny glass or plastic filaments which are bundled together to make up the fibre-optic cable. As explained above, digitisation is the conversion of signals into electrical pulses. The pulses are converted into light and transmitted through the fibre-optic cable at speeds close to the speed of light. Fibre-optic cable has certain important advantages over its traditional wire counterpart, the most important being greater bandwidth. Fibre-optic cable is also less susceptible to outside interference (a major problem with traditional cable) and the quality of the signal is better. However, fibre-optic cable is relatively expensive, and companies must have a clear business model for the revenue which they will earn before making the investment in these new networks. Many long-distance trunk networks are now fibre, but the local loop, that is the wire to the door of the home, remains largely copper.

The significance of the existence of these various, often competing, often incompatible, platforms for the licensor of rights in content is that, by licensing too widely to a particular platform or proprietary standard, the licensor may tie up his rights in a multimedia format which has limited commercial potential. We deal with licensing issues in full detail in Chapter 15.

• 2 •
GOVERNMENT AND POLITICAL ISSUES

As the move forward into the 'information society' has accelerated since 1992, multimedia has been forced on to the political agenda. This chapter provides a brief overview of how the UK and Europe have taken up the challenge of on-line multimedia in particular.

2.1 UK

2.1.1 GOVERNMENT POLICY

In 1984 the Government commenced the privatisation of British Telecommunications Plc (BT), the then monopoly telephony supplier, at the same time granting Mercury a licence to compete with BT and establishing the so-called 'duopoly policy'. In 1991, as a result of a White Paper entitled 'Competition and Choice. Telecommunications Policy for the 1990s' (commonly known as the 'Duopoly Review'), the government concluded that termination of the duopoly policy would increase competition to the benefit of the consumer and announced that applications for telecommunications licences would be considered from any person seeking to operate new telecommunications networks over fixed links in the UK. The Duopoly Review also ended certain line-of-business restrictions on cable operators. The government's view was that by allowing *new* operators to convey both entertainment and telecommunications services over their systems, the development of competing local networks would be encouraged. Cable companies were free therefore to provide voice telephony, other telephony services and broadcast entertainment services, on obtaining a local delivery licence under the Broadcasting Act 1990, awarded by the ITC on a local franchise basis. This measure had an immediate positive impact on the sector and has led to considerable new investment in cable networks. At the same time the government restricted certain national PTOs, including BT, from *providing* entertainment services and BT, Mercury and Hull from *conveying* entertainment services.

Trade and Industry Committee report
Although this policy achieved the aim of kick-starting the cable industry in the UK, it is not without its critics. In July 1994 the House of Commons Trade and Industry Committee delivered a Report entitled 'Optical Fibre Networks', addressed to what it termed 'a communications revolution'. The introduction of the report makes clear that the

Committee's enquiry in fact focused on broadband networks, and upon broadband services, primarily in the local loop.

Among the recommendations of the report were that:

- The government should direct Oftel and the ITC to review licences for current franchise areas with a view to allowing competition on a franchise-by-franchise basis. In suitable cases, PTOs would have the restrictions on providing entertainment services lifted at specified future dates, being no less than seven years from the grant of the original licence.
- The government should make clear that all restrictions on PTOs on conveying or providing entertainment services would be lifted by the end of 2002.
- New franchise areas should be offered for franchising to any operator, including PTOs, by the end of 1995.

DTI Command Paper

The Department of Trade and Industry (DTI) published the Command Paper, 'Creating the Superhighways of the Future: Developing Broadband Communications in the UK' in November 1994. It examined the role of the regulatory framework for the telecommunications industry in providing for the development of underlying broadband networks; it concluded that the current regulatory environment remains the right one for the encouragement of broadband technology. A distinction is made in the paper between the development of *networks*, identified as the objective of telecommunications policy, and the development of *services* carried over networks. The government expressed satisfaction that existing policy is proving successful in stimulating investment in broadband infrastructure, but considered that the debate over the way broadband services should be developed is only just beginning.

The most important role for government, it stated, is the development and maintenance of a stable and effective regulatory framework, providing the economic benefits of competition and maintaining the confidence of investors in new communications technology. The government's approach to regulation will continue to aim for technology neutrality, subject to ensuring networks remain capable of interconnecting with each other over the full range of their services. To encourage local cable operators to build their networks to provide local competition in communication services, and provide the confidence necessary for the investment, the policy of not allowing PTOs to *convey* entertainment services nationally to homes at least until 1998 and the policy on not allowing *provision* until 2001 is not to be reviewed.

The government states that it wants all broadband operators to be able to develop and to gain market experience with the full range of new interactive services. From April 1994 national PTOs, including BT and Mercury, have also been able to apply in their own right for the new Local Delivery Operator (LDO) franchises for local broadcasting services from the ITC. The government has made it clear that it will also be prepared to issue these companies with a Telecommunications Act licence enabling them to supply entertainment services within the local franchise areas, to allow them to test new technologies alongside existing services, making use of the same infrastructure where possible. The Command Paper also confirms that the national PTOs are able to offer a wide range of interactive services, including video on demand, to individual residential customers. The prohibition which prevents BT providing 'entertainment services' relates to entertainment services for simultaneous reception in two or more dwelling houses.[1] In a press release in September 1993, the ITC stated its view that this prohibition did not cover video-on-demand services, on the basis that these services are not for simultaneous reception but are for reception at different times in response to individual requests.

2.1.2 LABOUR PARTY POLICY

The UK Labour Party has issued a policy document on these issues and, while acknowledging that the responsibility for building the networks rests with the private sector, looks to BT, and the other national telephony operators, to finance high capacity infrastructure nationwide. In this respect it backs the proposal of the Trade and Industry Select Committee for a rolling programme of entry by telephone operators into the cable franchise areas, beginning in 1998, and with full and open competition by 2002. In return, Labour would 'require' BT and the other telephone operators to establish a roll-out programme to cover the whole country, as far as technically practicable.

Labour points out that 'people do not buy wires; they buy programmes, services and information'. It proposes to revamp the regulatory watchdogs in the area along horizontal rather than vertical lines, so that Oftel would become Ofcom, regulating all communications infrastructure, and the ITC be revamped to regulate all content provision. There are signs already that Oftel and the ITC are manoeuvring to be the regulator of the superhighway. (See Oftel's Consultative Document, 'Beyond the Telephone, the Television and the PC', published in August 1995.)

The DTI Command Paper of November 1994 identified other, non-regulatory, roles for government in the promotion of information networks. Primary among these is the role of government as a user, and provider of, multimedia broadband services. Ian Taylor MP is to co-ordinate the DTI's interests in these fields, and a Multimedia Steering Group has been established. The government information technology consultancy and procurement agency, CCTA, has also been taking initiatives to promote the creation of information networks. The CCTA Government Information Service was launched in November 1994, to provide a range of information via the Internet. Clearly multimedia and the Superhighway will have important implications for cross-media ownership. However neither the existing UK media ownership restrictions nor the recent government proposals for change yet address the new issues arising from multimedia.

2.2 EUROPE

The Information Superhighway, as a concept, knows no geographical boundaries, and as such, sits easily within the ambit of the European Union (EU). The EU has for many years taken an active interest in the promotion of the media and technology-based industries in Europe as a source of funding for projects, as a regulator, as a legislator at the European level and as a co-ordinator for national governments. The European Commission (EC) takes a very active interest in the development of multimedia and information networks.

The EC's Discussion Paper (Impact 56/94) foresaw that the integration of information, communication, transaction and payment functions in multimedia services would create major new opportunities in both the consumer and professional marketplaces and that, while the creation of a European Common Information Area woud depend primarily on private-sector investment, the Community had the role of ensuring that the right conditions are created to stimulate this investment and help overcome fragmentation arising from linguistic, cultural and regulatory barriers. The Paper called for a stable, transparent and harmonised legal framework at EU level. This move towards an information-intensive society was seen as requiring a regulatory response in key areas such as intellectual property, data privacy and data security, media ownership and access to government information.

2.2.1 BANGEMANN REPORT

In January 1990, the European Council issued a Resolution concerning Trans-European Networks (TENs). This Resolution argued that the development of trade, the free movement of persons and the requirements of economic and social cohesion made it necessary both to improve and to extend *existing* communications networks, and to develop wholly *new* networks, with special priority given to the development and interconnection of, among others, telecommunications networks, in particular to the linking of the main Community conurbations by broadband telecommunications networks. Two initiatives are under way: ISDN as a TEN, and, at a discussion stage, ISDN for Europe-wide Broadband Communications Networks (IBCNs).

The Council established two TEN committees, one of which, chaired by Vice-President Martin Bangemann, produced the Bangemann Report, the document with the most impact in this area of information society policy. The Bangemann Group, composed of 20 'eminent personages' with expertise in the area of information infrastructures, was set up with the express purpose of creating an impetus for examining the Community's response to the new developments in multimedia, digital and broadband technologies. The Group's report was presented by Bangemann, now the European Commissioner for Industry, to the European Council at its Corfu meeting in June 1994.

The Bangemann Report provided a wide-ranging survey of the conditions necessary to create a partnership between the private and public sectors to carry Europe forward into the information society. The report took as its starting-point the idea that information and communication technologies are currently generating a new industrial revolution, as significant and as far reaching as any of the past: a revolution based on information. It identified a need to seize the opportunity of the information society, to create jobs, and to improve the quality of life of Europe's citizens. It recognised that risks are involved and that a great deal of effort should be put into securing widespread acceptance and use of new technology, with education, training and promotion playing a key role. It identified keen competition between Europe and the rest of the world, but clearly felt Europe to be well placed to succeed. It saw that the revolution is to be driven by the market and private investment: the prime task of government is to safeguard competitive forces and to give a 'strong and lasting political welcome' to the information society. The emergence of the new information market necessitates a new regulatory environment, to allow for full competition, a prerequisite for mobilising private capital to fund the revolution.

The Bangemann Report highlighted a number of key areas.

Telecommunications

Telecommunications provide the basis for the establishment of a true Information Superhighway, and the Report recommended the acceleration of the ongoing process of liberalisation: the opening up to competition of infrastructure and services that remain the subject of monopolies, and the removal of non-commercial political burdens and budgeting constraints imposed on telecommunications operators.

By the time the Bangemann Report was presented, substantial progress in liberalisation of telecoms in Europe had already taken place, but there was much still to do. In 1987 the telecommunications market in Europe was still dominated by state-owned operators and broadcasters enjoying national monopolies. The EC published a Green Paper in that year which had two policy goals: liberalisation and harmonisation, and aimed to create an internal market by breaking down monopolies, lowering barriers to entry and establishing equivalent trading conditions across the Community, enabling undertakings to compete on equal terms. The corner-stone of EU telecommunications law is the 1990 Services Directive, issued under art 90 of the Treaty of Rome. The Directive provided that Member States must withdraw all special or exclusive rights for the supply of telecommunication services, other than for voice telephony, and take all necessary steps to enable other operators to provide services over public networks. Further liberalisation was resisted by some Member States.

Following the Bangemann Report, however, the political climate changed and, at the meeting of the Telecommunications Committee in November 1994, the Council of Ministers decided to abolish all telecommunications monopolies by 1 January 1998, including monopolies on infrastructure. (Spain, Portugal, Greece and Ireland having an option to delay opening their markets until 2003.)

Notwithstanding this decision, the Commission has pushed ahead with further interim liberalising measures including the draft Commission Directives, under art 90 of the Treaty of Rome, on the liberalisation of:

- cable television networks;
- telecommunications services and infrastructure and, in particular, 'alternative infrastructure'.

The combined impact of these two draft Directives will be to liberalise the provision of infrastructure including cable and 'alternative infrastructure' of utilities such as railway companies throughout the EU by 1 January 1998 and to enable all network providers to carry any telecommunication services other than public switched voice telephony, and entertainment services by 1 January 1996.

Regulation

The Report called for the establishment of:

- a European authority to identify and establish the minimum regulation needed to ensure the rapid emergence of an efficient European information infrastructure and services;
- a kind of 'Euro-Oftel' to enforce this regulation.

Standards

Standards are of primary importance to the construction of the Superhighway, for the seamless interconnection of networks and the interoperability of the services that run on them. The Report called for operators to establish memorandums of understanding to set themselves specifications for specific application objectives which they would then input to standardisation bodies. This has successfully been done with GSM digital mobile telephony.

Intellectual property rights

The Report recognised that high level protection of IPR should be maintained in the face of the challenges of globalisation and digitisation, but that the stimulation of new multimedia products and services may necessitate the re-examination of existing legal regimes to see how appropriate they are to the information society. The ease with which digitised information can be transmitted, manipulated and adapted will require protection for the content provider, but flexibility and efficiency in obtaining authorisation for multimedia exploitation is also felt to be necessary for the creation of a dynamic European industry.

Data and privacy

Protection of data and privacy issues will be of crucial importance as detailed information on individuals is increasingly stored and potentially manipulated by new technology. The Bangemann Group believed that without the legal security of an EU-wide approach, lack of consumer confidence will have a detrimental impact on the information society. Digital security systems and encryption will be important:

- in ensuring that only those who pay for services receive them; and
- in the protection against misuse of personal data.

Competition

In its discussion of media pluralisation and competition the Bangemann Report displayed the tension between established competition policy and the need in the development of multimedia for convergence and joint ventures. It recommended that the notional global, rather than EU-wide, market should now be used in assessing European competition issues such as market status, joint ventures and mergers.

Building blocks

The Bangemann Report identifed the 'building blocks' of the information society. It saw ISDN as being at the forefront, but identified integrated broadband communications as providing the premier technological opportunity to combine all media in a flexible way, allowing for the development of new multimedia services. In these high quality video communication is crucial. The Report identified ATM as the technology to implement this. The Report also identified new basic services which should be required to be carried upon these new networks, such as e-mail, file transfer and interactive multimedia, while pointing out that new services could not take off until a certain number of customers have subscribed, thereby achieving a critical mass, pointing to the example of the Internet.

In addition the Report identified ten applications to 'blaze' the information society trail, providing a demonstration function and helping to promote wider use, and as a test bed for suppliers. Priority applications were also required to contribute to a number of macroeconomic objectives:

- to strengthen industrial competitiveness and job creation;
- promotion of new forms of work organisation;
- the improvement of quality of life and environment;
- the response to social needs; and
- the raising of efficiency and cost effectiveness of public services.

The following applications were identified:

- teleworking;
- distance working;
- university and research networks;
- telematic services for SMEs;
- advanced road traffic management;
- air traffic control;
- health care networks;
- electronic tendering;
- trans-European public administration networks;
- city information highways.

2.3 THE G-7 NATIONS

Of course the information society is in principle borderless, global. The Bangemann Report recognised that the taking of steps to guarantee equal access across the world is of paramount importance for Europe.

The G7 is an informal organisation of the leaders of the major industrialised nations: Canada, France, Germany, Italy, Japan, the UK and the USA. At their Naples summit in July 1994, the G7 leaders agreed that they should encourage the development of a worldwide 'information society'. A G7 ministerial conference was held specifically on the information society in February 1995, where senior politicians met with leading industrialists to discuss both underlying policy aims and the necessary economic and regulatory framework for the Information Superhighway.

The G7 ministers agreed that the information society should aim to integrate all countries into a global effort. Countries in transition and developing countries should be provided with a chance fully to participate in the process and be given the opportunity to leapfrog stages in technology advancement and to stimulate social and economic development. To succeed in this, it was agreed that governments should facilitate private initiatives and investment and ensure an appropriate framework that would both stimulate such private involvement and allow usage of the network for the benefit of all citizens. They should also create a favourable international environment by co-operating within the relevant international organisations such as World Trade Organisation (WTO), International Telecommunications Union (ITU), World Intellectual Property Organisation (WIPO), International Standards Organisation (ISO), and Organisation for Economic and Commercial Development (OECD).

The G7 ministers agreed a set of eight principles based upon this common vision of the global information society, aimed at striking a balance between the need for a competitive, profitable environment for businesses and the importance of ensuring fair and universal provision of services and access to networks:

- promoting dynamic competition;
- encouraging private investment;
- defining an adaptable regulatory framework;
- providing open access to networks;
- ensuring universal provision of and access to services;
- promoting equality of opportunity to citizens;
- promoting diversity of content, including cultural and linguistic diversity; and

- recognising the necessity fo world-wide co-operation, with particular attention to less developed countries.

It was intended that these principles apply to the global information infrastructure by means of:

- promoting interconnectivity and interoperability;
- developing global markets for networks, services and applications;
- ensuring privacy and data security;
- protecting intellectual property rights;
- co-operating in research and development and in the development of new applications;
- monitoring the social and societal implications of the information society.

The ministers also set up a number of pilot projects, including projects in the fields of electronic libraries and museums and the development of the global emergency management system, all aimed at putting the above principles into practice and encouraging demand. However no detailed policy document was produced and questions remain over the regulatory detail of liberalisation, as well as how privacy and security of data and intellectual property should be protected. The G7 ministers are relying on the relevant international organisations, especially WIPO and WTO, to agree suitable standards.

---

[1] This policy frustrates BT, which argues that the most effective way for the UK to gain a national, seamless broadband network would be for it, as dominant market player, to build it. BT is not, as yet, prepared to make the investment in a national fibre-optic network while these restrictions preventing it from supplying valuable broadcast entertainment services are in place. However, the government points out that any PTO, including BT or Mercury, may convey and provide entertainment or information services to homes on a local franchise basis by holding the relevant local delivery licence. (BT owns a cable franchise in Westminster through a wholly owned subsidiary, but has chosen to dispose of all other cable franchises in which it once had an interest.) BT and Mercury may not provide braodcast entertainment services over their national networks, but no other PTO can provide entertainment services nationally either. BT's licence sets out details of the services which may be provided over the BT national network; BT is permitted to convey all types of messages except cable programme services sent under a licence granted under s 58 of the Telecommunications Act 1984. Section 56 of that Act defines 'cable programme services' as 'the sending of sounds or visual images, or both, either for *simultaneous* reception in two or more dwelling houses or for reception at a place in the UK for presentation to members of the public or a group of persons' (our emphasis).

• PART 2 •
THE LEGAL AND REGULATORY FRAMEWORK

• 3 •

UK COPYRIGHT LAW

3.1 INTRODUCTION

This review of copyright law is not intended to be comprehensive but to flag the more important areas as they impact on multimedia. For fuller discussion on copyright law the reader is directed to the standard works. One of the problems in dealing with multimedia is that other countries approach copyright from a different perspective or provide varying levels of protection.

The main copyright legislation in the UK is the Copyright, Designs and Patents Act 1988 ('the CDPA'). This chapter considers the main provisions of this Act as they relate to multimedia.

3.1.1 MULTIMEDIA

'Multimedia', or the dealing with different categories of works by electronic means (ie, using a computer) is in fact just a new way of dealing with material. The primary restricted acts are the rights to:

- copy;
- issue copies to the public;
- perform, show or play work in public;
- broadcast a work or include it in a cable, programme service;
- adapt a work.

Forged in a pre-electronic era these restricted acts have been stretched to include electronic dealing.

The inclusion, in the CDPA, s 17, of the expression 'storing' within the definition of 'copy' has in practice caught almost any dealing with electronic rights: the data have to be stored, even if only transiently, in the computer's memory. Accordingly, permission from the copyright owner is needed: and that is the basis for the copyright owner's protection.

Copyright is a national right. Protection in the UK is given by the CDPA. Protection for an 'English' copyright in other countries requires reliance on one of the two main copyright treaties, the Berne Convention or the Universal Copyright Convention. International protection of neighbouring rights eg, sound recordings is afforded by the Rome Convention. These are discussed in Chapter 5.

In the context of the European Union (EU), English law is being amended as a result of the series of Directives which have become known as the Harmonisation Directives (*see* Table 3.1).

Table 3.1 Copyright Harmonisation Directives

	Directive	Adopted	UK Implementation
1.	Software Directive	14/5/91	1/1/93
2.	Satellite Directive	27/9/93	1996(?)
3.	Rental and Lending Right Directive	19/11/92	1996(?)
4.	Duration Directive	29/10/93	1/1/96
5.	Database Directive	1996	1998

The Green Paper, 'Copyright and Related Rights in the Information Society', issued by the EC in July 1995 argued that while traditional notions of copyright and related rights, being limited in their territorial application, might need review, and that digital technology may require multimedia works to have a separate status, nevertheless copyright is sound as a concept. This is a view with which the authors currently agree.

3.1.2 ELECTROCOPYING

A narrow definition of electrocopying is the 'use of a scanner allowing the user of printed materials to scan the text and to store it in character encoded form in an electronic store'. Once it is in the store it can be searched and reproduced at will whether on a screen or on hard copy, and once scanned, material can be manipulated: the text changed; whole, parts or excerpts selected; annotations added and edited; and changed material reproduced. A broader definition would allow copying from one electronic store to another.

3.2 CATEGORIES OF WORK

Copyright is a creature of statute. It is recognised as a proprietary right; it has been described as a bundle of rights; it can be dealt with as property: it can be sold, licensed, divided up, mortgaged etc.

To obtain copyright protection, not only does the author have to be a qualified person, but the work has to fall within one of the categories of works set out in the CDPA as works to which copyright protection is given. Copyright is a national right. The CDPA applies only to works:

- first published in the UK;
- created by qualified persons, that is by British nationals, persons resident within the UK or by companies registered in the UK; also by legal persons to whom the CDPA has been extended whether by statutory instrument or by international convention.

Table 3.2 sets out the categories of work covered by the CDPA, identifies who is regarded as the author of the different categories of work and indicates the duration of copyright under the existing legislation and under the Duration Directive.

Each of the categories of separate work in Table 3.2 is entitled to protection in slightly different ways and copyright will not subsist unless certain pre-conditions are satisfied.

3.2.1 LITERARY, DRAMATIC, MUSICAL AND ARTISTIC WORKS

In the case of literary, dramatic and musical works, it is specifically provided that copyright will not subsist until the work is recorded, whether in writing or otherwise; and it is not material whether the recording was done by or with the permission of the author. An artistic work cannot, of course, exist until it has been created in some medium.

Public performance of literary, dramatic and musical works is protected. There is no performance right in an artistic work.

> **Example 1**
>
> If I write a speech and then deliver it more or less verbatim, the speech is protected as a literary work as a result of my having written it in the first place. However if I deliver the speech extempore it is not subject to copyright protection because it is not recorded in material form. But if someone writes my speech down or records it on a tape recorder, the work will have been recorded and will be capable of copyright protection.
>
> The person who wrote it down will have recorded the work in material form but I will still be the owner of the copyright in it. The person who wrote it down will not have any rights unless he or she has applied sufficient originality to the creation of the notes. For example, if in an interview a journalist uses particular skill in picking out just the relevant highlights of the interview or speech, his work may be capable of copyright protection. Because his work will have been based on the interviewee's, he will not be able to use that material without permission (which may be deemed to have been given in the circumstances).
>
> If my extempore speech was recorded on a tape recorder, that recording would have its own copyright (*see* Table 3.2) but once again, while I could not copy that recording, the person doing the recording could not use the recording without my permission, since the copyright in the recording is based on my copyright.

> **Example 2**
>
> I suggest the idea for a series of interactive CDs to you during a conversation in a pub: you go away, develop the concept and produce the series. You own the copyright; I have no copyright claim. There is no copyright in ideas, only in the form in which the ideas are expressed and then only when reduced to material form. (I may, however, have a claim for misuse of the information if it was disclosed under conditions of confidence—unlikely in a pub!)

3.2.2 SOUND RECORDING AND FILM

A sound recording or a film cannot exist until it has been created in some medium. The recording of sound on, say, a CD will be protected as a sound recording under the CDPA, s 5(1).

The definition of a 'film' (*see* Table 3.2) is so wide that it could, and probably does, include a multimedia work—which is (electronically) nothing more than 'a recording (on say a CD) from which a moving image may . . . be produced' (*see* further discussion at 3.2.6). If it is a film, consider whether the provisions of the Video Recordings Act 1984 may apply.

It is clear from the CDPA that some measure of originality applies in respect of a sound recording or film, in the sense that it is specifically provided that copyright will *not* subsist in a sound recording or film where it is a copy taken from a previous sound recording or film. However, the CDPA does not otherwise require that a film or sound recording should be original (as it does for literary, artistic, dramatic or musical works). A film (or multi-media work) is usually based on or derived from some other works and therefore cannot be 'original' (and where those works are in copyright, permission to use them will be required).

There can be, and usually will be, two or more copyrights in a sound recording, a film or a broadcast. There will be the copyright in the sound recording, film or broadcast; and also the copyright in the underlying works, that is the copyright works that go towards making the sound recording, film or broadcast, such as the screenplay.

3.2.3 BROADCAST

Excluded from the definition of 'broadcast' are services run for a business (or by a single individual where all the apparatus is under his control and the images, sounds or other information conveyed by it are for his own purposes); or where the apparatus is all within premises under single occupation. (In both the above cases the system must not be connected to any other communication system.)

Also excluded are services run for the service providers themselves.

3.2.4 CABLE PROGRAMMES

Copyright does not subsist in a cable programme if it is included in a cable programme service by reception and immediate retransmission of a broadcast or to the extent it infringes the copyright in another cable programme or in a broadcast.

3.2.5 PUBLISHED EDITION

It will be a question of fact on each occasion whether the incorporation of a typographical arrangement into a multimedia work will be an infringement of the typographical copyright (ignoring for these purposes whether the text itself is in copyright). The restricted act is making *an identical* copy: if the copy in the computer's memory and the copy reproduced from that memory are not identical to the original, it is submitted that there will be no infringement of the typographical copyright.

> **Example 1**
>
> A publisher publishes a new edition of a work which is out of copyright, eg, a Dickens' novel. The publisher cannot prevent anyone else publishing that novel but he can (for the copyright period in the typographical right, ie, 25 years from the end of the calendar year in which the new edition was published) prevent them producing film from his new edition in order to print their own edition. The other publishers would have to re-set the work themselves.

> **Example 2**
>
> The other publisher scans the same text into a computer. There is no infringement of the text (as it is out of copyright); there is no infringement of the typographical right while it remains in the computer memory (where it is represented by electronic zeros and ones and is not a facsimile copy); and there is no infringement if it is then printed out with different typeface and pagination (again, there is no facsimile copy).

3.2.6 IS MULTIMEDIA A 'WORK'?

There is no specific category of work in the CDPA into which a multimedia work naturally falls. The expression 'multimedia' does not appear anywhere in the CDPA. From the legal point of view, a multimedia work is comprised of a bundle of other works, whether literary, dramatic, artistic or musical, or all four. Published editions have their own copyright under English law. A multimedia work does not. Accordingly a multimedia work will fall to be protected in one or more of the following groups:

(1) As the sum total of its parts.
(2) To the extent that it is a sound recording or a film, it can be protected as such. On the subject of 'film' the definition under the CDPA is wider than in many other countries, where legislation is inclined to talk of 'cinematograph works' (as do the Berne Convention and TRIPS). Thus in France it is questionable whether a film of eg, a sporting event is a 'film' for copyright purposes.
(3) To the extent that it is a compilation, there would be the possibility of a compilation copyright (a literary work): that is the skill, effort and labour that has gone into combining the various underlying works into the multimedia work. A literary work is sufficiently widely defined to include a table of information and a compilation; so why should it not include a compilation made up of a mixture of literary, artistic, musical and dramatic works? 'Literary' work is the category which the CDPA uses to extend copyright to compilations. It should not matter what categories of work comprise a compilation: there is no practical problem even if there is a conceptual challenge to overcome. Under the Berne Convention, the position is still less satisfactory since 'collections of literary or artistic works' are only protected if they constitute 'intellectual creations'.
(4) To the extent that it is a database, it may be protected as such (*see* databases and the discussion of the *Feist* case (at 4.5)).

3.2.7 PROTECTION: A PUBLISHER'S RIGHT

Many feel that a developer and publisher of a CD-ROM must have a clear and separate right of copyright in the product of his work, and one that he can enforce directly against infringers. If it is a film or a database, it will enjoy a publisher's right. If not, the position is much less certain and the developer must presumably fall back to any statutory or contractual rights enjoyed as an assignee or a licensee of the underlying works, which must surely be unsatisfactory.

Discussion continues as to the nature of any possible publisher's right in a multimedia work. Should the work itself be protected or the exploitation of it? In Switzerland there is an *unfair competition* concept to the effect that it is unfair 'to take over and use the marketable product (the published edition) of another by technical means of reproduction (photocopying or electrocopying) without incurring costs'.

From an international perspective, it can be seen that there are potential problems with compilation, database and film as the basis for copyright protection of a multimedia work because of the variance of protection in other territories for these categories.

What else should the publisher do to protect his investment? He should work out a complete framework of protection. Protection should be achieved by a partnership of technology and law; technology can perhaps prevent unlawful copying, manipulation and retransmission (which is so simple with digitised material) or reuse of the works. It can also tag or identify material contained in the CD-ROM to make it easier to identify unlawful copies. Law should then plug the gaps of the technology, using tagging as evidence in any infringement proceedings.

> **Note**
> In the USA, CD-ROM games can be registered as films.

3.3 ORIGINALITY

The CDPA requires that a literary, dramatic, musical or artistic work has to be 'original' before it is capable of protection. The same requirement does not apply to sound recordings, films, broadcasts or cable programmes nor to typographical arrangements of published editions (but it *does* apply to copies of them).

By 'originality' (which is not statutorily defined) is meant that the work originates from the author and that it is not a slavish copy of a previous work.

Originality must be distinguished from quality: quality is not a requirement of UK copyright protection to the extent that mundane works, such as a timetable, are (if original) protectable. A straight line is unlikely to be protectable because of itself it is too mundane but a series of them in a particular pattern could be. It is also believed that titles (of eg, books or films) are not sufficiently original to be capable of copyright protection (but *see* passing off at 7.3.3).

> **Example**
> A multimedia work will not be original if it is a simple copy of another multimedia work but it *will* be original if the producer, in collecting together and compiling the new work, uses sufficient skill, effort or labour (*see* discussion of *Feist* at 4.5) in choosing the component parts.
>
> One should query the position if there is no such skill, effort or labour and it is the *user* (or the software program) who effectively makes the compilation. *(Cont'd)*

> Note that continental European law requires a greater intellectual input into originality than Anglo-Saxon law does; and that the Database Directive will introduce those continental concepts into UK law. (*See* Database Directive and *Feist* at 4.5.)

3.4 AUTHORSHIP

In copyright terms, the expression 'author' applies to the creator of a work, whether he or she be photographer, sculptor, artist or writer.

> **Example**
> A cameraman is the author of the photograph which he takes unless his role is simply mechanical—eg, where someone else sets the whole shot up and all he does is to press the trigger.

The author must be distinguished from the owner of the copyright (*see* ownership at 3.5) who must in turn be distinguished from the owner of the physical object. They may not necessarily be the same person.

> **Example**
> I buy a painting from the artist. Unless we agree in writing that I shall own the copyright, the artist remains the copyright owner but I own the physical property in the painting (without the right to copy it). Accordingly if I want to incorporate a reproduction of that painting into, say, an electronic work, I need to acquire the relevant rights *from the copyright owner*. If I do not own the painting, I need also to obtain permission to get access to the physical painting.

In certain circumstances the CDPA provides who is to be taken to be the author (*see* Table 3.2).

3.4.1 AUTHOR OF A MULTIMEDIA WORK

Who is the 'author' of a multimedia work? Under English law in the case of a film, the author is the person who made the arrangements for the production of the work: usually the producer, whether an individual or a company.

It is necessary to distinguish between the author of the work and the separate authors of the constituent parts. To the extent that a multimedia work is a film or a sound recording, the CDPA makes the producer the author. To the extent that it is neither, one has to look to the individual authors of the constituent parts and, here, the contracts pursuant to which the rights were acquired or the services rendered will be crucial in determining the producer's rights. *See* the discussion of the Duration of Copyright Directive at 4.3 and the Rental and Lending Rights Directive at 4.4 for forthcoming changes to UK law.

3.4.2 JOINT AUTHOR

There are provisions for works of joint authorship (ie, work produced by the collaboration of two or more authors in which the contribution of each author is not distinct from that of the other author or authors).

3.5 OWNERSHIP

3.5.1 FIRST OWNER

The author of a work is usually the first owner of any copyright in it. However where a literary, dramatic, musical or artistic work is made by an employee in the course of his or her employment, it is the employer who is the first owner of any copyright in the work. This applies unless, and to the extent that, the parties make an agreement to the contrary.

Examples

A multimedia production company *employs* a scriptwriter: the copyright in the script will belong to the company by operation of law (unless the parties agree otherwise and in writing).

The same company *engages* the writer as a freelancer (or commissions him or her): the copyright will belong to the writer unless the parties agree in writing otherwise (which they usually will).

Recommendations: Review your contractual practices carefully; consider whether contracts with freelancers (anyone *not* an employee) are sufficient to pass the rights you need. Consider whether the work your employees are doing is being carried out in the course of their employment. Also review your contracts of employment.

Sample clause: The assignment of copyright in a freelance contract

The following are suggested forms of wording for the assignment of copyright in a freelance contract:

> You acknowledge that any copyright and all other rights of whatever nature subsisting in or attaching to the products of any of the services provided by you hereunder will belong to the Company absolutely to the fullest extent permitted by law. To such end you undertake at the request and expense of the Company, to do all further acts and execute all further documents as the Company may from time to time require for the purposes of further assuring the performance of your services hereunder and of giving effect to the assignment of rights herein contained.
>
> You hereby assign to the Company the entire copyright and all other rights of whatsoever nature in and to all products of your services provided to the Company (and where such products are not in existence at the date hereof, by way of present assignment of future copyright) throughout the world for the full period of copyright and all renewals and extensions.

DURATION OF COPYRIGHT 3.6

> **Example**
>
> An employee whose job is to write advertising copy for magazine advertisements writes advertising copy in his spare time, on a freelance basis, for a multimedia company; the employer is probably the owner of the copyright in it, but the definitive answer may depend on whether, and if so how, the contract of employment deals with the issue.
>
> The same employee writes a novel or script in his spare time: the employee is probably the copyright owner (but with the same caveat: look at what the employment contract actually says).

Sample clause: The ownership of copyright in an employment contract

The following is a suggested form of wording for inclusion in an employment contract to cover assignment of copyright:

> You acknowledge that any copyright and all other rights subsisting in or attaching to the products of any services provided by you during the course of your employment shall belong to the Company absolutely to the fullest extent permitted by law. To such end you undertake at the request and expense of the Company, to do all further acts and execute all further documents as the Company may from time to time require for the purposes of vesting such rights in the Company.

Different rules apply to Crown and parliamentary copyright.

- Crown copyright: the Crown is the first owner of copyright in a work made by the Sovereign or by an officer or servant of the Crown in the course of his duties.
- Parliamentary copyright: the relevant House (Commons or Lords) is the first owner of a work made by or under the direction or control of either House.

See CDPA, ss 163–7 for more detail.

3.5.2 WHO IS THE OWNER OF THE COPYRIGHT IN A MULTIMEDIA WORK?

If the multimedia work is a film, under existing English law the producer is currently the author and therefore the first owner of the copyright in it. Otherwise the position will depend on the contracts pursuant to which the producer/publisher has acquired the rights in the underlying works (ie, the works that are contained in the multimedia product).

3.6 DURATION OF COPYRIGHT

The area of UK law concerning the duration of copyright will be amended following the implementation into UK law of the Duration of Copyright Directive with effect from 1 January 1996.

Table 3.2 shows the present standard periods and the changes which will be made by the Duration Directive.

A number of points may be made about the duration of copyright

- Copyright in literary, artistic, dramatic and artistic works is calculated by reference to the life of the author(s). It makes no difference whether the author was employed or was a freelancer.
- No unauthorised acts trigger the start of the copyright period. Thus, if a pirate publisher copies an unpublished multimedia work and sells it in quantity, these sales do not count as publication or release of the original for any copyright purpose.

As there is no formal 'multimedia' category of works in the CDPA, there is no formal copyright period in such a work *except* to the extent that it falls into a different category such as a film, a sound recording, a literary work or compilation or a database.

> **Example**
>
> A multimedia work recorded on CD comprises:
> - literary material which is in the public domain;
> - music specially composed by a composer who died 20 years ago;
> - artwork by a living artist;
>
> and was produced by an employee of the CD company
>
> The whole work is recorded on CD and published on 15 July 1994.
>
> The copyright position in the UK (assuming all the authors qualify for protection) is as follows:
> (1) To the extent that the CD is a sound recording, the recording of the sounds is protected for 50 years from 1 January 1995. This prevents persons copying the recording (but does not prevent them re-recording the underlying works if they can get a licence from the respective copyright owners—possibly not required in the case of the literary material). If they copy the selection itself, they run the risk of infringing compilation copyright.
> (2) To the extent the CD is a film, the whole CD is protected from copying for 70 years from the end of the year in which the last of the relevant authors died.
> (3) The literary material is out of copyright (but may come back into copyright if the author died less than 20 years ago).
> (4) The artwork is protected by copyright and will be protected for the life of the author plus 70 years.
> (5) If the CD is a film, the director of it will be an author—*see* the Rental and Lending Rights Directive—and thus his contribution is protected. The Rental and Lending Rights Directive will also give him a rental right.
> (6) To the extent that the CD is a joint work copyright will not expire in it until 70 years after the death of the last of the joint authors to die.
>
> It is important to note the moral rights of all those entitled to them. (*See* the discussion of moral rights in Chapter 8.)

3.7 WARNING WORDING

It is necessary for multimedia works to carry warning wording concerning unauthorised reproduction or transmission. Suitable wording is:

> No part of this product may be reproduced or transmitted in any form or by any means without the express prior written permission of [   ].

The usual copyright notice wording is:

> © [name of owner] 19 [Year of first publication]. All rights reserved

3.8 RESTRICTED ACTS

3.8.1 PRIMARY INFRINGEMENTS

Under the CDPA, ss 16–21, in the UK, the copyright owner has the exclusive right to:

(a) copy the work;
(b) issue copies of the work to the public;
(c) perform, show or play the work in public;
(d) broadcast the work or include it in a cable programme service;
(e) make an adaptation of the work;

or to do any of the above in relation to an adaptation.

Adaptation
An adaptation is made when the work is recorded. 'Adaptation' has a limited definition under the CDPA and means:

(a) in relation to a literary work or dramatic work (other than a computer program):
  (i) a translation;
  (ii) a conversion of a dramatic work into a non-dramatic work or vice versa;
  (iii) a version in which the story or action is told by means of pictures in form suitable for reproduction in a book, newspaper, magazine or similar periodical;
(b) in relation to a musical work: an arrangement or a transcription of the work;
(c) in relation to a computer program, an arrangement or altered version of the program or a translation of it. Translation includes a version of the program in which it is converted into or out of a computer language or code into a different computer language or code.

Copying
Copying in relation to a literary, dramatic, musical or artistic work means reproducing that work in any material form. The CDPA specifically says that this includes storing the work in any medium by electronic means (which includes making copies which are transient or incidental to some other use of the work).

Publishing
Publishing means:

(a) issuing copies to the public. This includes renting sound recordings and films to the public but otherwise does not prohibit subsequent distribution, sale, hiring or loan

of copies. In other words the concept is putting into circulation copies not previously in circulation;
(b) making a work available to the public by means of an electronic retrieval system (CDPA, s 175(1)).

3.8.2 SECONDARY INFRINGEMENTS

According to the CDPA, ss 22–27, secondary infringements are:

- importing an infringing copy;
- possessing or dealing with an infringing copy;
- providing means for making infringing copies;
- permitting use of premises for an infringing performance;
- providing apparatus for an infringing performance

and knowing or having reason to believe that a copy is an infringing copy. Note that knowledge is not a requirement for primary infringement.

Infringing copies

Under the CDPA, s 27, an article is an infringing copy if its making constituted an infringement of the copyright of the work in question; and if:

- it has been imported into the UK; and
- its making in the UK would have constituted an infringement of the copyright in the work.

Note that exhaustion of rights applies to a computer program which, if previously legitimately sold in any other Member State, is *not* an infringing copy if imported into the UK.

3.9 PERMITTED ACTS

A number of provisions in the CDPA (ss 28–76) set out what may be done without infringing copyright.

3.9.1 FAIR DEALING

Research or private study

Fair dealing with a literary, dramatic, musical or artistic work for the purposes of research or private study does not infringe copyright (s 29). 'Fair dealing' has, deliberately, not been defined statutorily: it is up to the courts to judge each instance.

Criticism or review

It is not an infringement of copyright to deal with a work for the purposes of criticism or review provided there is 'sufficient acknowledgement', defined as an acknowledgement identifying the work (by its title or otherwise) and the author (s 30(1)).

PERMITTED ACTS 3.9.1

> **Example**
>
> Channel 4 included 12 minutes of material in a 30-minute television documentary about Stanley Kubrik's film, *A Clockwork Orange* and its 'suppression' in the UK. The clips used comprised 8 per cent of the film as a whole and made up 40 per cent of the documentary. The documentary was made at a time when the film's director had effectively withdrawn the film from the UK market. Channel 4 claimed that its use of the clips constituted fair dealing under CDPA 1988, s 30(1) since the documentary criticised and reviewed not only the decision to withdraw the film but also the film itself. The court decided in *Time Warner Entertainment Co Ltd v Channel 4* (1994) EMLR (1)1 that s 30 was concerned with the treatment of material rather than the manner in which it was treated and that Channel 4's use was fair. The judge seems to have come to his decision on the basis of 'impression' and that quality rather than quantity was relevant.

Reporting current events

Fair dealing with a work (other than a photograph) for the purpose of reporting current events does not infringe any copyright in the work provided (in certain cases) there is sufficient acknowledgement (s 30(2)).

> **Example**
>
> BSkyB transmitted in its sports news programmes excerpts—varying in length from 14 to 37 seconds—taken without licence from BBC broadcasts of international football matches. The excerpts were accompanied by a verbal report and by an acknowledgement of the source of the film. BSkyB defended itself on the grounds of CDPA 1988, s 30(2). The court decided that the use was fair in the context—again an 'impression' test was used; *British Broadcasting Corporation v British Satellite Broadcasting Ltd* (1992) Ch 141.
>
> Note that it was in *Hubbard v Vosper* (1972) 2 QB 84—the Scientology case—that the view was established that fair dealing was a question of degree and 'must be a matter of impression'.

> **Example**
>
> A company makes multiple copies of a selection of copyright literary works for its workforce as part of an exercise reviewing competitors' works. The copies acknowledge the publications from which they are taken. This is insufficient acknowledgment; the names of the authors should have been acknowledged also. The copying is likely to be an infringement of copyright.

Computer programs

It is not an infringement of copyright for a lawful user to make a back-up copy of a computer program (CDPA, s 50A). Decompilation provisions are contained in CDPA, s 50B.

A 'lawful user' is a person who has a right to use the program.

See also the Software Directive discussed at 4.2.

Incidental inclusion

Incidental inclusion of copyright material in an artistic work, sound recording, film, broadcast or cable programme is not an infringement (CDPA, s 31).

> **Example**
>
> Paintings on the walls of a room are included in a film. They amount to background only and are incidental to the plot. Even if the paintings are recognisable, there is no infringement of any copyright. It would, of course, be different if the film was about the paintings or one or more of them was 'involved' in the plot.

In respect of a musical work, words spoken or sung with music are not to be regarded as 'incidentally included' in another work if they are deliberately included.

> **Examples**
>
> Background music included in the soundtrack at the choice of the producer is not 'incidentally included'.
>
> However, if the film is made in a place where, incidentally, music is being played, and can be heard on the soundtrack, there will be no infringement of copyright.

Education and library exceptions

There are a number of exclusions relating to education and to copying by librarians (CDPA, ss 32–44).

Electronic form

Section 56 of the CDPA provides that where a copy of a work in electronic form has been purchased on terms which expressly or impliedly, or generally, allow the purchaser to copy the work or to adapt it or to make copies of an adaptation in connection with his use of it then, if there are no express terms prohibiting the transfer of a copy or providing the terms upon which the transferee may do things, anything which the purchaser could do, a transferee can do. However, any copy, or copy of an adaptation, made by the purchaser which is not also transferred is to be treated as an infringing copy after the transfer. For further details on the transferability of a licence to use, refer to 14.2 on exploitation.

There is provision for the Secretary of State to order that the rental of sound recordings, films and computer programs shall be deemed to be licensed provided a reasonable royalty is paid (CDPA, s 66). This will not apply if there is a relevant licensing scheme certified by the Secretary of State under CDPA, s 143. The Rental and Lending Rights Directive (*see* 4.4) proposes an amendment of this provision.

3.10 TRANSFER OF COPYRIGHT

Ownership of copyright can only be transferred by written instrument signed by, or on behalf of, the copyright owner. Note, however, that it is possible to *agree* to assign copyright (which agreement does not have to be in writing) and that the beneficiary of that agreement can call for a formal assignment in writing.

> **Example**
> A commissioned contributor to a multimedia work promises to deliver his contribution in return for a fee and agrees that he will on delivery assign his copyright. He delivers but fails to assign; then he dies. As the author, he was the first owner of copyright which on his death vested in his estate. The executors or beneficiary can be compelled to enter into a formal assignment of copyright.

An exclusive licence also has to be in writing; a non-exclusive licence can be oral.
Copyright ownership can be transferred in whole or in part.

> **Examples**
> In the film industry (which multimedia producers can be expected to follow) it is usual for all contributors to be required to assign their entire interest in copyright and to waive any moral rights, the argument being that the film company invests so much money in the project that it wants to own everything lock, stock and barrel.
>
> In book publishing, practices differ: scientific, technical and medical publishers usually require an assignment of copyright; with trade publishers (novels, autobiographies, crime thrillers, cookery books, etc) the practice is more often to accept an exclusive licence.
>
> If you assign, or grant an exclusive licence over, rights in a work you are no longer able to exploit those rights yourself, or to assign or grant them to anyone else. The grant of a non-exclusive licence allows the grantor to continue to exploit such rights himself or to permit one or more third parties to do so.

Table 3.2 Copyright in different categories of work

Category of work (CDPA section)	Definition and exclusions	Author (CDPA section)	Existing duration	Duration Directive
Literary work (s 3(1).)	Any work (apart from a dramatic or musical one) which is written, spoken or sung including: a table or a compilation; a computer program and preparatory design material for a computer program.	The person who creates it (s 9(1).).	50 years from the end of the calendar year in which the author dies (irrespective of whether the author was employed or a freelancer). For joint authors the period runs from the end of the year of the death of the last of them to die. Note also that copyright in a work of unknown authorship expires 50 years from the end of the calendar year in which it is first made available to the public. *See* CDPA, s 12(2), for detail.	70 years from the end of the year in which the author (or in the case of joint authors the last of them) dies. Note also that copyright in a work of unknown authorship expires 70 years from the end of the calendar year in which the work was made or, if the work is made available to the public before the end of that period, at the end of the period of 70 years from the end of the calendar year in which it is first so made available.
Dramatic work (s 3(1).)	Includes a work of dance or mime.	As above.	As above.	As above.
Musical work (s 3(1).)	A work consisting of music (exclusive of any words or action intended to be sung spoken or performed with the music).	As above.	As above.	As above.
Artistic work (s 4.)	A graphic work or a photograph, a sculpture or	As above.	As above.	As above.

Table 3.2 *Continued*

Category of work (CDPA section)	Definition and exclusions	Author (CDPA section)	Existing duration	Duration Directive
	collage (and artistic quality is immaterial); also a work of artistic craftsmanship; a graphic work includes a painting, drawing, diagram, map, chart or plan; and a photograph means a recording of light or other radiation on any medium on which an image is produced or from which an image may by any means be produced (and which is not part of a film).			
Sound recording (s 5(1).)	A recording of sounds from which the sounds may be reproduced or a recording of the whole or any part of a literary, dramatic or musical work from which sounds reproducing the work or part may be produced and that is regardless of the medium on which the recording is made or the method by which the	The person by whom the arrangements necessary for the making of the recording of the sound recording were made. (s 9(2)(*a*).)	50 years from the end of the year in which it was made. If released (ie, first broadcast) before the end of that period, 50 years from the end of the year of release. *See* CDPA, s 13(1).	No change.

Table 3.2 Copyright in different categories of work

Category of work (CDPA section)	Definition and exclusions	Author (CDPA section)	Existing duration	Duration Directive
Film (s 5(1).).	sounds are reproduced or produced. A recording on any medium from which a moving image may by any means be produced.	The person by whom the arrangements necessary for the making of the rewording of the film were made (s 9(2)(a).).	As above, in this case release meaning first shown in public.	70 years from the death of the last survivor of: The principal director, the dialogue author, the author of the screenplay or the composer of specifically created music. In the event that there is no one falling within the above categories, copyright will expire at the end of the period of 50 years from the end of the calendar year in which the film was made.
Broadcast (s 6.)	A transmission by wireless telegraphy of visual images, sounds or other information which either is capable of being lawfully received by members of the public or is transmitted for presentation to members of the public. A transmission is not a broadcast if it is encrypted	The person making the broadcast or, where relay of another broadcast is involved, the person making the other broadcast. (s 9(2)(b).).	50 years from the end of year in which the broadcast was made or the programme was included in a cable programme service. *See* CDPA, s 14(1). Copyright in a repeat broadcast expires at the	No change.

COPYRIGHT IN DIFFERENT CATEGORIES OF WORK 3.10

Table 3.2 Continued

Category of work (CDPA section)	Definition and exclusions	Author (CDPA section)	Existing duration	Duration Directive
	and decoding equipment has not been made available to the public by or with the authority either of the person making the transmission or the person providing the contents of the transmission.		same time as copyright in the original. Cannot 'roll over' copyright period by re-broadcasting.	
Cable programme (s 7.)	Any items included in a cable programme service. A cable programme service means a service consisting wholly or mainly in sending visual images, sound or other information by means of a telecommunication system (otherwise than by wireless telegraphy), for reception either at two or more places or for showing to members of the public.	The person providing the service in which the programme is included. (s 9(2)(c).)	As above. Same proviso as above as regards repeating programmes.	No change.
Published edition (s 8.)	There is copyright in the typographical arrangement of the published edition of eg, a book. This prevents the making of a	The publisher. (s 9(2)(d).)	25 years from end of year of publication.	No change.

47

Table 3.2 Copyright in different categories of work

Category of work (CDPA section)	Definition and exclusions	Author (CDPA section)	Existing duration	Duration Directive
	facsimile copy (ie, an identical copy which may be reduced or enlarged in scale (CDPA, s 178) of the printed page. The right does not apply to the extent that the published edition reproduces the typographical arrangement of a previous edition; and it only prevents the making of a facsimile copy.			
A computer-generated work (s 178.)	Work generated by computer in circumstances such that there is no human author.	In the case of a literary, dramatic, musical or artistic work, the person by whom the arrangements necessary for the creation of the work are undertaken. (s 9(3).)	50 years from the end of the calendar year in which the work was made.	Depends on how the work is categorised. If it is a 'film', the period will be 70 years from the death of the last of the specified to die; otherwise, no change. The UK does not consider this type of work to be covered by the Directive.
Performance (s 180.)	A live dramatic or musical performance; a live reading or recital; or a live performance of a variety act.	Performer. (s 180.)	50 years from the end of the calendar year in which the performance takes place.	No material change: 50 years from the end of the calendar year in which the performance takes place or if during that period a recording of the performance is released, 50 years from the end of the calendar year in which it is released (first published, played, shown in public, broadcast or included in a

• 4 •

EU COPYRIGHT LAW

4.1 HARMONISATION

As part of its level playing field policy, the European Commission (EC) has been seeking to harmonise many aspects of intellectual property law. It has not sought to do this by creating, for example, a European Copyright Act but rather by specifying in the various Directives, in the tradition of international treaties, minimum copyright standards, leaving individual nations to legislate to incorporate these minimum standards into national law. This may be the best that anyone could expect could be achieved in the short term, but it will leave standardisation and detailed harmonisation at the mercy of national legislators, with the possibility of substantial discord between Member States instead of the intended harmony.

The Directives do not currently seek to harmonise other issues such as originality, although attempts are being made in the Database Directive (and have been made in the Software Directive) to define that expression. Details of the Directives are set out in Table 3.1.

Among the reasons for harmonisation has been a desire:

- to avoid the current situation where goods manufactured in one Member State can be prevented from being imported into another by reason of different copyright laws;
- to maintain or increase protection currently enjoyed by rightsholders in the EU;
- to make copyright more valuable to protect the increasingly heavy investment that is now often required before there is any return, eg, in the field of classical music.

4.2 EC SOFTWARE DIRECTIVE

The European Council Directive on the Legal Protection of Computer Programs of 14 May 1991, 91/250/EEC [1991] OJ L122/42 (the 'Software Directive') was the first EC measure to harmonise aspects of national copyright law.

The Software Directive was implemented in the UK by the Copyright (Computer Programs) Regulations 1992 (SI No 3233) (the 'Regulations') which came into force on 1 January 1993 and apply to all computer programs whenever created and to contracts entered into after that date.

From a multimedia perspective the Software Directive has substantive relevance, concerned as it is with a product which as an 'engine' or 'backbone' supports all multimedia applications and is of fundamental importance to their practical and commercial development. The Software Directive attempts to deal with the creation, loading, transmission and use of software and as such tackles most of the acts associated with both on- and off-line multimedia products.

4.2.1 PROTECTION OF ALL ELEMENTS OF A COMPUTER PROGRAM

It confirmed that a computer program is protected by copyright as a literary work if it is the author's own intellectual creation. Protection is granted to all natural or legal persons eligible as authors under national copyright legislation as applied to literary works. This protection is extended to preparatory materials, such as graphs or flow diagrams which lead to the production of computer programs. In the absence of a licence, there is no automatic right for a person to use a computer program, because the act of running the program on a computer will necessarily involve its reproduction. The Regulations introduced a number of new rights for lawful users of software, in some cases in the face of express prohibition in a licence.

4.2.2 LAWFUL USER RIGHTS

A lawful user is defined as a person who has a right to use a program whether under a licence 'or otherwise'. This is understood to include a licensee or someone deriving title under a licensee (such as an employee or contractor or someone entitled to use a program by some other, for example statutory, authority). A lawful user of a computer program may make backup copies of that program without permission from the copyright owner provided that the copies are necessary for the lawful use of the program. This right exists even if there is a term in the user's licence which purports to restrict or prohibit the right to make backup copies.

Decompiling a program

A lawful user has, in certain circumstances, the right to 'decompile' a program (ie, to convert it from a low-level to a higher-level language and in so doing, to copy it) provided that:

- It must be necessary to decompile in order to obtain the information necessary to create an independent program which can be operated with the decompiled program or with another program.
- The information so obtained may not be used for any purpose other than the permitted objective.

These conditions will not be met if the information is readily available to the user, eg if it is freely provided by the program's licensor, as is commonly provided for in software licences.

For the limitations on decompiling, please refer to the Regulations.

Studying a program

A lawful user also has the right, which cannot be prohibited or restricted by licence, to use 'any device or means' to observe, study or test the functioning of a computer program in order to understand the ideas and principles which underlie any element of it.

Copying or adaptation

The copying or adaptation of a computer program by a lawful user is permitted provided that it is necessary for his lawful use and it is not prohibited under any term or condition of an agreement which permits his use of the program.

Exhaustion of rights

Under CDPA 1988, s 19 the copyright owner's right to restrict the issue of copies to the public is exhausted once copies of the work are put in to circulation in the EC. This right is extended to other copyright works by the Rental and Lending Rights Directive (*see* 4.4).

4.3 DURATION OF COPYRIGHT DIRECTIVE

The EU Directive on Duration of Copyright (93/98/EEC of 29 October 1993) has now received implementation in the UK. Implementation did not happen by the deadline of 1 July 1995 set by the EU Council of Ministers. The original draft Regulations were withdrawn following consultation and replaced in November by a new Statutory Instrument which became law on 1 January 1996 (*see* SI 1995 No 3297).

The Directive is a mandatory guideline to relevant European countries. It applies not only to Member States of the EU (including Austria, Sweden and Finland which joined the Union on 1 January 1995) but also to Iceland and Norway as members of the EEA. Each relevant European country has a degree of discretion as to the manner of its implementation of the Directive.

4.3.1 HARMONISATION UPWARDS

The Directive requires the harmonisation *upwards* of the term of copyright to the longest term employed in any of the European nations. This is 70 years, as employed in Germany.

One of the main consequences of the Directive is that the basic term of copyright for literary, dramatic, musical and artistic works must last for at least 70 years after the end of the calendar year of the death of the author. On the other hand, for audio-visual works, the basic term of copyright must last until 70 years after the end of the year of death of the last survivor of a relevant group of people, ie:

- the principal director;
- the author of the screenplay;
- the author of the dialogue;
- the composer of music specifically created for the audio-visual work (as opposed to pre-existing music that is used).

The position is likely to be extremely complicated where a multimedia work qualifies in part as an audio-visual work and in part does not.

4.3.2 EXTENDED OR REVIVED COPYRIGHT

Which works will have their copyright extended, or indeed resurrected? It was originally thought (but not now) that only the following would be subject to the provisions of the Duration Directive:

- works that were written by German nationals or a resident of Germany;
- works which were first, or simultaneously, published in Germany, in France (which in many instances has a 60-year period and a number of war extensions) or in Spain, which had an 80-year period but currently has 60 years.

This would have had a reasonably limited effect on English copyright works because the Berne Convention (*see* 5.3.1) contains, as one of its few exceptions to national treatment, a provision which allows a Member State not to give protection to a foreign work for a longer period than is given to it in its 'home' state. Accordingly, while Germany *could* accord protection to foreign works for 70 years from the death of the author, it does not.[1] Thus, English copyright works which are in the public domain because the author has been dead for over 50 years are *not* currently protected in Germany.

The *Phil Collins* case

Perhaps it would be more correct to say *were not*. The previous understanding of the law was turned on its head by the *Phil Collins* case (Case C-92/92 joined with Case C-326/92) which (essentially) seems to have decided that as a matter of European law, German courts are *not* allowed to distinguish between German nationals and nationals of other EU states. Phil Collins had originally been refused copyright protection in Germany in respect of pirated musical works (from a concert in America) on the grounds that German law gave protection to a German national but (because there was no relevant treaty) not to this particular work. The European Court of Justice (ECJ) decided that it was illegal within the EU to distinguish between nationalities; accordingly, where German nationals were entitled to protection, the German courts were required to give protection to nationals of other Union countries.

Extrapolate from that and it will be apparent that, since the Duration Directive requires any work that is protected in any Member State to have its copyright extended or revived throughout the Union, *all* works written by nationals of EU states may (provided Germany is required to extend copyright protection to those works) now be subject to the increased term. There must be some doubt about the extent of this because Phil Collins was (and still is) a living author and it is not clear whether the ECJ judgment applies to eg, beneficiaries of dead authors (although the current thinking appears to be that it does).

A communication was expected from the Commission regarding the implications of the *Collins* judgment but it now appears the Commission intends to leave individual states to work it out themselves.

> **Example**
>
> A distributor of a film based upon a public domain novel may find that the UK copyright in the novel is revived, making it necessary to acquire rights to exploit the novel in other audio-visual forms.

The longer term of copyright will apply to works in which copyright subsisted immediately before commencement of the Statutory Instrument, that is 31 December 1995. Those other works which, although they may now be in the public domain in the UK but which were still subject to copyright protection in at least one Member State of the EU as at 1 July

DURATION OF COPYRIGHT DIRECTIVE 4.3.2

1995, will enjoy a *revival* of protection in those other states in which they had in the meantime fallen into the public domain. For both types of work, the copyright period will now be 70 years from the end of the year of the author's death. Accordingly, some revived periods will be short: for an author who died in 1926, his work fell into the public domain in the UK on 1 January 1977. The revised copyright will run from 1 January 1996 and will expire 70 years from death, ie, 31 December 1996.

There are important distinctions between *extended* and *revived* works. The effect of the Statutory Instrument is to give the extended copyright to the person who is the owner of the copyright in the work immediately before the commencement date. Any copyright licence subsisting at the commencement date which was for the full original period of copyright will continue to have effect during the extended copyright period.

So far as revived copyrights are concerned, it is in general the person who was the owner of the copyright when it expired who will own the revived copyright.

It will not be an infringement to exploit works in which there is revived copyright where those works were made before 1 July 1995 or indeed to do anything in pursuance of arrangements made before 1 January 1995 (at a time when copyright had already expired) for the exploitation of the work in question. Where it is not reasonably possible to find out the name and address of the person entitled to the copyright it is not an infringement to do anything after commencement which would conflict with the revived copyright.

Where moral rights were waived (or asserted) before expiry of the original copyright period, those waivers and assertions continue to have effect after revival.

In the case of revived copyright there is deemed to be a licence of right to do, after 31 December 1996, any of the acts restricted by copyright. This licence of right is subject only to the giving of reasonable notice of intention to carry out a restricted act and to payment of a reasonable royalty. Failure to agree the fee or royalty will not invalidate the licence but application can be made to the Copyright Tribunal to fix the royalty or fee.

It is interesting to note that the UK government does not regard computer-generated works as falling within the scope of the Directive.

As far as works which are not of EU origin are concerned, the UK government has further underlined that the UK will apply the new rules on duration of copyright to non-EC works only on condition that the country of origin grants reciprocal protection to works of UK origin.

> **Example**
>
> The term of protection for a literary work under current US copyright law falls short of the new longer term harmonised by the Directive; in the USA, it is currently 50 years. Thus, a US literary work which is in protection in the UK on 1 July 1995 will not enjoy the new longer term of the author's life plus 70 years, but will instead only be protected for the current 50 years. Similarly, if such a work were in protection, say, in Austria but not in the UK on 1 July 1995, there will be no revival of protection in the UK. The position may be different in the different EU Member States where it will depend upon each state's own legislation.

4.4 RENTAL AND LENDING RIGHTS DIRECTIVE

The Rental and Lending Rights Directive, 92/100/EEC, once implemented, will extend the existing UK law which currently includes rental, but only of sound recordings and films, as a restricted act. The much wider spread of benefits which will be available once the supplementary legislation passes into law include the following:

- Rental rights will be extended to virtually all copyright works.
- Those entitled to benefit will be extended from film and record producers to all authors.
- Performers will have an exclusive right to authorise or prohibit the rental of works containing their performances.
- Rental rights owners will have a legal right to a 'reasonable proportion' of rental income.

Where there is a contract, except where the contrary appears, the rental rights are deemed to be assigned to the producer or publisher; and in any event, the author or performer will have an unwaivable right to 'equitable remuneration'.

Whether a CD-ROM is a 'work' entitled to rental rights will depend upon whether it is a film or not. The right to equitable remuneration is unwaivable and not readily capable of definition ahead of time. Accordingly, while the contract may seek to specify, for example, that the basic fee payable includes any future right to equitable remuneration, such a provision may not be effective. What is 'equitable' may have to be judged in hindsight.

Sample clause: Rental rights

You hereby acknowledge that the Fee is inclusive of full consideration for all rights in the Performance and if under the provisions of any legislation adopted by any member state of the EU in compliance with the Directive on Rental and Lending Right, dated 19 November 1992 or of any legislation which complies with any such Directive you are or become entitled to any additional payment, then we shall be entitled to make a fair and reasonable apportionment of the sums payable hereunder between the amount which will be deemed to be a payment of or on account of such additional payment on the one hand and an amount for the remainder of the rights granted by you hereunder on the other hand and you will accept the first apportioned amount as being equitable and adequate to satisfy your said entitlement.

NB: This clause should be treated with care: it may not work, since the objective of the Directive is to give a continuing interest in income.

4.5 THE DATABASE DIRECTIVE (96/9/EEC)

The CDPA, an Act drafted in 1988, does not mention the word 'database'. The Database Directive, 96/9/EEC, (OJ 1995 C156) attempts to harmonise EU law on the protection of databases. Currently, the UK has a higher level of protection than continental European countries because it sets a low threshold for the originality required. The UK has a 'sweat of the brow' test, whereas continental Europe, in the main, requires there to have been an author's own intellectual input, generally a higher test of intellectual creativity. Accordingly, English law protects the compilation of a database of otherwise public domain material such as addresses. Someone who goes to the trouble and effort of compiling a list of addresses is entitled to protect not the addresses themselves, but the *compilation* of them.

DRAFT DATABASE DIRECTIVE 4.5

Continental European laws would, in general, not protect such a compilation. It is in part on that difference that a strong UK database industry has developed.

> **Example**
>
> The USA, having an Anglo-Saxon legal tradition, is a subscriber to the 'sweat of the brow' test. However, a recent US case, the *Feist* case, 111S C1282, 20 IPR 121 (1991), has thrown doubt on that (although others say there has been no change in the law as a result of *Feist*). In this case, a telephone company was held not to be able to prevent a rival using its directory as the basis for its own work. The facts were somewhat special in that the telephone company had a statutory duty to produce the directory. In essence the court said that an alphabetical listing of essential public domain material in those circumstances was not capable of protection: *some* originality of selection or arrangement was required.

The law in England is quite clear: the *Waterlow Directory* case (*Waterlow Directories Ltd v Reed Information Services Ltd* (1992) FSR 409) confirmed the 'sweat of the brow' test. The defendant used Waterlow's directory to mail out to the persons listed in it, with the intention of creating his own directory from the replies. The judge held that it was clear that a person could not *copy* entries from a directory and use such copies to compile his own directory. Emphasis is placed on the word copy because that was the issue before the court: it might of course be possible to *use* the information in a directory in compiling another one provided legally defined copying did not take place.

The Commission recognises that the publishing community, whether traditional print publishers or the new electronic publishing, is unlikely to be willing to invest heavily in the future of new electronic highways, new services and new products unless it has adequate legal protection which will enable it to secure a return on the investment. The legal system has to be able to protect against piracy, to ensure security and to enable record and reward systems to work. It therefore proposed a new Council Directive to strengthen protection on databases.

The Council of Ministers reached a common position on this proposed Directive on 10 July 1995. The Directive was adopted by Council on 26 February 1996 and is to be implemented in national laws by 1 January 1998.

The Directive applies to databases.

> **Database**
>
> - A database is defined as a 'collection of works, data or other independent materials arranged in a systematic or methodical way and capable of being individually accessed by electronic or other means'.
>
> This definition therefore includes both electronic and certain manual databases.

Two rights are provided:

(1) Copyright to protect any original selection or arrangement incorporated into the database. It is the *selecting* or *arranging* which is protected, not the contents.

> **Restricted acts under art 5 of the Directive**
>
> (a) temporary or permanent reproduction by any means and in any form in whole or in part;
> (b) translation, adaptation, arrangement and any other alteration;
> (c) any form of distribution to the public of the database or of copies. (The first sale within the EU of a copy of the database by the rightholder or with his consent exhausts the right to control resale within the EU of that copy);
> (d) any communication, display or performance to the public;
> (e) any reproduction, distribution, communication, display or performance to the public of the results of the acts referred to in (b) above.
>
> Exceptions permit a lawful user to do any of the restricted acts which are necessary for the purposes of accessing the contents of the database and normal use of those contents. Other optional exception items, which Member States may adopt, are:
>
> (a) reproduction for private purposes of a non-electronic database;
> (b) use for the sole purposes of illustration for teaching or scientific research, to the extent justified by the non-commercial purpose;
> (c) use for the purposes of public security or for the purposes of the proper performance of an administrative or judicial procedure;
> (d) other exceptions to copyrights which are traditionally permitted by Member States, without prejudice to points (a), (b) and (c).
>
> None of these points may be interpreted so as unreasonably to prejudice the rightholder's legitimate interests, or to conflict with the normal exploitation of the database (Berne Convention).
>
> Many will, however, be worried that allowing these exceptions opens the door to much wider exceptions than currently exist for other protected works.

(2) An independent unfair extraction right. This is a new 15-year year *sui generis* right to restrict unauthorised transfer or distribution of copies by any means of transmission, taking or reuse of all or a substantial part of the contents of any database. To obtain the protection of this second right the database maker must show *substantial investment in obtaining, verifying or presentation* of the contents.

The owner of the new unfair extraction right will be the maker responsible for obtaining, verifying or presenting the contents. Where there is more than one company there will be more than one owner.

Database makers looking for protection under the Directive must show that they are EU nationals or corporations or that reciprocity rules apply. Databases produced outside, but imported into, the EU will not enjoy protection of the unfair extraction right but will, of course, enjoy copyright protection for any original selection or arrangement.

> **Database 'Maker'**
>
> - The makers, or their successors in title must be EU nationals or corporations.
> - An EU corporation is one formed in accordance with the law of a Member State, having its registered office, central administration or principal place of business within the EU. (If only the registered office is in the EU, the corporation's operations must possess an effective and continuous link with the economy of a Member State.)

4.5.1 FOREIGN COMPANIES

Protection under the Directive is proposed to be given to databases 'whose makers are nationals of a Member State or who have their habitual residence on the territory of the Community'.

Article 3(4) of the Directive proposes that an employer will have exclusive rights to exercise all economic rights in a database which is created by an employee in the execution of his duties or following instructions given by the employer (unless there is provision to the contrary in any contract).

Any company or firm incorporated pursuant to the legislation of a Member State which has only its registered office within the Community will only get protection under the Directive if its operations 'possess an effective and continuous link with the economy of one of the Member States'.

The Council will be empowered, on a proposal from the Commission, to enter into agreements, presumably reciprocal in nature, in respect of databases produced in third countries and falling outside the above provisions. No reciprocal protection may exceed the 15-year term of protection offered to databases within the Community under the Directive.

If the foregoing proposals are enacted into the Directive there will be no protection for databases created by foreign companies with no economic, legal or residential connection with the Community. It is too early to say how foreign companies should or could protect their databases within the Community. The obvious suggestion is to create or maintain an 'effective and continuous link' with a Member State; but what 'effective' means and how it is to be measured remain to be seen.

4.5.2 MATERIALS

The Directive specifically provides that it does not derogate from any separate subsisting rights in the materials incorporated in the database. The copyright owners of the materials incorporated in the database therefore retain their rights. Accordingly there will in effect be three layers of protection:

- the copyright in the materials;
- the copyright in the original selection or arrangement of the materials; *and*
- the *sui generis* right.

The Council of Ministers has deleted the compulsory licensing provisions in the previous draft. These compulsory licensing proposals worried the UK database industry, which was concerned not to lose its current protection. All is not safe: the European Parliament may try to reintroduce them.

There is no exhaustion of rights arising from on-line transmission of the contents of a database (a service), but exhaustion of rights does apply where a material copy is sold (which is not defined).

The copyright period will run for the life of the individuals responsible for producing the database and for 70 years following the death of the last of them. Member States will be entitled to choose who those authors are and the UK is expected to continue to allow a company to be the author of a database.

The *sui generis* unfair extraction right will last for 15 years and, if and to the extent that there is any substantial change (evaluated qualitatively or quantitively) to the contents of the database, the amended database will enjoy a further 15 years of protection from (each) such change. It seems the 'old' database(s) will be unprotected once the 15 years has expired. Exactly how the courts will evaluate quantity and quality remains to be seen.

UK databases which are in existence on the date when the Directive is implemented will continue to enjoy full copyright protection for the remainder of the copyright term so long as they were, when created, 'original' in the sense of the old 'sweat of the brow' test. UK databases produced after the implementation date will become subject to the new regime.

Recommendations

Database makers should keep an audit trail of:
- the work done in obtaining, verifying and presenting the database;
- the criteria used to determine selection, arrangement and presentation;
- (separately) the investment made in putting it all together.

Exhaustion of rights will not apply to providers of databases to on-line services as each transmission will require their consent. Database providers must, however, ensure that contracts in favour of on-line suppliers contain strict contractual conditions on use and reuse of the contents by the on-line supplier and its customers. Exhaustion of rights *does* apply to the first sale of a material copy, eg, a CD-ROM. Providers should consider whether it is practical not to sell the CD-ROM but to supply it by way of rental or, as in the software industry, by way of licence, in order to have a better chance of avoiding exhaustion of rights.

Points of interest

- Because the compulsory licensing proposals have been dropped, a refusal to license will be subject only to EU and national competition rules. *See Magill,* Case C241 and 242/P 1995 at 4.7. *(Cont'd)*

> - A number of exceptions to copyright and *sui generis* protection are available and Member States can choose from a menu of them.
>
> The *sui generis* right will only be available to non-EU databases on the basis of reciprocity.

4.6 EC GREEN PAPER

The European Commission has recently published its Green Paper on Copyright and Related Rights in the Information Society which deals with intellectual property rights in a multimedia context (COM(95)382), adopted on 19 July 1995. Although the Green Paper is primarily a discussion document for the purpose of developing EU policy in this area, it highlights a number of issues which are, or which are becoming, increasingly significant. A very brief synopsis of these issues can be found at Appendix 11.

4.7 COMPETITION LAW AND COPYRIGHT (*MAGILL*)

One question many copyright lawyers will be seeking to answer in the future is whether the *Magill* case C241 and 242/P 1995 represents the high-water mark of the European tide flowing against copyright or whether the competition issues raised in that case will lead to the undermining of the principles of the Berne Convention and the author's right to determine when, where and how to put his or her work on to the market and thus to the prising open of the Pandora's box of compulsory licensing.

The *Magill* case involved an Irish company which sought to break the monopoly which the BBC and the RTE exercised over information about forthcoming programmes. Both broadcasters published their own magazine (in the BBC's case the *Radio Times*) and licensed, without charge, newspapers to produce minimal information only up to two days ahead. There was a total refusal to license the provision of weekly scheduling.

Magill decided to publish its own TV and radio listing and was sued by both the BBC and the RTE. In Dublin, the plaintiffs were successful in obtaining an injunction prohibiting Magill from continuing the practice. Magill thereupon complained to the EC which, subsequently supported by the Court of First Instance in Luxembourg, determined that the BBC and RTE were abusing a dominant position and that in such circumstances art 36 of the Treaty of Rome was overridden by the provisions of art 85 of the EC Treaty.

RTE appealed to the ECJ which, going against the argument of its own advocate general (who supported the right of a copyright owner to determine when, where and how his copyright work was published), upheld the Commission and the CFI. The reasoning was expressed to be that:

(a) the BBC and RTE were the sole source of this information; and
(b) they were using this exclusivity, without justification, to prevent the arrival on the market of a competing magazine.

Many observers have concluded that the case was decided on such special facts that it will serve as no precedent for the future, but there are others who are concerned that the anti-copyright and pro-competition elements in Brussels will use the case as a wedge further to reduce the scope of copyright.

---

[1] There does exist a bilateral treaty between Germany and the USA dating from the last century pursuant to which Germany gives US works 70 years' protection in Germany. The current undertaking of the British government is that the Directive will not require the UK, therefore, to give US works 70 years' protection in the UK. The UK will remain free to require reciprocity.

• 5 •

INTERNATIONAL COPYRIGHT

5.1 COPYRIGHT IS A NATIONAL RIGHT

UK copyright can only be enforced within the UK. Accordingly, if the owner of a UK copyright wishes to enforce his rights outside the UK he has to rely on local law and one of the international conventions (*see* below). Conversely, the owner of a French copyright cannot, unless he is a UK qualified person or the work is a UK qualifying work, enforce his right in the UK unless he can establish that one of the international conventions and UK law give him a right to protection.

5.2 DIFFERENT APPROACHES OF CIVIL AND COMMON LAW

The civil law (*droit d'auteur*) approach to copyright assumes paramount importance of the author. The author can only be an individual; civil law cannot contemplate a company being an author. Common law considers the author to be a mere part of the process and has no difficulty in allowing a company to be an author.

Civil law assumes that while an author can part with his economic rights, he cannot part with his moral rights. Common law has compromised in its recent introduction of moral rights into English law by allowing an author to waive his rights, effectively to part with (the right to exercise) them.

These two separate approaches of civil and common law are inevitably going to converge as harmonisation of laws progresses. The UK is, with Ireland, one of only two Member States with a common law tradition. Already it is possible to see the civil law approach in, eg, the Rental and Lending Rights Directive which provides that there will be a number of authors of a film. Individual countries can decide which of a number of individuals will be authors but one of those must be the director. Accordingly, if a multimedia work is a film one of the authors will be its director (if there is one).

5.3 CONVENTIONS

The three major copyright conventions are the Berne Convention of 1886, the Universal Copyright Convention (1952) and the Rome Convention (1961). The signatories to these conventions are listed in Appendix 10.

5.3.1 BERNE CONVENTION

Article 1 states that the purpose of the Convention is: 'the protection of the rights of authors in their literary and artistic works'. Article 2 describes these as 'every production in the literary, scientific and artistic domain, whatever may be the mode or form of its expression' and gives examples.[1]

The protection of the Convention does not apply to news of the day, nor to miscellaneous facts giving the character of mere items of news.

Articles 14 and 14(*bis*) extend the protection given under art 2 to cinematograph films but without prejudice to the rights of the authors of any underlying works.

The Convention was signed in 1886 and appears to have difficulty in matching advances in technology; for instance it does not unequivocally require its 100 plus signatories to protect computer programs or databases.

WIPO has before it a proposal for a protocol to the Berne Convention.

5.3.2 UNIVERSAL COPYRIGHT CONVENTION

The Universal Copyright Convention provides that each contracting state shall give adequate and effective protection to the rights of authors and other copyright proprietors in literary, scientific and artistic works, including writings, musical, dramatic and cinematographic works, and paintings, engravings and sculpture.

The Convention does not describe the details of protection which is to be afforded by the contracting states, but sets certain minimum standards.

5.3.3 ROME CONVENTION

The International Convention for the Protection of Performers, Producers of Phonograms and Broadcasting Organisations (1961) (the Rome Convention) gives international protection to the makers of sound recordings, performers and broadcasting organisations.

5.4 GATT/TRIPS

The General Agreement on Tariffs and Trade/Trade Related Aspects of Intellectual Property Rights (GATT/TRIPs) Accord is an ambitious free trade agreement. The benefits to the new technology industry from reduction in tariff and non-tariff trade barriers and from the provisions which strengthen intellectual property protection are wide-reaching; but it is the structural changes to the legal standards for the protection of intellectual property which we concentrate on here.

The TRIPs part of GATT was driven by the Americans who are very keen to protect their computer and technology industries. It was inspired by the growing realisation that existing laws were not protecting the new technology intellectual property owners: the software developers and the developers of biotechnology products.

The two important general principles of protection are national treatment and most favoured nation treatment. The former requires countries to give nationals of other member countries no less favourable treatment than it gives its own nationals (save only as permitted by the Paris, Berne and Rome Conventions, which exceptions recognise the right of a country not to give protection to nationals of other countries which do not provide adequate protection to its own nationals).

GATT/TRIPS

Most favoured nation treatment is the principle that any advantage, favour, privilege or immunity given to nationals of one member should be given to nationals of other members with similar exceptions as above. There are anti-competitive savings allowing Member States to adopt appropriate remedies or controls, including exclusive grant back conditions, conditions preventing challenges to validity and coercive package licensing.

Moral rights were excluded from TRIPs at the insistence of the USA. Copyright protection follows generally in accordance with US copyright law and computer programs, both source and object code, are recognised as literary works enjoying the exclusive rights given to such works. Databases and data compilations, to the extent they constitute intellectual creations, are also protected as to the compilation but not to the data itself.

5.4.1 ENFORCEMENT

Members must set up adequate and effective enforcement procedures provided they do not create new trade barriers or anti-competitive weapons. There must be access to fair and equitable administrative or judicial proceedings. The reasoned decisions of these proceedings must be given in writing. The minimum power must be to injunct infringement, to award damages, expenses and lawyers' fees and to order an account of profits and payment of damages, delivery up of infringing goods and disclosure of third party infringers. There must also be criminal penalties for wilful trade-mark, counterfeiting or copyright piracy on a commercial scale.

It will take anything from two to ten years to get the GATT/TRIPs provisions implemented into national laws but it does provide a basic floor of protection.

A new set of dispute settlement procedures has been set up to deal with disputes between members. Ultimately the penalty against the offending country is an order to pay compensation with trade retaliation left as a measure of last resort.

---

[1] The works cover:
- books, pamphlets and other writings;
- lectures, addresses, sermons and other works of the same nature;
- dramatic or dramatic-musical works, choreographic works and entertainments in dumb show, musical compositions with or without words;
- cinematographic works to which are assimilated works expressed by a process analogous to cinematography;
- works of drawing, painting, architecture, sculpture, engraving and lithography;
- photographic works to which are assimilated works expressed by a process analogous to photography;
- works of applied art, illustrations;
- maps, plans, sketches, and three-dimensional works relative to geography, typography, architecture or science.

• 6 •

COPYRIGHT PROBLEMS AND POSSIBLE SOLUTIONS

6.1 SOFTWARE COPYRIGHT

Unlike other literary works, computer programs exist at several levels, both in eye-readable form as:

- design documents—flow charts, etc;
- high-level language, eg, BASIC or C+;
- assembly code;
- (in use) screen displays and format;

and also in a form understood only by the computer hardware as:

- machine or object code;
- microprograms;
- flows in the digital logic circuit.

Establishing when elements of a computer program have been copied and when this amounts to copyright infringement has proved to be a difficult task. In the software field building and improving upon the products of others is a far more common and legitimate practice than in the more traditional domains of literary works. Further, while consideration of structure, function and visual display are of limited relevance in book publishing, these elements go towards the crucial 'look and feel' of a software product. It is possible to copy the structure or even the visual displays of a computer program without slavishly copying the code used to create them in the original program (or vice versa), and the definition of this so-called 'non-literal' copying has proved particularly problematic. Thus some argue that the experience of protecting computer programs as literary works has been unsatisfactory, leading to confusing and uncertain case law as the copyright principles of traditional literary works are made to fit uneasily with computer technology.[1]

These points are of course highly relevant for multimedia.

6.1.1 STATUTORY FRAMEWORK

The CDPA (*see* Chapter 3) attempts no definition of computer program or computer. Sensible pragmatism in an age of fast-moving technological change this may be, but it leaves the difficulty of distinguishing between hardware and software, and in the multimedia field, where software is interlinked with other elements and copyright works. The key protection afforded to computer programs by copyright is the restriction on copying, unlicensed use and the making of adaptations. 'Copying' of a literary work is defined as a reproduction in any material form; including storage in any medium by electronic means and making transient or incidental copies (CDPA, s 17). 'Electronic' is defined widely as any means activated by electric, magnetic, electro-magnetic, electro-chemical or electro-mechanical energy but does not explicitly extend to light or optical technology (CDPA, s 178). The CDPA, s 21(3) defines an adaptation of a computer program as an arrangement or altered version of the program or translation of it. For computer programs, a translation includes:

> A version of the program in which it is converted into or out of a computer language or code or into a different computer language or code [otherwise than incidentally in the course of running the program]. (s 21(4))

In addition, the Software Directive (*see* 4.2) introduced further provisions. It does not define computer programs but does make clear what should be within, and what beyond, the scope of protection. Included are preparatory design materials and programs incorporated within hardware. Excluded are user or maintenance manuals; ideas and principles underlying any element of a program or its interfaces; and program logic, algorithms and languages in so far as they too are merely ideas and principles.

The ideas behind a computer program are not as accessible as those contained in traditional literary works. To understand how a program operates, the relevant elements of machine or object code first need to be translated into human-readable form, which in itself constitutes an infringing act. As a result the Software Directive allows the lawful users of protected computer programs to do certain acts without infringing copyright in the program: a lawful user may decompile a program, ie convert it into higher-level language, in order to obtain information necessary to create a new program, within given limits; he may also make backup copies of the program, and further copy or adapt it if necessary for his lawful use of the program (CDPA, s 50(A)–(C)).

While the statutory framework for copyright protection of computer software has existed in the UK for a number of years there have been few decisions in this country with which to assess its application. Most commentators have looked to the large body of USA case law for further guidance on the boundaries of copyright protection for computer software.

> **Note**
> A number of these decisions involve defendant software programmers who, having originally produced software for the plaintiff, are sued for infringement when they produce similar programs for themselves or others. In such cases, whether software or multimedia products, it should be noted that trade secrets, confidentiality, contract and employment law may in practice be as relevant as copyright for controlling the situation.

It is well established in most legal systems that copyright will not protect a mere idea or principle. As the Software Directive states at art 1(2):

> Protection in accordance with this Directive shall apply to the expression in any form of a computer program. Ideas and principles which underlie any element of the computer program,

including those which underlie its interfaces, are not protected by copyright under this Directive.

Indeed this already represented the position under UK law and no amendments to the CDPA were considered necessary to deal with this aspect of the Software Directive. Yet computer programs are defined widely in the Software Directive, to include preparatory design materials, so the practical scope of this exception is not as wide as it first appears.

This is not the case in the USA, where particular emphasis is placed upon this distinction that while ideas as such are not protectable by copyright, the expression of them is, through what is known as the 'idea/expression dichotomy'. It attempts to define a precise dividing line between protected material and material which is too abstract and therefore unprotected. However determining this with software has proved to be a difficult task and moreover this approach is not now accepted at least by some judges under English law (*see* below).

Problems have arisen from the fact that functional works have traditionally received limited protection under USA copyright law and that, under the so-called 'merger doctrine', it has been argued that where there is only one way of expressing an idea, that expression will be considered to be in the public domain and unprotectable. As a result, complex and contradictory case law covering copyright in computer programs has arisen in the USA.

6.1.2 CASE LAW

One case (*Whelan Associates v Jaslon Dental Laboratory* [1987] FSR I) dealt with these issues by holding that the idea behind a program should be considered to be its purpose, in that situation running a dental laboratory. It said that if there are several ways of running a dental laboratory then each of these may be considered to be expressions of that underlying idea and hence protectable by copyright.

Other cases (eg, *Computer Associates International Inc v Altai Inc* (1992) 23 IPR 385) rejected this approach and proposed an alternative which attempted to 'filter out' a 'core of protectable expression'.

This latter method was adopted in one of the first English cases to deal with the non-literal copying of a computer program, *John Richardson Computers Ltd v Flanders* [1993] FSR 497 at 527. Copyright had been held to subsist in the overall structure of a computer program as a form of literary expression (*Computer Aided Systems (UK) Ltd v Bolwell* [1990] IPD 13051) and *Richardson* confirmed this, also holding that copyright did not subsist in the screen display as a literary work since the screen display was not the program but just a product of it.[2] *Richardson* held that a court could, and should, look beyond the program's structure and organisation or screen display in claims of copyright infringement. The correct test to follow was to decide whether the plaintiff's program as a whole was entitled to copyright and then to decide whether any similarities between it and the defendant's program, which were attributable to copying, formed a substantial part of the plaintiff's program. Controversially, it was held that in evaluating what constituted a substantial part, a similar, if less complex, approach to that taken in the USA (*see* eg the *Computer Associates* case above and *Sega Enterprises Ltd v Accolade Inc* 997 F 2d 1510 (1992)) should be adopted. This would involve a court discovering the original program's 'abstraction levels', ie, analysing each stage of the development of the product, from the basic concept behind each section to the actual code used, in order to identify the key elements on which it was based. These abstractions must then be filtered to disclose a 'core' of protectable material. This process of filtration will exclude from consideration:

- elements dictated by efficiency, that is those elements which result from the expression of an idea where there is only one way to express the idea;
- elements dictated by external factors, that is elements which result from the description of the same facts, which can only be described in a particular way;
- elements taken from the public domain or those elements in which the plaintiff does not own the copyright.

A comparison must then be made between what is left—the 'protectable core'—and the defendant's program to determine if copying has taken place and if so whether of a substantial part.

This test was strongly criticised in the case of *Ibcos Computers Ltd v Barclays Mercantile Highland Finance Ltd* [1994] FSR 275. The court in *Ibcos* warned that it was both dangerous and unnecessary to try and apply US decisions in the UK since, as we have seen, the US law of copyright differs from that of the UK. It proposed an alternative 'back-to-basics' approach, starting from the UK position that if the idea embodied in the plaintiff's work is sufficiently general, the mere taking of that idea will not infringe. If, however, the idea has been developed in detail in the plaintiff's work and the defendant reproduces that then he would infringe. As a result, the court should ask the following questions:

(1) What are the work or works in which the plaintiff claims copyright?
(2) Is each such work 'original'?
(3) Was there copying from that work?
(4) If there was copying, has a substantial part of that work been reproduced?

It was acknowledged that the answer to these questions would be a matter of degree in each case, but a good guide was to consider whether there had been 'an over-borrowing of the skill, labour and judgement' which had gone into the original copyright work. Like all questions of copyright infringement, this would involve a value judgement, helped especially by expert evidence.

Ibcos stressed that, under English law, if skill, labour and judgement had been used to produce a program, the fact that it was functional or could only be expressed in one or a limited number of ways did not prevent it enjoying protection. By contrast there might be no protection for design features which, although of interest and value to the user, did not require skill, labour or judgement on the part of the programmer. The concept of a 'core of protectable expression' merely complicated the matter and ignored the fact that, in the UK, copyright may subsist in a collection of non-copyright material if skill, labour or judgement had gone into its compilation. If a defendant takes from a plaintiff something which is original and detailed enough to be an 'original literary work' in its own right, then the defendant has appropriated a copyright work and not an unprotected idea.

It has yet to be seen whether this rejection of specific US-style tests will be maintained in this country.[3] However, even under the 'traditional' UK copyright approach of *Ibcos*, determining just which elements of a program's function, structure or appearance are actually protected and the true scope of copyright protection for computer software is currently far from certain. There is a reluctance to stretch the traditional principles behind copyright[4] to provide what might be a more appropriate approach to copying protection in the software field.[5] This is clearly important for multimedia and the implications are examined further below.

6.2 DATABASE/COMPILATION COPYRIGHT

Electronic databases are important to multimedia since, like computer programs, they are digitised products that have been exploited commercially under the protection of copyright for a number of years. This category of work may perhaps be applied to a multimedia product on the basis that it too is a collection of different sets of digitised data. Indeed the Database Directive (*see* 4.5), recognises databases as 'the hypermarkets of the future for the products of intellectual activity'. The concept of an electronic database in its widest form—the storage of a large body of information by computer which can be processed and retrieved as required—applies just as well to new multimedia works as to more mundane and established products such as electronic telephone directories.

There is currently no mention of databases in the UK's copyright legislation. Instead, as has been discussed above (*see* 4.5), protection has traditionally been afforded to databases either as literary works in their own right as texts or as 'compilations', which are included within the definition of a literary work under the CDPA, s 3. It is important to note that although a compilation is classified as a literary work for the purpose of defining the rights of the owner, a compilation need not consist merely of text, and a variety of works have been classed under this head including maps (*see Geographica Ltd v Penguin Books Ltd* [1985] FSR 208) and a trade catalogue of illustrations (*Maple & Co v Junior Army and Navy Stores* (1882) 21 ChD 369). The CDPA states that a literary work means 'any work, other than a dramatic or musical work, which is written, spoken or sung' and defines writing as 'any form of notation or code, whether by hand or otherwise and regardless of the method by which, or the medium in or on which, it is recorded', and 'written' shall be construed accordingly. This is quite a wide definition but still might be seen as a restriction on what may qualify as a compilation (*see* an article by Monotti [1993] 5 EIPR 156). Alternatively, a court might be more flexible and consider that the category 'literary work' is merely the particular copyright peg upon which the concept of a compilation is hung. Thus, whether the works incorporated into a multimedia work are literary and artistic works or films, sound recordings or otherwise, the skill and labour used to select, collect and arrange them will be recognised and protected. *See also* the discussion of the *Feist* case and the Database Directive at 4.5.

6.3 COPYRIGHT PROTECTION FOR MULTIMEDIA WORKS

The content of the product may well be protected as a whole by compilation copyright, or the regime introduced to replace it by the Database Directive.

6.3.1 PROTECTION OF ELEMENTS OF MULTIMEDIA PRODUCTS

As mentioned above, there are other categories that may afford protection to multimedia works both as a whole and to particular aspects. Individual elements of a product that are original will be afforded protection, irrespective of the fact that they form part of a multimedia work. Copyright protection for computer programs and compilations/databases will obviously be relevant to the protection of multimedia products. The software engine used for search and retrieval of material will be protected as a literary work under the CDPA as amended by the Software Directive. Where a multimedia product has original film, graphics, sound, and text, these will each have their own separate protection as individual copyright works. The copyright in an on-screen display created by a program must be distinguished from the literary copyright in the program itself. The screen displays of a program or multimedia work could be protected as artistic, though probably not photographic,[6] works or perhaps as films, but this again only provides a partial protection. The whole point of multimedia is that these elements have been brought together to form one product, so should that product—the creative work of a multimedia producer—be protected as a whole?

The producer of a multimedia product has an important creative and production role. Typically, he has first of all originated the concept for the product, then developed the outline and produced or acquired the different elements of the product, brought them together as the finished product, and finally distributed it.

The end product has a number of unique features:

- the selection of the material contained in the product;
- the screen displays: the functionality displayed on the screens, the design of icons and other screen elements and the positioning of the individual screen elements;
- the architecture of the product, the hierarchy of the material and the way in which it is organised.

The individual elements incorporated into the product, the video clips, music, photographs, illustrations and so on are all protected by copyright in their digital format. The software which enables the search and selection of material will also be protected. The whole, however, is greater than the sum of the parts.

In creating the product, the producer has undoubtedly added economic value as well as exercised his creativity. The product has distribution and other exploitation rights which are worth considerably more than that of the individual elements going to make up the program. Should there be special protection for the producer of a multimedia product? The analogy with copyright in a film is indisputable and the history of the protection of film is instructive.

Protection of films

Although the use of cinematograph films as an entertainment was well established at the time the Copyright Act 1911 was drafted, that Act only afforded protection to film through the copyrights existing in the underlying works: as a series of photographs, for the screenplay as a literary work, artistic copyright in the sets of animation, dramatic copyright, and musical copyright in the musical accompaniment on the soundtrack. It was not until the Copyright Act 1956 that UK law created a separate copyright for film.

The Gregory Committee (in its White Paper, 1952) thought it not 'sensible', though 'scientifically exact', to see film as a set of graphic works, or as a collective work, compilation, or work of joint ownership. Instead, it recognised the manner in which a film was, and is, actually produced, namely that a producer takes an idea for a film, develops it, perhaps by setting up a specialist company, secures finance and the appropriate rights, hires personnel and produces the film, perhaps through a second company, and then finally licenses the rights to distribute and exploit the film. The producer who initiates and manages this process, the person 'by whom the arrangements necessary for the making of the film are undertaken', adds clear economic value to the project and deserves his own copyright protection in the finished film. As a result, the author and first owner of the new film copyright was, and still is under the CDPA, defined in these terms (though authorship and copyright ownership of films will be extended once both the Rental and Lending Rights and the Duration of Copyright Directives have been implemented in the UK—*see* 4.4 and 4.3 respectively).

COPYRIGHT PROTECTION FOR MULTIMEDIA WORKS · 6.3.1

Are multimedia products protected as films?

Against this background, an important question arises as to whether there is actually protection for a multimedia product as a film already. The key definition is CDPA, s 5(1). This provides that:

> film means a recording on any medium from which a moving image may by any means be produced.

There is an argument that many multimedia products fall within the CDPA definition of a 'film'.

Multimedia products combine computer-generated displays and digitised pre-existing information to form its images, which are far more diverse than the images that appear in what we currently recognise as a film. In addition, this material is not shown in one single, unchanging sequence, like a film. The choices of the viewer will dictate the sequence in which they appear. This could present a difficulty in fitting a multimedia CD-ROM into the film definition.

There are also many images on a typical CD-ROM that do not move. Clearly the use of text may be far more prevalent in a multimedia CD-ROM than in a feature film: text may make up a much higher percentage of the screens displayed than the opening and closing titles for a conventional film.[7]

A further complication is that the definition of film takes no account of the interactive element of a multimedia product. This does not exist in a normal film, but the definition is wide enough to encompass this element.

Ultimately, whether a multimedia product is protected as a 'film' will depend upon the flexibility of the courts in their interpretation of the CDPA and their willingness to adopt the old copyright adage that something worth copying is worth protecting. If they do, they may squeeze multimedia works, on a case-by-case basis, into the film definition. Three recent decisions suggest the courts might adopt such an approach, but there has not yet been a case directly on the point.[8]

There are a number of important practical consequences.

(1) Should 'film' rights be acquired alongside 'multimedia' rights? If film rights are not acquired, should the multimedia producer at least obtain a film quit claim, ie, that exercise of the multimedia rights will not infringe the film rights?
(2) Will the separate existence of the film rights cause material difficulties down the line?

Suitable wording for a sample clause for the acquisition of electronic including film rights for a multimedia work is provided at 12.1.1.

Examples

- Are multimedia producers acquiring the correct rights in pre-existing works which are to be incorporated into a product? Most do not think in terms of acquiring the film rights in pre-existing material; rights are usually obtained by reference to the production of the specific work in question, or possibly by more wide-ranging terms such as 'electronic rights'. There is an issue as to whether this kind of rights acquisition is in fact sufficient for the purpose if a multimedia CD-ROM is categorised as a film. *(Cont'd)*

> - What is the impact of this approach on existing arrangements for the exploitation of copyright works? Take, for instance, the ancillary rights to a children's book. If a television series or a film is made out of the book, it is possible that the grant of the rights for this purpose will (inadvertently) have been drawn too widely, so that the publisher will have granted CD-ROM rights (as a 'film') to the film or TV producer. It will become a matter of chance, depending on the precise wording of the grant of rights, whether the rights to produce a CD-ROM remain with the publisher or have gone to the TV or film producer. Of course, in many contracts the intention of the parties will be very clear and no problems will arise. In addition, in cases of ambiguity the courts will look first to the ordinary and natural meaning of words at the time the contract was made. Nevertheless there will be disputes which will come to court where the position will not be easily established.[9] Tensions already exist between authors, agents, publishers and producers over how far rights have been granted for the exploitation of materials in traditional media and, certainly in the short term, multimedia will not make things easier.
> - What, technically, does film copyright protect? If a director copies the action from another movie into his own production—eg, re-shooting some of the scenes—he may infringe the underlying rights in the original movie, ie the literary copyright in the screenplay, the artistic copyright in the sets etc, but has he infringed the film copyright as a whole? Some copyright texts (Copinger, Laddie *et al*)[10] argue that only mechanical copying of a film is an infringement of the film copyright. If this is the case then a CD-ROM would be denied protection from a competitor product that copied its 'look and feel' but did not reproduce any of its contents directly.[11]

6.3.2 ON-LINE COPYRIGHT ISSUES

Where multimedia products are made available on-line, whether via the Internet or another Information Superhighway, other issues arise. The rights to upload a work if available over a network, sometimes also called a diffusion right, can be defined as:

Sample clause: Diffusion rights

> the right to store, or authorise the storage of, the work on any electronic, magnetic or optical medium now known or hereafter devised and to transmit the work by any wired or wireless telecommunication systems or other means now known or hereafter devised for presenting the work to members of the public and for enabling them to view [and make copies of] the same.

Making a copyright multimedia work available over an on-line network involves the loading of the work on to a computer server, the transmission of the material via the network involved and the downloading, storage and potentially the copying in hard form by the end user. All these elements involve restricted acts under copyright law:

- copying the work;
- issuing copies of all works to the public;
- performing, showing or playing the work in public;

- broadcasting the work or including it in a cable programme service (*see* below);
- making an adaptation of the work or doing any of the above acts in relation to an adaptation.

Clearly then, licences to carry out these activities will be necessary for on-line transmission of copyright works, but will the transmissions over the on-line network themselves be protected by copyright, and if so how? Transmissions may enjoy additional copyright protection, over and above the copyright in the works, if they fall within the definition of a 'cable programme service' (*see* Table 3.2).

Most on-line multimedia transmissions will probably remain cable programme services and attract copyright because the only return signal is likely to fall within the exclusion contained in CDPA, s 7(2). The scale of the exclusion is debatable, however, since it may not always be clear whether the messages received from the end user are merely for the control of the application. There is also uncertainty over how the phrase 'essential feature' will be interpreted. Whether an interactive application would be excluded, or whether a separate copyright will subsist in the service provided over a network, therefore, determine all the facts pertaining to the particular on-line system.

Clearly, whether a distributor of a multimedia product over networks enjoys a separate right of copyright in his on-line transmissions will be vital if and when he tries to enforce rights directly against a person retransmitting or copying the transmissions or otherwise misusing the on-line system. If there is no separate copyright in the transmission, the producer, or others, must instead rely on the separate copyrights in the individual works transmitted over the system and on the contractual arrangements made between those copyright owners.

It is too early to tell whether copyright will turn out to be wholly effective for protecting computer works in general and multimedia works in particular. For the various reasons given above—and specifically because copyright is recognised and already has a network of international treaties in place—copyright is the most promising medium. In the meantime, it is the authors' view that a multimedia product, where it is not already a film, should be offered its own copyright protection.

Please refer also the EC Green Paper, 'Copyright in the Information Society' (summarised in Appendix 11).

---

[1] Despite the international acceptance of computer software as a form of literary copyright *see* eg, EC Software Directive and GATT/TRIPs, there is a growing interest in patent protection for programs—*see* 7.3, *below*.

[2] The possibility of using other categories of copyright to protect a screen display instead are dealt with elsewhere.

[3] Ferris J has approved his own judgment in *Richardson* in *ZS Associates Inc and Another v Nazis Ltd and others* (1994) unreported, 17 March.

[4] *See* recent discussion on TV Format rights in connection with the protection of ideas.

[5] Other policy issues are relevant (eg, a possible restriction on competition by the author—*see Ibcos*).

[6] Defined by the CDPA, s 4(2) as 'a recording of light or other radiation on any medium on which any image is produced or from which an image may by any means be produced, and which is not part of a film'.

[7] Though such works as Derek Jarman's *Blue*, which consists of a blue screen with accompanying track, are classed as a film. And note that many would argue that if you scroll through text on the screen, you create a moving image, even if the characters do not move in relation to each other.

[8] *Kent County Council v Multi Media Marketing (Canterbury) Ltd and Another* (1995) *The Times*, 9 May held that a computer game was a 'video work' for the purposes of the Video Recordings Act 1984, s 1(2) which defines 'video work' as 'any series of usual images (with or without sound) (a) produced electronically by the use of information contained on any disc or magnetic tape, and (b) shown as a moving picture'. *Nintendo Co Ltd v Golden China TV Game Centre* [1994] 1 ELR E-8, a South African case decided on a similar definition of film

under the South African Copyright Act, held that the visual displays of video games are capable of copyright protection as films. However, cf *British Amusement Catering Trades Association and another v Westminster Borough Council* [1989] AC 147, HL, which held that video games were not 'an exhibition of moving pictures' for the purposes of the 1909 Cinematograph Act.

9   *See Hospital for Sick Children v Walt Disney Productions* [1968] Ch 52 and *Lee v Walt Disney Co* Cal 1d BO 58897 (Sup Ct No C705414). In the former case a grant of rights referred to all 'literary and dramatic works existing and future of whatsoever nature for the terms of the respective copyrights thereof in cinematographs or moving picture films' but was made before the development of films with sound. One of the judges who heard the case thought sound films should be included whilst the other three thought they should not. In the absence of clear wording it was held that it was necessary for a court to determine what was in the contemplation of the parties at the time the contract was made.

10 See the Australian case *Telmak Teleproducts Australia Pty Ltd v Bond International Pty Ltd* (1985) 66 ALR 118.

11 However, it may be argued that since s 16(3)(*b*) of the CDPA restricts any copying whether directly or indirectly this view is incorrect.

• 7 •

PROTECTING AND ENFORCING RIGHTS IN MULTIMEDIA WORKS

7.1 COPYRIGHT INFRINGEMENT

As previous chapters have shown, a copyright owner has the right to prevent unauthorised persons from doing a number of restricted acts or from committing a number of secondary acts in respect of his or her copyright work. There has to be an original copyright work, a qualifying author and a restricted act. Nothing done which is not one of the restricted acts, primary or secondary, is an infringement of copyright, even if it is done with guilty knowledge.

What is done must be done to a 'substantial' part of the work. 'Substantiality' is to be decided qualitively rather than quantitively. There are also the fair dealing exceptions dealt with in 3.9.

> **Checklist for infringement**
> - Is there a copyright work?
> - Was the author a qualifying author?
> - Has there been a restricted act or an act of secondary infringement?
> - Was what was done, done to a substantial part?
> - Do any of the fair dealing exceptions apply?
> - If the act was a secondary act, was there an intention, or element of knowledge, to infringe?
> - Is the work still in copyright?
> - Has the unauthorised person had access to (or was he aware of) the original work?
> - What damage resulted? (proof of damage is not necessary).
> - Is the producer entitled to sue in his own name or does he require any or all of the contributors to join in? Only copyright owners and exclusive licensees can sue for infringement of copyright.

7.1.1 PRIMARY INFRINGEMENT

Knowledge of infringement is not necessary, although it must be shown that the infringer did, in fact, reproduce the original copyright work.

> **Example**
>
> A publisher incorporates a picture into a CD product believing that the picture is out of copyright. The publisher is wrong; the illustration is still in copyright. Result: Infringement.

7.1.2 SECONDARY INFRINGEMENT

Secondary infringement requires knowledge or reason to believe. 'Had reason to believe' was introduced as a concept by the CDPA. Prior to that it was necessary to prove actual knowledge, which is a much more difficult issue.

> **Example**
>
> S is a shopkeeper selling CD-ROMs incorporating infringing copyright material. He cannot be successfully sued for copyright infringement unless the copyright owner establishes that the shopkeeper knew or had reason to believe that the CD-ROM was an infringing copy.

7.1.3 LIABILITY

The person who performs or authorises the performance of the restricted acts without the authority of the copyright owner is the person liable.

7.2 ENFORCEMENT

There are both civil and criminal remedies for infringement of copyright.

7.2.1 CIVIL REMEDIES

Civil remedies include: damages, an injunction, an account of the profits gained as a result of the infringement, and delivery-up of the infringing articles. Conversion damages (ie the right to a proportion of the value of the work in which the infringing article was incorporated) were abolished by the CDPA.

Where the infringer did not know and had no reason to believe copyright subsisted in the work, damages are not available: only an account of profits. Where the infringement was flagrant, a court has power to award additional damages.

Who may sue

The original copyright owner or the person to whom an exclusive licence has been granted may sue.

7.2.2 CRIMINAL REMEDIES

Criminal remedies require knowledge in order to establish liability. In the circumstances set out in the CDPA, ss 107–10, it is a criminal offence to manufacture, deal in or possess in the course of business articles which the defendant knows or has reason to believe infringe copyright.

Powers of Customs and Excise

The copyright owner of a published literary, dramatic or musical work can apply to Customs and Excise requesting it to treat as prohibited goods printed copies of the work where they are infringing copies.

In addition, the owner of the copyright in a sound recording or film may notify Customs and Excise that infringing copies are to be imported into the UK and request Customs and Excise to treat the copies as prohibited copies, in which event the goods may be seized and not released into free circulation.

Liability of companies and directors

A company can be liable for copyright infringement. A director may be liable if he has ordered or procured the infringement of copyright by his company.

Section 107 of the CDPA provides that where an offence is committed by a company and the copyright owner can show that the director or manager or secretary or other officer consented to or connived with the offence, the individual as well as the company is guilty.

International protection

Copyright being a national right, a copyright owner has to rely upon local law—ie, the law of the country in which he seeks to enforce the right, for protection. Under the international conventions, protection is usually given on the basis of national treatment, ie, the other jurisdiction will give the foreign copyright owner the same protection as it gives to its own nationals but it will not give more protection than the copyright owner has in his own country. *See* the discussion at 4.3.2 of the effect of the *Phil Collins* case on this within the EU. *See* also GATT/TRIPS at 5.4.

7.3 OTHER LEGAL PROTECTION

A range of other legal mechanisms may offer additional protection to multimedia works.

7.3.1 PATENTS

A patent gives to its owner a monopoly for a term of years, now a maximum of 20, to exploit an invention. The aim of the patent system is to encourage technical and commercial development generally by providing for the inventor to be rewarded with a monopoly of exploitation in exchange for a full disclosure of the invention which is publicly available. This public disclosure raises the general level of technical expertise and knowledge and thereby contributes to further development.

Patent law in the UK is regulated by statute; the Act now in force is the Patents Act 1977 ('PA 1977') as amended by the CDPA. The procedures for seeking patent protection and prosecuting the application to grant is laid down in the Patents Rules 1990 (SI No 2384) ('the Rules'), issued under the authority of the PA 1977. The procedures are administered by the Patent Office, which is part of the Department of Trade and Industry (DTI).

A patent may be granted, subject to various exclusions set out below, for an invention that is:

(a) novel;
(b) involves an inventive step; and
(c) is capable of industrial application (PA 1977, s 1(1)).

The following are specifically excluded from patent protection:

(a) a discovery, scientific theory or mathematical method;
(b) a literary, dramatic, musical or artistic work and any aesthetic creation whatsoever;
(c) a scheme, rule or method for performing a mental act, playing a game or doing business, or a program for a computer;
(d) the presentation of information (PA 1977, s 1(2)).

A patent granted under these provisions will only be valid in the UK (and other territories as the PA 1977 allows). In contrast to the network of international copyright treaties, there is no world-wide scheme of patent protection. However a number of international agreements do provide a large measure of assistance, so that virtually all significant markets are covered by one agreement or another. There are four such agreements.

The Paris Convention
Signed by 96 states, the Paris Convention provides that submission of an application for patent protection in one signatory state will serve to establish priority for the applicant in the event that equivalent applications are submitted in other signatory states within 12 months.

The Patent Co-operation Treaty
The Patent Co-operation Treaty, which came into force in 1978, allows an applicant to file a single 'International Application' for a patent. The application is subject to a single international search, and, on the applicant's request, a single preliminary examination, before the application is forwarded to the National Patent Offices which have been specified.

The European Patent Convention
An applicant may file a single application for a patent, specifying for which of the contracting states the applicant wants protection. British subjects may only apply at the UK Patent Office. An application under this Convention results, if successful, in the grant of a bundle of national patents, one in each of the states designated in the application.

The Community Patent Convention
The EC signed the Community Patent Convention in 1975 in order to introduce the concept of a single patent having effect in all Member States. However, introduction of the Community patent has been delayed.

Exclusion of computer software from protection by patenting
It can be seen that where one of the elements of a multimedia product satisfies the statutory requirements for inventiveness and novelty the grant of patent protection will be possible. Computer software, usually the most likely candidate for patent protection, is however excluded from protection. Under UK law there are two exceptions to this general restriction:

(1) A computer program to perform an inventive, novel function of industrial application can be the basis of a valid application. In such a case it is the industrial

application which is protected, not the program itself, which is only a means to the end. If the novelty and inventiveness rest only in the program, the patent cannot be granted (*see Merill Lynch's application* [1989] RPC 561).

(2) A computer program is, in its machine-code version, a statement of a series of binary mathematical and logical switches. If this machine code is permanently fixed as a series of circuits in the memory of a semiconductor chip, this could form the basis of a valid patent application. A read-only memory (ROM) is not only a store containing the mathematical and logical instructions that make up a computer program, it is an article of manufacture, and even if the function of the ROM is within the prohibitions contained in the Act, as a novel product it can be considered for protection (*see Re Gale's application* [1991] RPC 305).

At the European level under the European Patent Convention, art 53(2) there is the same prohibition on the patenting of software as such, but the exceptions to this basic prohibition are formulated differently. Under both systems, the obtaining of a software-related patent, while not prohibited, will only be possible in restricted circumstances.

Obtaining a patent for software

A patent, if obtainable, offers better rights than copyright as it affords protection not just against copying but also any exploitation of the invention. As we have seen, copyright protects a multimedia product in the same way that it would protect any traditional work. It prevents an unauthorised copying of the original. Copyright does not stop a competitor producing a product which performs the same task as a copyrighted work using a different method.

USA

Unlike the UK and most other countries, the USA is more likely to permit patents for computer software and these are more widely sought. It has allowed companies that have invested considerable resources in product development to ensure that their products are protected in a stronger way than is possible under copyright law. This does, however, mean that when new products are produced for sale in the USA, developers must ensure that they have not infringed patent-protected software elements. Since a patented piece of software may consist of only a few lines of code and a multimedia product may run to several thousand, the checking process involved would be a significant task, particularly as one would have to check for patented inventions which cover the principles used in the product. The situation is not helped by the difficulties which have been experienced at the US Patent and Trademark Office, where software inventions are not all clearly categorised for searching purposes and objections can only be raised by other interested parties after a patent has been granted. Thus many in the US industry are split over whether the increasing use of patents rather than copyright to protect software and multimedia products is encouraging or harming innovation, investment and new products[1].

This situation has already had an effect upon the US multimedia industry; on both CD-ROM and on-line products. In August 1994 the US Patent Office granted a patent to multimedia producer Comptons New Media. Comptons had published an encyclopedia on CD-ROM and been granted a patent for their method of searching a content database of text, graphics and video, a method that was commonly used in the industry. The grant meant that other multimedia producers would need to pay royalties for the use of methods covered by the patent in the software engines being used in their own products.

Understandably, other US producers expressed extreme concern that a commonly used search technique could be protected in this way and raised so many objections that the US Patent Office re-examined the patent, an almost unprecedented step, and decided that the patent should not be granted after all.

In another case, the largest US on-line service provider, CompuServe announced in December 1994 that the popular Graphics Interchange Format (GIF) specification used for on-line graphics files incorporated elements for which the Unisys Corporation had previously obtained a patent. Unisys had obtained this patent several years previously, but its existence was not known to CompuServe or others using the format. CompuServe and Unisys executed a licence agreement for the patent and third parties can now use the technology by paying a royalty and obtaining a licence from CompuServe. Many developers who have incorporated the GIF format into their products assuming that it could be used free of charge are unhappy with this situation and it has been suggested that an alternative standard should be adopted for encoding graphics files which would not infringe the Unisys patent.

7.3.2 REGISTERED TRADE MARKS

A trade or service mark is any form of sign (*see* below) which is capable of distinguishing the goods or service of one trade from another. It is in essence a 'badge' which can be identified by both customers and traders. Registered trade marks are governed by statute. The Trade Marks Act 1994 reformed the law in the UK in line with the EC Trade Mark Directive 1988 (as well as the EC Regulation on the Unitary Community Trade Mark 1993 and the Madrid Protocol Relating to International Registration of Marks).

The proprietor has a monopoly of the use of the mark which can be exercised vicariously by permitting use by registered users and licensees. The proprietor can restrain others from infringing his rights in the mark, and can claim compensation from infringers for the harm suffered or the loss of profits. These monopolies last so long as the mark is validly registered. Provided that the validity of the mark is safeguarded, and the renewals regularly maintained, the registration can continue indefinitely. This protection is unique in UK intellectual property law; all other forms of protection have limited lives, determined by the statute (eg, a patent or copyright) or by events which might be outside the proprietor's control (eg, confidential information, trade secrets). Thus it can be seen that trade marks offer an important and strong method of protection to a multimedia producer.

The Trade Marks Act 1994

The Act expands the scope of what can be registered. Now not only words, names, logos and devices may be registered but also colours, the shape of goods and/or packaging, smells and sounds so long as the mark to be registered is capable of being represented graphically. The division of the trade mark register into two parts (A and B) has been abolished and marks now only need satisfy the lower threshold, ie they must be 'capable of distinguishing goods or services of one undertaking from those of other undertakings'. Once registered, they will now attract the same level of protection. The UK Trade Mark Registry no longer has a general discretion to refuse the registration of a mark, and so marks are now presumed to be registrable unless they fall within certain stated criteria.

The previous near-absolute bar on registration of certain geographical and personal names has been relaxed. The new provisions on infringement have been extended to cover use of marks on similar goods and services to those for which the mark is registered and use of similar marks on identical goods and services where there exists a likelihood of confusion or association between the two marks. This change again widens the protection of registered marks. Registrations will now be renewable every ten years.

Of particular importance is the additional protection provided by the Act for marks with a reputation in the UK. Thus, where a mark has a reputation in the UK, use of an identical or similar mark on goods or services which are not similar to those for which the mark is registered could still be an infringement if the use of the mark is without due cause and takes unfair advantage of or is detrimental to the distinctive character or repute of the well-known mark. For example, a 'Levis' multimedia product could infringe the well-known jeans manufacturer's trade-mark registration.

The definition of infringement has now been extended to include oral use of a mark. The effect of this change is that spoken use of the words in trade marks, for example on a CD-ROM, will be an infringement.

Under the Act there are provisions for owners of certain overseas trade marks to prevent the use of those marks, or their registrations, by an agent or representative in this country. The effect of this is to create an increased requirement to perform trade-mark searches abroad.

Registered owners must now be able to bring evidence of use of their marks; a failure to do so will be treated as an admission of non-use and could also lead to cancellation.

The Act sets out provisions for ratification of the Madrid Protocol and for adoption of the Community Trade Mark Regulations. Under the Madrid Protocol an application for registration of a mark in the UK can be extended to all Madrid Protocol countries upon payment of a fee. The Community Trade Mark Regulations will allow trade-mark registrations to take effect throughout the Community. Such registrations will be important for multimedia providers wishing to use trade marks internationally. When they are fully operative these schemes will mean, in many cases, that costly trade-mark registrations in each and every territory in which a product is distributed will be reduced. With on-line technology that is particularly useful.

7.3.3 UNREGISTERED TRADE MARKS

Common law

Common law recognises and enforces marks established by custom and practice in the absence of registration. A mark that fails in an application for registration may still protect the reputation of its proprietor in relation to part, or even the full range, of the proprietor's goods and services. It is for the proprietor to establish that the mark goes with his reputation, whether new or long established, in connection with the goods or services in question. However the protection afforded in this way differs greatly between countries and, as with registered marks, there is no harmonisation of the law in Europe.

At present, except for the UK, freedom to market products using a trade name is solely dependent upon that trade name not being registered in the country concerned by a third party. If the trade name is not registered by any party there is freedom to use but the user acquires no rights of continued use. Consequently, anyone marketing products in Europe under a given trade name may be forced to change that name if a third party decides to register it. Conversely registration of a mark allows an individual to continue marketing and stop others from using that mark.

The situation in the UK is different, in that use of an unregistered trade mark can generate an entitlement to continue to use it, even if a third party subsequently registers the mark. It is for this reason that UK companies have historically adopted the approach of being slow to register their trade marks in comparison to continental European companies. Nevertheless registration where possible, is recommended.

Passing off in the UK, unfair competition in Europe
Unlike other nations in Europe the UK has no concept of unfair competition. Instead the action of 'passing off' has developed in circumstances where:

(a) there is a misrepresentation that the defendant's goods or services are those of the plaintiff;
(b) this occurs in the course of trade or business;
(c) the direct or indirect customers or consumers are or are likely to be deceived; and
(d) as an actual or likely outcome the trade or business of the plaintiff will suffer loss.

The reputation must be established by use in this country, or even a limited part of this country where it is to be exploited. Use, even long established exclusive use, in another country will not usually establish a legal, as opposed to a real, reputation here. This common law remedy is more difficult and more expensive than relying upon registered trade-mark protection.

7.3.4 INTERNET ADDRESS NAMES

The address strings which locate sites on the Internet (whether e-mail eg, **denton@denton.co.uk** or on the World Wide Web eg, **http://www.gold.net/denton**) have raised particular trade mark issues. These addresses have traditionally been allocated on a first-come first-served basis with the result that addresses incorporating trade marks have been allocated to third parties rather than the trade mark owner. In some cases the third party has then tried to sell the address to the trade mark owner at a premium. This kind of activity has resulted in litigation in the US and in response InterNIC, the US body responsible for top level domain name registration, has introduced a new policy of reallocation if opposition is raised by a *bona fide* trade mark owner. Such abuses have not been as prevalent in this country and the UK Internet Naming Committee has not faced the same problems. However, action could be taken by a trade mark owner in the UK under both registered trade mark and passing-off law to prevent use of an address incorporating its mark. The pool of available addresses on the Internet is, however, finite and those wishing to use a certain name for their on-line multimedia service should seek to register that name sooner rather than later.

7.3.5 CONFIDENTIALITY

While the law has always protected the use of information imparted or held in confidence regarding any misuse as a breach of trust, there is no statutory recognition of rights in confidential information. Breach of confidentiality is therefore an equitable right based entirely on case law. It should be stressed that while general principles have emerged, every case is peculiar to its facts, and seemingly similar cases might be decided differently.

There are statutory provisions, however, which protect the confidentiality, or secrecy of certain types of information, principally the Official Secrets Acts 1911–22, the Data Protection Act 1984, and the rules about insider dealing contained in the Companies Securities (Insider Dealings) Act 1985.

Right to enforce

The right to enforce confidentiality arises as a matter of law from:

(a) the nature of the information;
(b) how it was obtained and disseminated;
(c) the relationship between the parties at the time of disclosure; and
(d) whether the disclosure of the information would damage the party claiming confidentiality.

The law of confidence does not protect any information in the public domain and for these purposes the public domain is wider than common knowledge. Information that can be gained by examination of any freely obtainable article is equally not protected. However, and again emphasising that decided cases offer guidance only, should a purchaser of a product by dismantling the article get information on its design, a person bound by an obligation of confidence in respect of that information might be held to it.

Further, information that has been made public as a result of a breach of confidence can still be regarded as confidential, at least between the parties, and an injunction to prevent further publication may be issued if the plaintiff can establish in the facts that his business interests can be further damaged by the publication.

Information genuinely and freely available to the public is not protected even though its disclosure may have resulted from a breach of confidence. The following examples will illustrate the types of information which may be protected by the law of confidence:

- industrial secrets;
- inventive ideas;
- future corporate plans and corporate strategy; and
- customer lists, contacts, pricing and discount tactics.

Scope

The right extends beyond the industrial and financial fields to concepts for books, plays, serials, advertising campaigns and the like. Further, the relationship between parties may sometimes give rise to a duty of confidentiality, for example solicitor/client, doctor/patient, and perhaps the most obvious example, employer/employee. During the currency of an employment contract there is an implied duty of good faith on the employee not to use for his own benefit or transfer to another any information acquired as a result of his employment which is of value to the employer. Case law, however, establishes that information must be sufficiently important to acquire the quality of trade secret to be protected by such an implied obligation. The test would seem to be whether disclosure of the information considered to be a trade secret would cause real or significant harm to the owner; and there is also a defence of genuine public interest.

The lack of statutory guidance in the area of confidentiality means that owners of information must find ways of protecting their information. This may be done by either entering into confidentiality agreements or imposing covenants in restraint of trade.

Under a confidentiality agreement parties to a venture may agree not to disclose information other than for the purposes of the venture. There is doubt, however, as to whether confidentiality obligations may be imposed on the party unwilling to accept them. Somewhat akin to the shrinkwrap licence (*see* 15.4.3), it is common for confidential information to be enclosed in a sealed package clearly marked that opening of the package is a deemed acceptance of the terms of the confidentiality agreement.

Covenant

A covenant in restraint of trade is generally not adequate to protect confidential information but where it protects a legitimate interest and covers areas such as non-competition, non-solicitation of customers and non-disclosure it may be of benefit to the owner of the information. The terms must, however, be reasonable as regards the geographical area and duration in time of all restraints.

If a contract, including an employment contract, includes express terms relating to confidentiality, no implied terms will be introduced to make up for any lack of those express terms. If these express terms then fail there will be no terms about confidentiality at all.

The enforcement of confidentiality clauses in a contract is no different from that of any other contractual provisions. As the clauses are restrictive in their nature they are construed against the person who wishes to rely on them, so clarity of drafting is essential.

Remedies

The remedies for breach of confidence consist of:

- injunctions;
- damages;
- accounts of profits and
- delivery up or destruction of property.

Quia timet injunctions may be issued to prevent an infringement which is threatened but has not yet occurred. However the owner of the information must be able to show a strong probability of infringement and that the ensuing damage will be of a very serious nature.

Confidentiality clauses, or variations introduced after the contract was first made, must be supported by valuable consideration to be enforceable. Considerations such as a promotion, if confidentiality is to be introduced for the first time, will suffice.

Confidential information and trade secrets can be:

- licensed;
- for development;
- to enter new or extended markets; or
- as a supplement to a patent licence.

It will benefit both parties to the licence and enhance the revenue of the licensor if the licence is supplemented with information on the most efficient and economical method of working. However great care is required. It is a human tendency to regard other's secrets as less important than one's own, and the licensee should be bound to observe the licensor's confidentiality requirements and be supervised in his compliance with these measures. This principle will apply equally to other forms of intellectual property licensing. A licensee will receive information for a limited purpose, such as the use of computer software, and may not otherwise use or disclose it.

Multimedia

Specifically as regards multimedia, the law of confidentiality may offer protection to various types of information during the development process of the multimedia product. This protection is usually lost once the product is launched or enters the marketplace. As regards hardware, it is advisable to keep secret the full functional specification of the various product elements. Should a pirate copy of the software then be developed it will be

7.3.6 DESIGN RIGHT

Registered design

In the marketplace, and particularly in the field of consumer goods, sales appeal can be enhanced by the appearance of the product, in addition to its functional value. The design leading to that enhanced commercial value can be registered, provided it appeals to the senses, particularly the sense of sight, and is distinct from the functional aspects of the product. In the more fashion-orientated world of multimedia this will be important—allowing, for example, games consoles and other hardware to be protected. Registration confers a monopoly on the designer, allowing him to prevent others in the same field of business taking (even inadvertently) the benefit of his artistic efforts. A registered design can be compared with artistic copyright which protects the shape of things, but registration goes further. Copyright only protects against copying; a registered design prevents independent creation. A registered design can be contrasted with a design right, in that a design right gives protection to the functional as well as the artistic. Registered designs are governed by statute: the Registered Designs Act 1949 as subsequently amended by the CDPA.

Unregistered design

The CDPA introduced a new intellectual property right—the unregistered design right. This gives a limited monopoly to the creator of original design, which may be both functional and artistic. The right is entirely statutory. As it is new, there is as yet little indication how a CDPA provision will be applied, and the authorities relating to copyright have been used for guidance.

Semiconductor topographies

The protection given to the design of semiconductor chips has been expanded in the UK to remove any doubt that the protection given by copyright was adequate and to secure reciprocal rights in other countries. The masks used to produce semiconductor chips are artistic works, and the copyright in them can prevent reproduction of the chips. However, it is difficult to discern by eye that the chip, a solid three-dimensional object, is a copy. The right to protect chips is defined in the UK (now under the Design Right (Semiconductor Topographies) Regulations 1989) so as to secure reciprocal protection under the equivalent legislation in the USA. Before then it had been assumed (probably rightly, despite the caution expressed here) that copyright law was already sufficiently flexible and powerful to provide protection in the field of semiconductors.

7.4 PRACTICAL PROTECTION

7.4.1 OBTAINING WARRANTIES

Get warranties on the ownership and licensing of all the content of the product, including the software. For a major product it is worth implementing a due diligence exercise on the rights involved before or shortly after contracts are signed and either acquiring any that are missing or substituting other content. It is much easier to sort out these problems before the project is under way.

7.4.2 REGISTERING INTELLECTUAL PROPERTY RIGHTS

Register intellectual property (IP) rights in those countries where this is necessary (most notably in the US) and it is likely that you may want to sue (or threaten to sue) to protect your rights from infringers. A copyright notice © is no longer a prerequisite for copyright protection in the US but it has the effect of warning of the existence of copyright and the fact that the copyright owner is prepared to enforce the copyright and can increase the likelihood of higher damages. It also assists in establishing knowledge of the existence of copyright upon an infringer. The notice should be set out on screen displays, packaging and any ancillary documentation or promotional material. Similarly trade-mark protection should be sought in key territories and the ® (for registered trade marks) and ™ (for unregistered trade marks) symbols used appropriately. Where patent protection has been granted or applied for this should be made clear.

7.4.3 BUILDING A STRONG BRAND NAME

Seek to build a strong brand name for the product line or service. This is good marketing anyway, but it also strengthens registered IP rights, helps establish unregistered rights and provides practical protection. The popularity of a CD-ROM or other product will depend primarily on its contents and the way in which the data is organised and retrieved; or, in the case of a game, its 'gameplay'. A popular product will spawn 'me too' rivals, which may have very similar contents, structure and organisation to the original. In the absence of direct copying there is no infringement of the copyright in the contents of a CD-ROM. Furthermore, with physical multimedia products such as CD-ROMs there are severe retail bottlenecks and in the commercial battle for shelf space product brand names are very important. With on-line services trade marks are still important as they form part of the critical look and feel of the product. It is difficult to establish, develop and maintain a strong brand identity which will sustain a reputation in the multimedia marketplace, providing both protection from infringers and important commercial user identification, with a multiplicity of weak and uncoordinated trade marks. Thus the use of marks in the look and styling of both the product and any packaging or marketing should be carefully and consistently applied.

7.4.4 FIGHTING PIRACY

Just as digitisation and new technologies allow opportunities for piracy to flourish, so they also offer a number of opportunities to fight piracy. As Charles Clark of the Publishers' Association has said, 'the answer to the machine is in the machine' and it is vital that the technicians and lawyers behind a multimedia product adopt an intelligent partnership. This is not only relevant in the protection of IP rights. It also has benefits for royalty collection. Technical measures used to fight piracy should therefore dovetail with those providing revenue streams to the rights holder. Those involved in multimedia production should consider the following:

Identification

Many are investigating the capacity of new technology to provide unique identification schemes for individual copyright works. There have been several different proposals for the digital equivalent of the publishing industry's ISBN system. For instance, WIPO and CITED have proposed the adoption of a wide-scale institutional numbering standard at an international level. Taking a different approach, several commercial firms are developing proprietary systems, often concentrating on particular industries. In addition to the incorporation of unique identification numbers into the digital product, there are already a variety of physical identifiers, such as holographic protection labels, which can be used as successful and sophisticated protective trade marks, whether on packaging or in the product itself.

Tracking

The ability to identify a work is linked with the ability to follow it and track its use on on-line systems. There is much debate on the technical ability to ensure that the distribution of works over the digital networks can be traced and tracked. Clearly such efforts at providing information of, and evidence on, piracy activities are more likely to succeed in commercial networks rather than the Internet but even then a perfect system of control may not be possible. The aim should therefore be to identify where tracking is most effective and exploit it fully to maximise its deterrent and investigative value to the full. Even with on-line products, piracy requires some off-line support and payment. Money, whether in the form of digital streams or cold hard cash, can be traced to both payer and pirate. The marketing and revenue collection for infringing services often still remain in the physical world.

Access denial

Various technologies also allow control over access to digital products. On-line encryption techniques aim to provide secure distribution of copyright works which, in addition to helping protect against piracy, support revenue collection. Indeed on-line payment and the development of electronic money systems will not be successful until proven encryption technology is fully developed. Off-line products can also be protected through encryption. For instance, use of CD-ROMs can be limited by:

- access-control mechanisms in PCs or other devices;
- use of security sensitive retrieval software; or
- controls in the disks themselves.

A number of companies offer a variety of proprietary encryption and restriction devices and these systems can be harmonised with commercial strategies to introduce metering, 'try and buy', time-sensitive releases, updates and other payment mechanisms.

Copy protection

An extension of these techniques is the inclusion of copy-limiting devices in both on- and off-line products. Successfully countering the public's appetite for home copying without making payment may be a difficult commercial strategy to develop but in technical terms a combination of controls in both software and hardware can be used to ensure that when an interactive multimedia title is released, whether in a CD or in an on-line format, the viewer is only able to make copies of that work if the distributor allows him to.

7.4.5 RESPONDING TO MULTIMEDIA PIRACY

It will require substantial efforts by both government and private groups to respond to the challenge of multimedia piracy. However, a number of national and international groups and initiatives already exist which may be able to provide such a response and it is important that lawyers be prepared to work with them.

(1) The Federation Against Copyright Theft (FACT) is a non-profit-making private company which was established in the 1980s by the major film and video companies in the UK in order to combat piracy of their product. It responds to complaints throughout the UK and, acting in conjunction with either the police or the trading standards authorities, takes steps to seize material which infringes members' copyright. FACT normally acts under general UK law (CDPA) and specific video legislation (Video Recordings Act 1984). In the software industry the UK Federation Against Software Theft (FAST) operates in a similar way. Recently the European Leisure Software Publishers' Association (ELSPA) set up its own crime unit to fight piracy of its members' products and has uncovered software piracy ranging from infringing bulletin board operators on the Internet to car boot sales of pirate software. Other organisations and bodies in other industries are also acting against piracy. For instance the UK record industry body, the British Phonograph Institute (BPI), has specific personnel to defend the music business against the threat of piracy on the Internet.

(2) On an international level, the International Chamber of Commerce formed the ICC Counterfeiting Intelligence Bureau (CIB) in 1985 as a focal point for industries and other affected interests world-wide to fight the growing piracy problem. It was the first international private business initiative to go beyond political lobbying with practical prevention and enforcement support for police and customs authorities. The Business Software Alliance (BSA) is also active in countering international software piracy. The International Anti-Counterfeiting Coalition (IACC) has a membership of trade mark owners, in-house counsel, private practitioners and investigators and is dedicated to promoting anti-counterfeiting legislation as well as providing the US Customs Service with information to help reduce imported counterfeits. It attempts to educate IP owners about state anti-counterfeiting laws and to uncover on their behalf pirate copies in their particular area.

Anti-piracy initiatives work most effectively when public enforcement agencies combine with private bodies and commercial firms to co-ordinate activities. Thus in the UK a lawyer can work with the following professionals:

(a) Trading standards officers, who have a public duty to protect both the consumer and legitimate business from pirates, and are employed by local government to enforce national legislation.
(b) Customs and Excise staff who, under the current EC anti-counterfeit importation regulations (recently extended to cover a wider range of goods, including exports) may apply to monitor and seize incoming goods.
(c) The police and the various anti-piracy and other squads which have been set up by police forces throughout the UK.
(d) National and international organisations such as CIB, FACT, FAST, ELSPA, BIMA or any other organisation of the type mentioned above.

What is important is that as the new technologies bring media industry convergence, the coordination of such anti-piracy teams is not lost through overlapping initiatives and industry uncertainty. Clearly the same goes for international links which will be even more necessary with on-line systems.

---

[1] *WIRED* July 1994 (US) p 104.

• 8 •

MORAL RIGHTS (*DROIT MORAL*)

The concept of moral rights in its broad application was introduced into English law by the CDPA. Prior to that an individual had under the Copyright Act 1956 simply a right not to have a work falsely attributed to him. He also had general rights of contract, defamation and the like to protect his position and his professional reputation. *Droit moral* is a civil law concept, most actively pursued by the French but present in various forms in most continental jurisdictions. Usually it is inalienable; being considered so much a part of the author and his creative effort that the author is unable to part with it in any way, even where he can part with the economic interest in his work. The continental concept of *droit d'auteur* concentrates more on the right of the author than, as Anglo-Saxon law tends to do, on the work itself and its economic potential.

The CDPA, ss 77–89 introduced three new rights:

(a) the right to be identified as author or director (the paternity right);
(b) the right to object to derogatory treatment of a work (the right of integrity); and
(c) the right to privacy of certain photographs and films.

With the usual English sense of compromise, while moral rights are (as required by the Berne Convention) inalienable, the author may consent to infringement or indeed waive the rights in whole or in part, conditionally or unconditionally and revocably or irrevocably.

8.1 RIGHT OF PATERNITY

Authors of copyright literary, dramatic, musical or artistic works and directors of copyright films have the right of paternity provided that they have asserted that right.

Authors are generally entitled to be identified whenever the work is published commercially, performed or exhibited in public broadcast or included in a cable programme service, or if copies of a film or sound recording including the work are issued to the public; and also in connection with any adaptation. Authors of literary, dramatic, artistic and musical works are each treated in slightly different ways. Refer to the relevant textbook(s) for more detail and for information on exceptions.

Directors have the right to be identified whenever the film is shown in public, broadcast or included in a cable programme service or copies of the film are issued to the public.

The paternity right is to be identified in or on each copy, or in some other manner likely to bring the identity to the notice of a person acquiring a copy, or to bring the identity to the attention of a person seeing or hearing the performance etc. In each case the identification must be clear and reasonably prominent.

> **Query**
>
> Will an author have the right to be identified each time his work or any part* is displayed (publicly) on the screen? Or will it be sufficient to have a credit 'menu' within the programme?
>
> The identification must be clear and reasonably prominent: whether identification matches this test will depend upon *how* the material in, eg a CD, is presented.
>
> *Note that the rights of paternity and to privacy of certain photographs and films apply in relation to the *whole or a substantial* part of the work whereas the right to integrity and the false attribution right (*see* 8.3) apply to *the whole or any* part.

The right is not infringed unless it has been asserted and the CDPA, s 78 sets out the situations in which the right is deemed to have been asserted, and the people bound by such an assertion.

> **Examples**
>
> - An assertion in the assignment of copyright signed by the author or director binds the assignee and anyone claiming through them whether or not he has notice of the assignment.
> - An assertion by notice in writing binds anyone to whom the notice is brought.
> - The court is entitled to take into account any delay in making the assertion.

The right does not apply to:

- a computer program;
- the design of a typeface;
- any computer-generated work;
- anything done with the authority of the copyright owner where copyright in the work originally vested in the author's or director's employer and where the work was created in the course of employment;
- a work made for the purpose of recording current events;
- a publication in: a newspaper, magazine or similar periodical; or an encyclopedia, dictionary, year book or other collective work of reference where the work was made for the purpose of publication or made available with the consent of the author for such publication.

> **Example**
>
> If a film director (or author) is *employed* to direct a film (or to write a script) as opposed to being *engaged* to do so, the paternity right does not apply to acts done with the copyright owner's authority; and the copyright owner will be the employer.
>
> **Note:** How this will be affected by the provisions in the Harmonisation Directives that a director is considered to be an author (*see* Table 3.2) (and therefore a copyright owner) remains to be seen.

The right is not infringed by virtue of any act falling within certain copyright 'fair dealing' provisions.

> **Example**
>
> A work is commissioned, or acquired from the author, for incorporation into eg an encyclopedia or database: the author has no paternity right.
>
> **Note:** If the author's work is used outside the work of reference (whether by the publisher or, say, by a user downloading it, the right may well then apply. In both cases there would also be copyright issues to consider, ie whether publisher or user had the right to use the work outside the encyclopaedia format).

The right does not apply to:

- Crown or Parliamentary copyright material;
- a work which vests in an international organisation (defined as an organisation the members of which include one or more states) unless the author or director has previously been identified as the author or director on published copies of the work.

8.2 RIGHT OF INTEGRITY

The author of a copyright literary, dramatic, musical or artistic work (and the director of a copyright film) has the right not to have his work subjected to 'derogatory treatment'.

It is important to consider what the statutory definition of 'derogatory treatment' is.

> 'Treatment' means any addition to deletion from or alteration to or adaptation of the work other than:
> (i) a translation of a literary or dramatic work; or
> (ii) an arrangement or transcription of a musical work involving no more than a change of key or register.

Treatment of a work is 'derogatory' if it amounts to distortion or mutilation of the work or is otherwise prejudicial to the honour or reputation of the author or director.

> **Example**
>
> There is very little case law so far. One example is that of the music publishing company in the *George Michael 'Bad Boys Megamix'* case, *Morrison Leahy Music Ltd v Lightbond Ltd & Others* (1993) EMLR 144. They produced a sound recording which was a medley of words and music from five of George Michael's compositions. The composer argued that among other infringements, his moral right of integrity had been infringed by the treatment given to the compositions in the course of mixing them on to the recording (specifically, that selecting parts of works, and playing them out of context, alters their character). An injunction was granted on the basis that there was a triable issue and that damages would be an insufficient remedy, but the judge took the view that a final decision must depend on the significance and quality of the parts taken in their original and their new contexts. This is an unsatisfactory example from which to draw many conclusions.

The right is infringed by a person who:

- publishes, performs or exhibits in public, broadcasts or puts into a cable programme service a derogatory treatment of a work; or
- issues copies of a film or sound recording to the public containing a derogatory treatment of the work.

Where one person has treated a work derogatorily, and another person uses or further treats part of such treatment, the right is infringed by that other person if the parts used or further treated are attributed to, or are likely to be regarded as the work of, the author or director.

> **Examples**
> - If I am the writer of a scholarly work on Islam, can I object to the reproduction of part of the text in a multimedia work against a background of film footage of rioting Muslim fundamentalists?
> - If I am a composer can I, on the basis of my moral rights, object if someone takes extracts of a number of my works and combines them into one recording? The answer may be 'yes': *see Bad Boys Megamix, George Michael's case, above.*

There are certain exceptions to the right; it does not apply to:

- a computer program;
- any computer-generated work;
- a work made for the purpose of recording current events; or in relation to
- publication of a work in a newspaper, magazine or similar periodical, or an encyclopaedia, dictionary, year book or other collective work of reference of a literary, dramatic, musical or artistic work made for the purposes of such publication or made available with the consent of the author for the purposes of such publication. The

right will not apply in relation to *any* subsequent exploitation of such a work without any modification of the published version.

> **Query**
>
> Is a newspaper delivered on-line or by CD-ROM still a newspaper or otherwise a 'similar periodical'? Or is it a collective work of reference? If not, moral rights may (re-) apply to the work so delivered. The answer to the question remains to be decided: time will tell what attitude the UK courts will take, or indeed the ECJ if the matter is taken that far!

The right does not apply in relation to anything done to a work with the authority of the copyright owner where the work originally vested in the author's employer (or in the director's employer) unless the author or director is identified at the time of the relevant act or has previously been identified in, or in published copies of, the work. However, where the right does apply, it is not infringed if there is a 'sufficient disclaimer'. The statutory definition of what amounts to a sufficient disclaimer is that it must be clear and reasonably prominent; given at the time of the act (and, where the author or director is then identified, appearing along with the identification); and it must state that the work has been subjected to treatment to which the author or director has not consented.

The integrity right is also infringed by anyone who deals in the course of a business with an article which is and which he knows, or has reason to believe, is an infringing article (this is analogous with secondary infringement of copyright). For these purposes 'an infringing article' means a work or copy of a work which has been subjected to derogatory treatment and has been or is likely to be, eg published commercially, issued to the public or shown to the public in circumstances infringing the right not to have the work derogatorily treated.

8.3 FALSE ATTRIBUTION

A person is entitled not to be called the author of a work if he or she is not the author; nor to have a film falsely attributed to him or her as director. There are no exceptions.

The right is infringed if the work bearing the false attribution is published or otherwise issued or shown to the public, or included in a cable programme service.

> **Examples**
>
> - A serialisation of an author's work is published in a newspaper with the wrong attribution. Not surprisingly, the author's right of paternity is infringed by such publication! But the author's right of false attribution is not infringed. This is because the right is not to have another's work credited as one's own. So, in this example, it is the unknown person who is wrongly credited with the author's work who would have a claim in false attribution!   *(Cont'd)*

> - An author's work is incorporated under the author's name into a multimedia work which can be manipulated electronically. It is then manipulated to such an extent that it becomes a different work but it is still credited to the author. In addition to any infringement of the author's right not to have the work treated derogatorily, there could be an infringement of the right not to have a work falsely attributed. (But note that there would be no infringement of the right of integrity if any of the exceptions mentioned above apply.)

8.4 RIGHT TO PRIVACY OF CERTAIN PHOTOGRAPHS AND FILMS

A person who commissions the taking of a photograph or the making of a film for private and domestic purposes is entitled to prevent copies of that work being issued to the public, or to have it exhibited or shown in public, or to have it broadcast or included in a cable programme service. There is no infringement of this right if the work is incidentally included in an artistic work, film, broadcast or cable programme. This right can be exercised only by the person who *commissions* the film or photograph, not by those (others) who appear in it.

> **Example**
> - A wedding photographer is commissioned by the bride's father to take photographs. In the absence of agreement to the contrary, the copyright in the photographs belongs to the photographer. However, *the bride's father* (not anyone else in the photographs) has the right to prevent publication.
> - A journalist taking photographs, uninvited, is not subject to this right; he, or his employers, will own the copyright in the photographs and will be entitled to exploit them.

8.5 DURATION

The paternity, integrity and privacy rights last as long as copyright lasts. The false attribution right continues until 20 years after the individual's death.

8.6 CONSENT/WAIVER

The owner of a moral right can consent to its infringement and indeed can waive his or her rights in their entirety, in whole or in part. Any such waiver should be in writing *signed by the person giving up the right*. It appears that a waiver signed on behalf of an author or director would *not* be effective.

> **Example**
>
> An author's agent signs a contract on behalf of his client. Any purported waiver of moral rights in that contract might not be effective to bind the author. (The agent may, incidentally, lay himself open to an action for misrepresentation.)

8.6.1 MORAL RIGHTS WAIVER CLAUSES

Full waiver of moral rights clauses follow:

Sample clause: Waiver of author's rights

> The Author hereby waives unconditionally and irrevocably the benefit of any provision of law known as 'Moral Rights' whether pursuant to Section 87 of the Copyright, Designs and Patents Act 1988 or similar laws now or hereafter prevailing in any part of the world, which might otherwise apply to any products of the Author's services hereunder and the Author agrees that he will not assert any moral right against the Company. In giving this waiver, the Author recognises the Company's need to be able to deal without restriction with any copyright work, the creation of which he has been involved with.

Sample clause: Warranty by company where author's rights waived

A warranty from a company that an author had waived his moral rights might be worded as follows:

> The [Company] hereby warrants that the Author has unconditionally waived in favour of the [Company] any rights in relation to his performance or the product of his services hereunder to which he may be entitled under Part I Chapter IV of the Copyright, Designs and Patents Act 1988 or any moral right or *droit moral* or similar right to which the Author might be entitled in any country.

The waiver can be specific, conditional or expressed to be subject to revocation. Any waiver made in favour of an owner or prospective owner of a copyright is presumed to extend to his or her licensees and successors in title.

Joint authors must each assert their right to paternity. Each joint author is entitled, separately, to the right of integrity.

> **Queries**
>
> - Will the makers of multimedia products want waivers (whether absolute or conditional) of moral rights by the providers of content? If the film industry is any measure, they will.
> - Can the concept of moral rights be sustained in 'made-for-electronic' works? In some cases, yes, but in the majority of cases, in our view no.
> - Is a waiver under an English law contract effective in other countries? Possibly not (*see* 8.9 for the position in France).

8.7 GENERAL AND INTERNATIONAL RIGHTS

There are no moral rights in a computer program (which is not defined in the CDPA) nor in a computer-generated work defined (in the CDPA, s 178) as a work generated by computer in circumstances such that there is no human author of the work.

> **Example**
>
> An example of a computer-generated work is a selection (made by the operation of a computer program) of data from a database, such as a list of individuals (whose preferences are listed on the database) who like going to the theatre.
>
> It is irrelevant for these purposes that there was human input into the design of the program or that the original database was compiled by human action. However, if a human hand then made further adjustments to the list, the work could, depending on the extent and/or originality of that human input, be a work of joint authorship. The human would then have moral rights in his or her input.

The list of countries (*see* Appendix 7) which are signatories to the Berne Convention provides an indication of those countries which offer some form of moral rights protection.

English law may not currently take moral rights as seriously as civil law generally does, but these rights are important and must not be ignored. The film industry requires waivers; multimedia products may also need the benefit of waivers, particularly if full use is to be taken of the interactive capacity of the medium.

Under French law, waivers of moral rights are not possible and yet the French have a burgeoning film industry. In France infringement of *droit moral* is usually regarded as raising questions of honour, which are remedied by judicial recognition of that infringement (often accompanied by an injunction and the award of a token one Franc in damages). Anglo-Saxon judges will be inclined (on the basis of tradition alone) to award large damages for injured feelings and loss of reputation.

8.7.1 *DROIT DE REPENTIR*

French law (along with a number of other civil jurisdictions) gives an author an additional right: *le droit de repentir*, ie, the right to recall his or her work and/or amend it. Exercise of this right requires the author to compensate the publisher and, if the author subsequently decides to reissue the work, to re-offer it to the original publisher on the original terms. This right is not often exercised.

8.7.2 *DROIT DE SUITE*

Many continental, civil law jurisdictions also offer a further moral right, the *droit de suite*. This right allows an artist to 'follow' any increase in value in his or her work and claim a share of that increase when the work is sold at auction (but usually not when sold by private treaty).

8.8 MORAL RIGHTS IN THE USA

The USA adhered to the Berne Convention in 1989; at the time there was a debate, which continues in some quarters, as to whether (and if so, how much) US law gives protection to moral rights[1]. It was contended by some that US law contained sufficient protection for authors without further amendment. US law is complicated by the duality of Federal and State law.

Nimmer says that while on the face of it US Federal and State judicial decisions may lead one to believe that 'moral rights are utterly alien to the fabric of US law', deeper examination suggests that there is an increasing accretion of case law, whether under the label of copyright or otherwise (such as unfair competition, defamation, invasion of privacy or breach of contract), which effectively is meeting artists' demands for moral rights.

It is Nimmer's view that moral rights, to the extent they exist in the USA, have tended to be for the benefit of fine art: painters, sculptors, photographers and the like. The Federal and State laws which do exist relate solely to protection for works of visual art and are limited in their scope even within that boundary.

Writers in favour of moral rights protection might argue that the USA, by ratifying the Berne Convention and joining the Berne Union, obligated itself to honour the Berne moral rights standards and in effect adopted art 6(*bis*) into substantive US copyright law. Even this article specifies that the means of redress for safeguarding moral rights is to be governed by the legislation of the country where protection is claimed. So it is back to the provisions of US law.

Many US lawyers will argue that what we call paternity and integrity rights are well recognised within the fabric of US law. David Land, the former Registrar of Copyrights, said in 1988 that courts faced with moral rights claims will in many cases look for guidance to Berne and the laws of those nations more familiar with moral rights.

The purpose of going into these issues even at this length has been to show that there is no substitute for taking US advice on these issues, that they are complicated in the sense that moral rights do not exist as such, but that most of the rights which are recognised in Europe under the title of moral rights can probably be found in one form or another under some aspect of US legislation, whether at State or Federal level.

Checklist

Before using any material consider these issues:
- (1) Is the work subject to, or does the author have, moral rights?
- (2) Has *consent* been obtained for the intended use or has the author *waived* his or her rights? If no, then:
- (3) Is the use one where moral rights apply?
- (4) Has the work been subject to *treatment*?
- (5) Is the treatment *derogatory*?
- (6) Has the paternity right been asserted? If so, has credit been given to all relevant authors and to the director?
- (7) Do any of the exceptions apply?
- (8) Is the work correctly attributed?
- (9) If the work is a film or photograph:
  - (a) Could it have been commissioned for private and domestic purposes?
  - (b) Was it made prior to commencement of the CDPA?

(Cont'd)

> (10) What is the international position? Where, as inevitably, rights need clearing for international use, what is the moral rights position elsewhere? In many jurisdictions, moral rights are inalienable and unwaivable.
> (11) If contracting with a party other than the author, have adequate warranties (and indemnities) been obtained that the work is free and clear of *droit moral* claims?
> (12) Is the grantor worth 'powder and shot' in support of those warranties and indemnities?
> (13) Ensure adequate restrictions on use by licensees are inserted into user licences in order to limit exposure to moral rights claims.

8.9 MORAL RIGHTS ABROAD (PARTICULARLY FRANCE)

The concept of moral rights causes anxiety, especially for those of the Anglo-Saxon tradition. In the US (and also in non-Anglo-Saxon Japan), producers have identified moral rights as a serious legal barrier, given the commercial and technical need to re-edit and change the source material at the time it is loaded in a CD-ROM. Any significant change in the nature of moral rights, however, would be resisted by many and would probably require changes to the Berne Convention.

> **Example**
>
> The French case brought by the Estate of John Huston against the French broadcaster La Cinq is a strong reminder of the value attributed by the French to the moral rights of creators. 'Asphalt Jungle' was a film made in black and white in 1950 by John Huston. It was produced by MGM and the rights were bought by Turner Entertainment in 1986; in 1988 they colourised the film and licensed La Cinq to broadcast the colourised version on French television.
>
> At first instance the French Court held that colourisation of the film was capable of modifying the perception of the film by a viewer and that accordingly the Estate could object to the colourisation. In 1989 the Court of Appeal in Paris overturned that decision, considering that American law should apply and that any rights that John Huston had had, had been assigned to Turner.
>
> In 1994 the Court of Appeal in Versailles to which the case had been referred quashed the judgment of the Court of Appeal in Paris and seems to have applied the same reasoning as had the Court of First Instance in 1988. The Versailles court said that the applicable law was that of the country where protection was being claimed and in that case was French law. Under French law the right of integrity could not be assigned and accordingly remained vested in the estate of John Huston. It went on to decide that colourising a black and white film amounted to an infringement of that right. *(Cont'd)*

> It is clear that there needs to be much more study of moral rights and indeed the European Commission does have in mind that it will prepare a directive aimed at harmonising moral rights laws in the EU. That does seem to be a long term project however particularly as many feel that moral rights fall outside the Commission's jurisdiction.

8.10 TRANSITIONAL PROVISIONS

Only acts done after 1 August 1989 (ie before commencement of the CDPA) are subject to moral rights protection. The provisions of the Copyright Act 1956, eg the right not to have a work falsely attributed, continue to apply to acts done before that date.

Moral rights are applicable to works in copyright at the above date; however they do not apply:

(a) where the author died prior to that date;
(b) to films made before that date;
(c) where copyright first vested in the author, to anything done pursuant to an assignment of copyright or a licence entered into before that date.

> **Example**
> Before commencement of the CDPA, an author assigned his or her rights in a screenplay to a film company. The film was made *after* commencement. The author has no moral right to object to any changes made even though the changes were made after commencement.

Finally, the moral rights question cannot be dealt with in isolation. The essence of many multimedia products is that they easily cross national barriers. Thus the fact that pursuant to an English law contract an author waives his or her moral rights (or does not have any rights in the first place), and purports to do so world-wide may only mean that he or she does not have those rights in the UK; they may remain enforceable in eg, France, where moral rights are inalienable.

> **Example**
> An English multimedia producer commissions a Frenchman to supply the soundtrack, an American to supply text and a Scotsman to supply animation, all for a CD-ROM to be published in the UK, the US and elsewhere in the world. The contracts are expressed to be governed by English law. What is the moral rights position? Assume, first, that each contract contained a waiver of moral rights. The contracts with the two UK persons would be effective to cause them to have waived their moral rights, certainly so far as English law is concerned, almost certainly so far as US law is concerned but possibly not under French law.
> *(Cont'd)*

> The *La Cinq* case is a reminder that French law will not necessarily recognise the attempt to procure anyone to waive his rights in France: under French law, moral rights are inalienable and the *La Cinq* case has established that a French court will be reluctant to give effect to the attempt to force a waiver (in respect of acts done in France) even if the relevant contract is governed by a law which either does not recognise moral rights or allows the waiver of them.
>
> Exploitation of the CD-ROM in France will therefore always be subject to the exercise in France of moral rights. The same consideration must apply to those other jurisdictions which do not accept the possibility of waivers.
>
> Exploitation in America and the UK should not give rise to problems. Both UK and US law recognise waivers and accordingly would not be inclined to uphold the waived rights.

---

[1] For a fuller debate on the US position, the reader is referred to *Nimmer on Copyright*, Vol II, Chapter 8D to which this section is indebted. (The authors take their own responsibility for their interpretation and condensation of Nimmer's learned contribution to this subject.)

• 9 •
RIGHTS IN PERFORMANCES

9.1 INTRODUCTION

The CDPA, Pt II brought performances for the first time within the scope of copyright legislation. Before its enactment the protection of performances was contained within the Performers Protection Acts which made it a criminal offence, without the written consent of a performer, to record performances or perform them publicly. There was doubt as to the extent of the civil remedies.

Now, in addition to criminal sanctions, performers have civil remedies including damages and injunctions, as does a person who is a party to and has the benefit of a performance contract.

9.2 RIGHTS IN PERFORMANCE

For the purpose of the CDPA a performance is:

(a) a dramatic performance, including dance or mime;
(b) a musical performance;
(c) a reading or recitation of a literary work;
(d) a performance of a variety act or similar presentation.

It is only *live* performances given by an individual that are protected. The individual claiming protection must be a qualifying individual, ie, a citizen or subject of, or an individual resident in, a qualifying country.

9.3 RECORDING RIGHTS

Recordings are protected if:

(a) they are made directly from a live performance; or
(b) they are made from a broadcast of, or a cable programme including, the live performance, or are made directly or indirectly from another recording of the live performance;

provided that the party claiming protection is a qualifying individual (*see* above) or a qualifying company and has the benefit of an exclusive recording contract.

A qualifying company must be incorporated in, and have a place of business in, a qualifying country (not necessarily the same one); and the place of business must be one at which a substantial business activity is carried on.

A qualifying country means the UK, an EU country or a country to which the UK has extended protection. As a matter of UK government policy, protection is only extended to countries which provide reciprocity.

> **Example**
>
> A multimedia CD manufacturing company—Multi-CD Ltd— is incorporated in England and has its principal place of business in France. Its entire production line is exported to the USA. France grants reciprocity; the USA does not. Multi-CD Ltd is *not* a qualifying company.

Appendix 6 provides a list of those countries to which reciprocal protection under Part II of the CDPA has been extended.

9.4 INFRINGING ACTS (CIVIL)

9.4.1 PERFORMER'S RIGHTS

The performer's rights are infringed by the following:

(1) The making of a recording of, or the live broadcasting of, a qualifying performance (including live performances in a cable programme service) without consent infringes the performer's rights, unless the infringer can show that at the time of the infringement he believed on reasonable grounds that consent had been given.
(2) Public performance, broadcasting or inclusion in a cable programme service, of recordings which have, and which the 'infringer' knows or has reason to believe have, been made without consent are also infringements.
(3) Importation, without consent, into the UK of an illicit recording of a qualifying performance except for private or domestic use, or the possession in the course of business, offering for sale or distribution of the same are all infringing acts, provided, also, that the 'infringer' knows or has reason to believe that it is an illicit recording.

9.4.2 RECORDING RIGHTS

The rights of the person having recording rights are infringed by the same acts as set out above with the exception of broadcasting the performance *live* or including it *live* in a cable programme service.

9.5 DEFENCES

A person making a recording has a defence if the recordings were made for private or domestic use; or if he had reasonable grounds to believe that consent had been given; the user of the recording has to show that he neither knew, nor had reason to believe, that the recording was made without consent.

9.6 EXCEPTIONS

Similar exceptions apply to rights in performance as apply to copyright.

> **Example**
>
> If an excerpt of a recording (to which, for instance, the fair dealing provisions of the CDPA apply in relation to copyright infringement) is broadcast, the broadcaster also has a fair dealing defence against any complaint by a performer that the recording infringed his or her performing rights.

9.7 DURATION

The period of the rights is 50 years from the end of the calendar year in which the performance takes place.

> **Example**
>
> A performer gives a live performance on stage. The performance is recorded. The performer repeats the performance (with nightly variations) for the next two years.
>
> There is no requirement for originality (where performances are concerned) in the CDPA. Accordingly, under the CDPA it seems the copyright period will run from the end of the *third* year. If the performer gives another performance ten years later, it seems he or she starts the period running again.
>
> It does not matter whether a film of the performance is subsequently released or not. (It can only be released with the performer's consent.)

This period will *not* be extended by the Duration of Copyright Directive (*see* 4.3) but its *measurement* may be. The Directive requires a 50-year period from first publication of a recording of the performance or, if none, from first dissemination or, if none, from the performance itself. However, what is the position of a performer who repeats the same performance throughout his working career? The CDPA will have to be amended to bring in the provisions of the Directive and then the position will be:

> **Example**
>
> On the facts of the previous example, the 50-year period will run from the end of the year of the date of the *first* performance. If the recording is published or disseminated 49 years later, the period will be extended for a further 50 years from such publication or dissemination. The precise position will depend on how the UK actually implements the Directive.

9.8 ASSIGNMENT

Performance rights are personal and may not be assigned or transmitted; they will, however, accrue to a deceased performer's estate.

9.9 CONSENT

Consent does *not* have to be given in writing: oral consent or consent by conduct is sufficient.

> **Recommendation**
> Always seek consent in writing. Do not rely on oral tradition—memories are notoriously short and proof is difficult.

Consent may be given in relation to a specific performance, a specified type of performance or all performances; and it may relate both to past and future performances.

9.10 REMEDIES

Infringements are actionable as breaches of statutory duty. Damages, accounts of infringer's profits and injunctive remedies are available. A court may order delivery up of the recordings; and statutory powers of seizure exist. There are also criminal sanctions contained within the CDPA, ss 198–205.

Sample clause: Grant of performer's rights

1. The Performer hereby assigns to the Publisher the entire copyright (by way of present assignment of future copyright and including all similar neighbouring rights such as rental and lending) in the Performance throughout the world absolutely for the full period of copyright and all renewals and extensions thereof.
2. The Performer hereby irrevocably grants the Publisher all consents pursuant to Part II of the Copyright, Designs and Patents Act 1988 and any amendment or re-enactment thereof for the fullest possible use of the Performance in all media throughout the world including without limitation the right to:
   (a) alter, adapt or make additions to or deletions from the Performance at the Publisher's sole discretion and the Performer hereby unconditionally and irrevocably waives any moral rights the Performer may have in any country relating to the Performance;
   (b) make, distribute and exploit and to authorise the making, distribution and exploitation of any recording or fixation of the Performance separately from or in conjunction with the Work including all further versions for all media and by any manner or means whether now known or subsequently invented and all related marketing materials and advertisements.

— • 10 • —

CONTENT REGULATION

10.1 REGULATORY BODIES

A large number of bodies in the UK exercise regulatory control over the content carried in different forms of media. However, many of these are media specific and regulate particular industries and forms of communication. Since multimedia necessarily involves a convergence of traditional media forms, this has a number of important consequences for multimedia products:

- there is no dedicated regulatory regime which applies to it;
- it is not certain which of the existing bodies do apply to it; and
- different levels of classification, control and censorship are exercised in each media industry by each regime and this makes the establishment of a multimedia standard difficult.

The very existence of multimedia makes it likely that these different bodies and standards will gradually converge in a similar fashion to the industries they seek to regulate. A unified regime—whether desirable or necessary—is not on the horizon but a process of amendment and, it is to be hoped, mutual co-operation will probably take place in the near future. The Government and the Labour Party are already developing plans for such convergence (*see* 2.1). This should result in a more coherent and compatible legal and regulatory regime for multimedia content than exists today.[1]

The following bodies may be, or may be likely to become, relevant in regulating content in multimedia products. (The addresses of these bodies are given in Appendix 4.)

10.1.1 OFTEL AND ICSTIS

Under the Telecommunications Act 1984 Oftel (the Office of Telecommunications) was set up as the regulator of the telecommunications industry in the UK. Oftel set up ICSTIS (the Independent Committee for the Supervision of Standards for Telephone Information Services) to supervise the content of, and promotional material for, telephone information services through the enforcement of its code of practice, with the support of network operators themselves. Exemption for certain live services can be gained directly from Oftel. Where multimedia on-line services are provided through the telephone network the regulatory restrictions of either of these bodies may be relevant.

10.1.2 INDEPENDENT TELEVISION COMMISSION

The Independent Television Commission (ITC) is the public body set up by the Broadcasting Act 1990 for licensing and regulating commercially funded television services provided in and from the UK. These include Channel 3 (ITV), Channel 4, public teletext and cable, local delivery and satellite service—as defined by the Act. Thus where a multimedia product or service falls within the relevant definition, or subsequent legislation affects such an inclusion, the ITC's extensive body of regulations on programme content, advertising and sponsorship will be relevant. When regulating cable, local delivery and satellite services, the ITC has recognised that a different approach from that imposed on traditional broadcasting service is suitable. It considers that there is no need to maintain a specific content mix in which information, education and entertainment are balanced. However, it still maintains that there is a need to curb possible abuses, eg, protecting children from unsuitable programmes and adults' susceptibilities from exploitation through the control of violent and sexually explicit material. Advertising and programme sponsorship must not result in the public being misled or deceived. Thus, extensive controls are still enforced. A recent paper by the ITC's Director of Cable and Satellite has stated that whilst Internet services may fall within the Broadcasting Act's relevant definitions, the ITC 'has not so far considered it necessary to institute arrangements for enforcement of licensing over Internet services', although it has granted licences to UK video-on-demand trials.

10.1.3 BROADCASTING COMPLAINTS COMMISSION AND BROADCASTING STANDARDS COUNCIL

Again under the Broadcasting Act 1990 the Broadcasting Complaints Commission (BCC) and the Broadcasting Standards Council (BSC) consider complaints against the content of programmes. The BCC handles complaints of unjust or unfair treatment or unwarranted infringement of privacy. The BSC deals with complaints over the portrayal of violence and sexual conduct, and standards of taste and decency in programmes generally. Their ability to handle complaints over multimedia products or services depends upon whether the product falls within the Broadcasting Act 1990. If it does not their jurisdiction is otherwise extended. Plans to merge the two organisations are currently being considered.

10.1.4 ADVERTISING STANDARDS AUTHORITY

The Committee of Advertising Practice is a self-regulatory body whose members include organisations that represent the advertising, sales promotion and media businesses, eg the Direct Marketing Association. The Advertising Standards Authority (ASA) is an independent body which publishes the British Codes of Advertising and Sales Promotion. The most recent edition of the codes, published in February 1995, was explicitly extended to cover 'advertisements in non-broadcast electronic media such as computer games'. However, whilst the ASA have stated that this includes the Internet, no steps have so far been taken to actively regulate Internet advertisements.

10.1.5 BRITISH BOARD OF FILM CLASSIFICATION

The British Board of Film Classification (BBFC) has for many years regulated the content of films distributed in the UK. In recent years it has also controlled the content of videos distributed in this country. Under the provisions of the Video Recordings Act 1984 certain video games have also been referred to the Board for consideration. On this basis many multimedia works may well also require reference to the Board (*see* 10.3.4).

10.1.6 EUROPEAN LEISURE SOFTWARE PRODUCERS ASSOCIATION

The European Leisure Software Producers Association (ELSPA) was set up to provide a self-regulating body for the software industry. This was seen as necessary to head off the potential for government legislation on the content of, in particular, video games. ELSPA has its own rating system (*see* 10.3.4) but works in conjunction with the BBFC, the VSC and Video Packaging Committee.

10.1.7 VIDEO STANDARDS COUNCIL

The Video Standards Council (VSC) was established in 1989 to develop and oversee a code of practice designed to promote standards within the video industry. It has subsequently expanded to promote standards in the computer and video games industry. It consequently works closely with both ELSPA and the BBFC.

10.1.8 DATA PROTECTION REGISTRAR

A set of guidelines are published by the Data Protection Registrar to inform individuals of their rights under the Data Protection Act 1984 and to help those who process personal data to understand their obligations. The nature of certain multimedia products may require reference to these guidelines.

10.2 DEFAMATION

Digital media will be subject to the same complaints in defamation as other media. Reputations need protection (whatever the medium of delivery of the message) and defamation has already aroused considerable interest in the multimedia field, particularly with on-line services. Traditionally the Internet has relied upon its users' own restraint—adhering to a code of 'Netiquette' in order to control on-line behaviour but as use increases this self-regulation no longer appears to be enough.

Netiquette

This informal code of behaviour was developed by users as a way of regulating on-line communication (particularly on BBS) while at the same time maintaining the jealously guarded independent and non-commercial culture of the Internet. It is somewhat unevenly enforced, and transgressors may be punished by:
- 'flaming'—flooding a user with a torrent of data (a famous recipient being a US law firm who used a BBS to advertise its services, an 'offence' known as 'spamming'); or
- more drastic measures such as hacking into the offender's computer, publishing their telephone number on-line or erasing their particular link to the network.

The bulletin board news group moderators and service providers who manage material which appears on-line may take steps to control behaviour or it may be left to other users, including so-called 'Net Vigilantes', to act. Increasingly, as on-line services such as the Internet start to become mainstream commercial tools, eg, through

(Cont'd)

> growth of the World Wide Web, and as more users go on-line a more effective form of regulation will be necessary. More active editing, whether by software or paid editors (as is proposed for Microsoft's Network) can, however, only go so far in regulating the large volume of material that appears on-line.

Defamation—a definition

A statement is defamatory if, in the circumstances of publication, it lowers the subject in the estimation of right-thinking people generally. To be actionable the statement must have been published; in other words, knowingly communicated to someone else other than the subject, whether in permanent form (libel) or transient form (slander). Most on-line communications should have a sufficient degree of permanence to be classified as the former. Thus, a statement will clearly have been published when included in the screen display of a CD-ROM or other multimedia product sold to the public. In the case of an on-line service such as the Internet, where a defamatory message has been sent to a bulletin board news group (BBS), open either to all users or just to subscribers of a particular on-line service provider, it can be seen that this will have been published where the BBS operates like a conventional notice-board and allows any user, who has access to it, to read all the messages on the board. Similarly, the sender of a defamatory e-mail will be liable where third parties read that message in the same way as more traditional mail[2] as will the sender of a defamatory statement appearing on the pages of the World Wide Web which is read by a third party.

On-line defamation

Until recently the use of on-line services had not resulted in wide-scale defamation litigation. While the Internet makes it easy to publish defamatory messages, whether intentionally or by simply forgetting in the midst of heated debate on-line that others have access to a message, it is also easy to type in a reply and set the record straight. Further, users can ask the service provider running a service to act if a specific message goes too far. Indeed on many BBS, users will see both the original message and the response it generates displayed together. However, as UK law stands at the moment, this does not make any difference to whether or not a plaintiff may bring an action for defamation, although it could have a bearing on any damages awarded. It would be a significant step for the courts or legislators to allow a different standard to develop for on-line communications from that applicable to other areas of life.

10.2.1 LIABILITY OF SERVICE PROVIDERS

The Internet also raises other issues. When a defamatory message is published it is not just the author who may be held liable. Under UK law everyone who takes part in the publication of a libel is theoretically jointly and severally liable. Over the years the parameters of this liability in traditional media distribution have become established through case law (though statutory changes are proposed by the Defamation Bill—*see* 10.2.3). So where the material complained of is contained in a CD-ROM a plaintiff could elect whether to sue all the parties responsible for its publication, from the creator to the retailer, or to sue any one or more of them separately. However the position on-line is not so clear; by the very nature of a service such as the Internet, the author of a libellous message may:

- be unidentifiable or untraceable. Various technical devices can be used to disguise or hide the true identity of an Internet user and it is far easier to reach a large number of people anonymously with the Internet than with other publishing media;
- be outside the jurisdiction of the victim's courts. The ease with which messages on the Internet may cross international borders in comparison with traditional distribution channels for books and magazines or CD-ROMs is of great importance. The victim of a libellous statement may find its author far from the jurisdiction of the UK courts and practically impossible to sue;
- if traceable, have insufficient funds to meet the claim. A plaintiff will pick out whom they perceive to have a 'deep pocket' and the author may simply not be worth suing.

Defamation—service providers

So if anyone taking part in the publication of the libel is theoretically liable, whom else may a plaintiff sue? The most likely candidates are the service providers that allow a user access to the Internet or the particular destinations such as a BBS. For this purpose 'service provider' could include anyone who provides a service or product that allows third parties to post material on-line including, for example, access to advertising space or other interactive services, and could extend to many multimedia producers. However, applying the laws of defamation to a service provider is not straightforward. If it can successfully argue that it operates a 'telematic' service, ie a communication system for the exchange of information in the same way as a telephone company or the Post Office, but simply using a different medium, a service provider should be no more liable for delivering a libellous message than the Post Office is for delivering a libellous letter or BT for defamatory comments made over the phone or sent by fax. Such an analogy seems valid for e-mail between individuals. If, however, facilitation or participation in sending a message to a BBS is more akin to, say, publishing a book, or broadcasting a television or radio programme in that the messages are necessarily disclosed to a section of the public should the service provider be liable?

The difficulty is that the level of involvement of different service providers in the control and editing of messages and content on their network varies considerably. A service provider may merely set up a system and not take an active part in controlling messages that appear, just as a company providing transmitters or satellites may play no part in the selection or production of programmes appearing on the television channels it broadcasts. From a practical perspective, it is certainly difficult for the larger service providers to vet the number of messages appearing daily on a BBS. While smaller service providers may be able to censor subject-matter—indeed they may advertise this service to users who do not wish to receive certain types of material—identifying whether or not a message is defamatory (as a book or CD-ROM publisher usually has to do) will usually be far harder than spotting pornographic or other controversial content. On the other hand, some material may obviously fall into the 'dangerous' category and thus require vetting by a careful 'publisher'.

Thus service providers' liability will depend on whether they fit into the traditional categories of publisher, printer, distributor or vendor. If the courts decide that service providers should be treated as publishers, they will only have the same defences as the author:

- proving the truth of the message;
- establishing that it was fair comment;
- establishing that absolute or qualified privileged attached to the publication.

There is a further defence for a person who has only taken a 'subordinate part in disseminating' the material and this has been held to apply to distributors and sellers but not to printers (but *see* below), nor, presumably, to CD-ROM manufacturers. It would appear that the role of most service providers corresponds best to that of distributor since they do not arrange or edit the text and, if a court agreed, this defence would apply if the service provider could show that:

(a) it did not know that the material contained or was of a character likely to contain libel complained of; and
(b) its lack of knowledge was not due to any negligence on its part.[3]

Service providers undoubtedly do know that there is likely to be defamatory material on the Internet, but they could argue that they did not know that a particular message contained the libel. Again, establishing what checks a service provider should be expected to carry out to avoid negligence would probably depend upon its size and the service offered.[4]

10.2.2 US CASE LAW

How have the courts so far dealt with on-line defamation? In the US case of *CompuServe v Cubby* 776F, Supp 135 (1991) large on-line service provider CompuServe used a third party to 'manage, review, create, delete, edit and otherwise control the contents' of an on-line journalism discussion forum which carried defamatory remarks against the plaintiff. Claims against CompuServe were dismissed since the court held that:

> CompuServe does not have any more editorial control over such a publication than does a public library, bookstore or news-stand and it would be no more feasible for CompuServe to examine every publication it carries for potential defamatory statements than it would be for any other distributor to do so.

However, another US service provider, Prodigy, was recently sued for libel and negligence by a firm of underwriters, Stratton Oakmount, for defamatory statements made by a Prodigy subscriber on one Prodigy on-line investment BBS. In that case, 23 Media L Rep 1794 (24.5.95), Prodigy was held to be liable for the defamatory statements because:

(1) It held itself out as an on-line service that exercised editorial control over the content of messages posted on its computer bulletin boards.
(2) Prodigy implemented this control through its automatic software screening program. By actively utilising technology and manpower to delete notes from its BBS for offensiveness and bad taste, it was held, Prodigy was clearly making decisions as to content and such decisions constitute editorial control.

The court made it clear that the general legal position of BBS is that they should be regarded in the same context as bookshops, libraries and network affiliates. However, it was Prodigy's new policies, the fact that it held itself out as exercising editorial control, and had the technology and staffing to do so, which altered the scenario and resulted in the finding that for the purposes of defamation Prodigy was a 'publisher'. These cases have no legal authority in the UK and the Prodigy case has now been effectively reversed in the US by the recent Telecommunications Act, but how far should service providers be liable for material which third parties place on their on-line system? The Prodigy case highlights the potentially difficult issue that service providers could be liable for defamation where they monitor in order to avoid either being negligent or liability in respect of obscenity.

10.2.3 DEFAMATION BILL

No UK cases on defamation on the Internet have yet been reported but there have been several out-of-court settlements (see, however, the Australian case of *Rindos v Hardwick* (1994 of 1993) re: BBS). However government legislation, the Defamation Bill, is being planned which would reform liability for publication and, as currently drafted, expressly covers electronic publishing. It would provide a defence to Internet service providers in so far as they are not primarily responsible for publication of a defamatory statement, have taken reasonable care and did not know or have reason to suspect that their acts contributed to the publication. However, this still fails to provide practical guidance on where the dividing lines between being neligent, exercising reasonable care and adopting editorial control lie.

10.2.4 DEFENCES

On a practical basis, defamation clearance for publishers is usually framed in terms of a balance of risk, ie who is actually likely to take action? It will be much harder for lawyers to advise clients where the traditional territorial controls of print publishing no longer exist, allowing on-line content to reach anywhere in the world and defamation actions to be brought in any jurisdiction. British defamation law is less favourable to defendants than the law of most other countries. On-line services could help to maintain Britain's reputation as the libel centre of the world for potential plaintiffs. Further, small service providers are unlikely to be willing to take the financial risk of losing a defamation action and, if sued, would probably decide to settle out of court. Such decisions will depend upon the availability of defamation insurance cover and, while insurance companies are currently quoting cover for service providers, they clearly will not want to be exposed to open-ended liability.

While it seems to hold the access providers liable for messages which they cannot possibly vet, it is likewise unfair if a person or company has no effective remedy for libellous allegations made against them which could have a profound effect on their reputation.

How far service providers should be held liable for material that appears on the Internet clearly extends beyond defamation. The appearance of obscene and pornographic material is currently the source of a great deal of debate, especially in the USA, over appropriate standards and regulations. Further in a US case of copyright and trademark infringement, *Playboy Enterprises v Frena* 839 F Sup 1552 (MD Fla 1993) the defendant service provider was held responsible for infringing pictures taken from the plaintiff's magazines which were placed by a third party on the defendant's BBS, even though the defendant removed them as soon as he became aware of their existence.

10.3 OBSCENITY AND CENSORSHIP

The availability of pornographic material both on computer disk and via on-line services such as the Internet has received considerable attention in press and political debate. The UK Parliamentary Home Affairs Select Committee Report declared computer pornography to be the 'new horror' and well-publicised prosecutions and legislative steps have taken place in the UK and elsewhere in response.

The legal framework in the UK covering obscenity is complex. The main items of legislation are listed below.

10.3.1 OBSCENE PUBLICATIONS ACTS 1959 AND 1964

The OP Acts define an obscene item as something which, taken as a whole, tends to 'deprave and corrupt persons who are likely, having regard to all relevant circumstances, to read, see or hear it'. In applying this definition courts require material to go further than merely shock. The definition of obscenity is much narrower than sexual explicitness. There are two separate offences:

(a) to publish an obscene article (ie, 'distribute, circulate, sell . . . record, show, play or project it'); and
(b) to have an obscene article for publication for gain.

Possession in itself is not an offence.

The 1994 Criminal Justice and Public Order Act (the 1994 Act) amended the definition of publication of obscene matter to include: 'where matter is data stored electronically (a person publishes where he) transmits that data'. In the context of the Internet it will be seen that the above wording means that not only the sender of obscene material but also any party providing access or computer facilities may also be liable whether a service provider or an employer. It is a defence to show that the person charged did not examine the material in question and that they had no reasonable cause to suspect that their publication of it would lead to liability. Thus if a party knows that obscene material is being published via their facilities they cannot just turn a blind eye and escape liability.

10.3.2 TELECOMMUNICATIONS ACT 1984

This Act makes it an offence to transmit over a public telecommunications network a 'message or other matter that is grossly offensive or of an indecent, obscene or menacing character'. This should extend to Internet and on-line transmissions in so far as they are on a public network but no case law has yet emerged.

10.3.3 PROTECTION OF CHILDREN ACT 1978

The Criminal Justice Act 1988 amended the Protection of Children Act 1978 so that mere possession of an indecent (wider than obscene) image of a child is now an offence (in addition to distribution, sale etc). The 1994 Act introduced the concept of 'pseudo photograph' as a way of catching images in digital rather than hard copy form 'faked' to look like a child. There is, however, a defence where possession of the image was not requested and the image was not kept for an unreasonable length of time: this could protect the innocent Internet user receiving child pornography by error.

10.3.4 VIDEO RECORDINGS ACT 1984

The Video Recordings Act 1984 (as amended) ('VRA') was introduced to regulate video distribution and requires anyone who supplies or offers to supply or possesses for the purpose of supply a video work (to which the VRA applies) to ensure that the work has been classified by the BBFC and that its carrier has been labelled in accordance with the statutory labelling regulations. Given that the terms of the VRA refer to 'any series of visual images' that are produced electronically by the use of information contained on a

OBSCENITY AND CENSORSHIP 10.3.4

disk or magnetic tape the BBFC interprets the VRA to apply beyond merely video recordings distributed on VHS tape (unless they are 'exempt works'—*see* below)

> **BBFC Classification**
>
> Under the VRA multimedia works on CD-ROM, or similar disk format, which contain a video work caught by the Act must be classified by the BBFC and packaged correctly in order to be legally distributed in the UK. The BBFC guidelines for classification under the VRA are different from those for theatrical release as they take into account use in the home. The BBFC classifies a 'work', so a work once classified can be released in other formats as long as it has not been amended in any way.
>
> A video work is exempted from classification if, taken as a whole:
> (1) it is designed to inform, educate or instruct; or
> (2) it is concerned with sport, religion or music; or
> (3) it is a video game
>
> However exempted status is forfeited if the video work to a significant extent depicts:
> (a) human sexual activity or acts of force or restraint associated with such activity; or
> (b) mutilation or torture of, or other acts of gross violence towards, humans or animals; or
> (c) human genital organs or human urinary or excretory functions; or
> (d) images designed to stimulate or encourage anything within paragraph (a) to a significant extent or (b) to any extent
>
> The decision on whether a work is exempt or caught by the VRA rests with the multimedia producer and advice should be taken. See the recent case of *Kent County Council v Multi Media Marketing* (1995) *The Times*, 9 May—*see* 6.3.1.
>
> If so classified, certification symbols should appear on the packaging of the product in accordance with the Video Recordings (Labelling) Regulations 1985 (the 'Regulations') and the BBFC's own recommendations, in a similar way to video film cassettes. The Video Packaging Review Committee will approve the packaging as a whole in accordance with the Regulations and other criteria such as the British Code of Advertising Practice, again in a similar way to video film cassettes.

> **The European Leisure Software Producers Association**
>
> In an attempt to respond to concern over violent and sexual content in video games European video games producers agreed a rating system for software under the auspices of the European Leisure Software Producers Association (ELSPA). Games are rated for suitability in four age categories: 0–10, 11–14, 15–17 and 18+. The packaging is marked accordingly. The system is self-regulatory and joined through membership of ELSPA.   *(Cont'd)*

> Members of ELSPA also agree to be bound by the Video Standards Council (VSC) Code of Practice which sets out a mixture of law and recommended trading practices designed to ensure that games are supplied to the public in a responsible manner, as it does for video film cassettes.

There have been many prosecutions for obscene content over on-line services. Forty people were arrested in the UK following a major police operation to monitor material being carried on various on-line services. Similar cases in the US incited Senator James Exon to propose a Bill to establish legal protection against the transmission of 'obscene, lewd, lascivious, filthy or indecent' images on e-mail, text files and any other form of on-line communication. The Bill has been very much criticised by opponents including the American Civil Liberties Union, the Electronic Frontier Foundation and the Internet Business Association. The debate is very similar to the more general debate on censorship and on the problem of drawing a legal line between moral outrage and individual freedom.

10.4 ADVERTISING AND SPONSORSHIP

Many restrictions on advertising and sponsorship are media-specific rules introduced by the regulatory bodies listed at 10.1. The ninth edition of the British Code of Advertising and Sales Promotion released in 1995 explicitly applies for the first time to 'advertisements in non-broadcast electronic media such as computer games' and will therefore be the main body of controls regulating off-line multimedia services—*see also* 10.5.6. The ASA has however so far not moved to regulate the Internet although authorities in the US have.

As described at 10.2, Netiquette has its own restrictions on where advertising on the Internet is perceived to be acceptable. Areas such as the World Wide Web are far more suitable than BBS or other sites where commercial activities may be resisted.

10.5 PRIVACY AND PUBLICITY

The area of privacy and publicity raises two separate issues:

(1) What rights do individuals have to prevent others invading their privacy?
(2) Do individuals have a right to exploit their personality for commercial gain and prevent others from doing so without their consent?

While other countries recognise such rights expressly, there are at present no such laws in the UK. There are, however, various laws that afford limited protection and therefore multimedia producers, as with any other content creators, need to be careful when using material which may involve these issues.

10.5.1 BREACH OF CONFIDENTIALITY

As detailed in 7.3.5, there can be an action for breach of confidentiality and this may be of some relevance in protecting an individual's privacy but this is a more limited concept than that which is usually thought of as a right of privacy.

10.5.2 INFRINGEMENT OF COPYRIGHT

The owner of the copyright in, for example, a photograph may bring an action for copyright infringement in respect of publication of the photograph without his consent. However, this provides no protection for the subject of the photograph (unless, of course, he also happens to be the copyright owner) or the commissioner (under the moral right of privacy).

10.5.3 DEFAMATION

One defence to a defamation action is that the statement complained of is true (and the truth can be *proved*). Therefore, if a person makes a statement about an individual's private life which he can prove to be true, it may amount to an invasion of privacy, but an action in defamation will not lie (but the position may be different in eg France).

10.5.4 HARASSMENT AND PHYSICAL INTRUSION

Existing laws of trespass to land and nuisance protect the possession and enjoyment of land and, therefore, indirectly that aspect of privacy described as seclusion or solitude. However, since they are dependent on ownership of land (or certain other interests recognised in law), they cannot offer protection to everyone.

10.5.5 PASSING OFF AND TRADE-MARK PROTECTION

In order to protect what American law would define as a right of publicity, eg, where a famous individual wishes to prevent a multimedia producer from releasing a product in which the individual appears since that individual wants to endorse, and receive payment for, another product the individual could try to establish a case of passing off (*see* 7.3.3). This may be difficult where the individual has no established reputation in connection with the product involved. Some have actually tried to obtain protection by applying to register a likeness or name as a registered trade mark.

10.5.6 REGULATORY BODIES

It is important to note that the bodies regulating advertising and content in certain media do have regulatory controls on privacy and publicity. As discussed above their application to different multimedia is unclear. However the ASA's British Code of Advertising Practice will be relevant. This contains restrictions regarding privacy and, effectively, publicity and the ASA regularly rules on complaints on these matters.

10.5.7 PROPOSALS FOR REFORM

A Consultation Paper published in July 1993, proposed the implementation of legislation to create a civil remedy for infringement of privacy. However, although subsequent events highlighted this whole issue again, there is no indication as yet that these proposals will be taken any further and indeed, in July 1995, the National Heritage Secretary, Virginia Bottomley, ruled out legislation to deal with newspaper invasions of privacy. She opted instead for tougher self-regulation.

10.6 DATA PROTECTION

Multimedia works may include databases of information. However, to the extent that this information constitutes personal data, it will be subject to legal control aimed at ensuring adequate levels of protection to safeguard the interests of those individuals whose details are kept by others. Ease of access and manipulation highlights the need for this.

10.6.1 DATA PROTECTION ACT 1984

The Data Protection Act was the first piece of legislation in the UK to address the use of information stored on any database which allows automatic processing of data. The DPA applies only to 'personal data', ie, information relating to individuals.

The DPA focuses on three closely linked areas:

- establishing a registration scheme for data holders;
- conferring rights on individuals to whom the personal data held relate: these are the 'data subjects';
- laying down requirements relating to what sort of data may be held and what may be done with them.

Data subjects have the right to:

- receive a copy of any personal data held on them;
- challenge any information if the data subject believes it to be wrong and, where appropriate, have it rectified or erased;
- claim compensation for damage (and any associated distress) arising from the loss or unauthorised destruction or disclosure of any personal data relating to the data subject, or arising from any inaccuracy in the data.

Most data holders need to register. Exemptions exist but are very narrow: they include an exemption for payroll, accounts and pensions, and mailing lists, designed to enable businesses to keep a list of the names and addresses of their customers. If, for example, a record is kept of a person's status in a company, or a particular interest, that would be enough to bring the data user outside the scope of the exemption.

Merely processing the text of documents automatically does not amount to processing data for the purposes of the DPA: word processing is not covered, nor is receiving text on-line or in disk format and extracting the data in hard copy form. However, as soon as additional functionality is asked for, eg, to prepare a standard letter to all individuals on a list living outside London, the DPA will apply.

Registration is not difficult or expensive but it requires somebody who knows how the organisation works to ascertain exactly what personal data are used and what they are used for. The Data Protection Registry provides a registration pack with pre-printed forms and guidance notes on how to fill in the forms. A registration must identify the *purpose* for which data are to be used; for each purpose it must be stated:

- the types of individual about whom data are to be held;
- the type of data;
- the sources;

- the information; and
- disclosures.

If data are to be transferred overseas then the destination countries must be specified. For example, if, within a company data were transferred on-line to any of its overseas offices to be incorporated in their databases, this would be a transfer, whereas sending a fax would not. It would, however, be a disclosure.

If there is any doubt as to which categories apply, it is worth seeking the views of the Registry. The staff are extremely helpful and generally able to give good clear advice, although the decision, at the end of the day, is with the applicant.

Upon registration, there is an ongoing obligation only to use personal data in accordance with the DPA, ie making sure that the business operates within the scope of its registration and complies with the data protection principles contained in the DPA.

The data protection principles

The relevant principles are:

- **First principle:** obtaining fairly and lawfully. The Registrar's view is that individuals need to be informed, when they give information, of any other organisations, uses or disclosures which are proposed and which they could not reasonably be expected to anticipate. Similar types of issues arise under the second and third principles.
- **Fourth principle:** information should be adequate, relevant and not excessive in relation to the purpose or purposes for which it is held.
- **Seventh principle:** individuals have the right to be told what data are held and where appropriate have the data corrected or erased. It is particularly important to make sure that records are regularly updated and checked and also that information no longer required is deleted.
- **Eighth principle:** security measures. This principle requires that appropriate security measures should be taken against unauthorised access, alteration, disclosure or destruction. Some guidance as to what security measures are appropriate is given by the Act: eg, account should be taken of how sensitive the data are, where they are stored, how passwords are used and the reliability of staff.

A producer of a multimedia work which includes personal data will need to ensure that the data are collected, processed and used according to and within the scope of the data protection regime. This may mean:

- examination of the producer's own internal procedures;
- registration with the Data Protection Registrar;
- the taking out of warranties from any provider of the relevant information that the data are supplied in accordance with the data protection principles and with the information supplier's own registration under the DPA.

Warranties can act as a checklist to make sure that key obligations have been complied with. For example, warranties could be required that:

(a) information has been fairly obtained;
(b) the provider has copyright in the list given;
(c) specific uses and disclosures are in accordance with the provider's registration;
(d) information is kept up to date with regular checks;
(e) the principles have been complied with.

While obviously such warranties give a contractual claim in the event that there is a breach, they also serve to make sure that the provider of information is aware of the DPA requirements.

10.6.2 PROTECTION OF PERSONAL DATA DIRECTIVE

Personal data protection is also a concern of the EU. The Commission drafted a Directive that took into account its concerns to:

- increase the levels of protection afforded to individuals in relation to data held about them by others;
- harmonise laws among Member States; and
- assist, and provide safeguards for, the free flow of data between Member States, and between Member and non-Member States.

The Directive was adopted on 24 July 1995.

Member States will have three years to implement the Directive in national legislation.

The object of the Directive is that Member States must protect the fundamental rights and freedoms of natural persons, and in particular their right to privacy, with respect to the processing of personal data.

- **personal data** means 'any information relating to an identified or identifiable natural person; an identifiable person 'the Data Subject' is one who can be identified, directly or indirectly, in particular by reference to an identification number or to one or more factors specific to his . . . identity';
- **processing** means 'any operation or set of operations which is performed upon personal data, whether or not by automatic means, such as collection, recording, organization, storage, adaptation or alteration, retrieval, consultation, use, disclosure by transmission, dissemination or otherwise making available, alignment or combination, blocking, erasure or destruction';
- **filing system** means 'any structured set of personal data which are accessible according to specific criteria, whether centralized, decentralized or dispersed on a functional or geographical basis and whether alone or with others';
- **controller** means 'the natural or legal person, public authority, agency or any other body which determines the purposes and means of the processing of personal data'.

To be lawful, processing of personal data must comply with certain data quality principles. Personal data must be:

- processed fairly and lawfully;
- collected for specified and legitimate purposes;
- not excessive;
- accurate and kept up to date; and
- kept in a form permitting the identification of data subjects.

Personal data may only be processed in certain limited situations, which are specified in the Directive:

(a) if the subject has given his unambiguous consent; or
(b) if it is necessary for the performance of a contract; or
(c) if it is required by law; or

DATA PROTECTION

(d) if it is necessary to protect the subject's interests; or
(e) if it is in the public interest to do so; or
(f) if it is necessary in the legitimate interests pursued by the controller or by the recipient of the data.

Special restrictions apply to special categories of data which reveal racial or ethnic origin, political opinions, religious or philosophical beliefs, trade union membership, health or sex life, subject to a limited set of exceptions. Processing through journalistic or artistic or literary expression is exempted only in so far as there is no conflict between the right to privacy and the right of freedom of expression.

Certain information must be given to the data subject, including the identity of the controller and the purposes of the processing and the timing. The extent of the information to be given differs according to whether the data were obtained from the data subject himself or not.

The data subject is to be guaranteed right of access to the data, so that he can verify the accuracy of the content and the lawfulness of the controller's purpose. This access is to be provided without excessive delay or expense. Data subjects must also have a right to demand the rectification, deletion or blocking of any inaccurate data or data which are processed in breach of the Directive, and to demand that the controller notifies any third party to whom the data had been disclosed of its inaccuracy.

Data subjects will have the right to object at any time on 'compelling legitimate grounds' to the processing of data relating to them. This is an entirely new requirement not currently contained in the DPA. Quite what is envisaged by 'compelling legitimate grounds' is not yet clear.

Safeguards must be put in place in relation to data which are processed for 'automated individual decisions', ie for the purpose of evaluating personal aspects of the data subject such as performance at work, creditworthiness, reliability or conduct. Processing in such cases is not allowed if it is carried out in order to reach an individual decision which significantly affects or produces legal effects for the data subject and if it is based solely on automated processing, subject to suitable measures being laid down by national law to protect the data subject's legitimate interests.

Any person acting under the authority of the controller or processor, and who has access to personal data, must not process the data except on instructions from the controller. Certain minimum standards of technical and organisational security measures must exist.

Some of the more important differences between the DPA and the Directive are as follows:

- The Directive sets out a limited range of cases where processing of data is permitted. These are substantially more restrictive than those permitted under the DPA.
- The Directive sets out a list of information which must be given to a data subject when data are being collected, including the intended purpose of the processing, recipients of the data, right of access to and rectification of the data. This will be an administrative burden on data collectors.
- Data subjects will have a right to object at any time on 'compelling legitimate grounds' to the processing of data relating to them. This is an entirely new requirement, and it is not yet known what will constitute 'compelling legitimate grounds'.
- The data user must ensure that where data have not been obtained directly from a data subject, the subject is given certain information concerning the proposed processing. In the case of direct marketing, he must have been given the opportunity to

have the data erased before their disclosure to third parties or use for third party direct mailing.
- The Directive extends the degree of control a data subject has over the processing of personal data, and will therefore add to the compliance burden for processors.

---

[1] See also UK, EC and other international development on cross-media ownership and regulation.
[2] Recently a UK police officer won a 'substantial' out-of-court settlement over a libellous e-mail message circulated *within* a company.
[3] *See Emmens v Pottle* (1885) 16 QBD 354, CA; *Vizetelly v Mudie's Select Library* [1900] 2 QB 170; *Sun Life Assurance Co of Canada v W H Smith & Co Ltd* (1933) 150 LY 211.
[4] For a discussion on whether pressure on distributors inhibits freedom of speech *see Goldsmith v Sperrings* [1977] 1 WLR 478.

• PART 3 •

PRODUCING A MULTIMEDIA WORK

— • 11 • —

ACQUISITION OF RIGHTS

11.1 FIRST ESSENTIALS

In Europe, at least, there are still no established benchmarks for multimedia licensing, production or distribution deals, although many of the big players are trying to create them. Some may claim otherwise, but there is no right or wrong way to do a multimedia deal—the industry is still too young and too much is still changing. Content providers and developers in multimedia licensing, whether large or small, have expressed the same commercial concerns over the inherent uncertainties of their deals. Obviously, the established industries which are converging on this new market each have their own traditional clearance and payment structures and other established industries can be looked to for guidance. However, the processes and the economics of producing and distributing a film or a TV series are very different from those of a book or magazine and, as a result, the contractual framework is also very different. Video games producers and software houses work to a different set of parameters from those of other producers (and from each other).

The contractual structures which are largely taken for granted in each industry are colliding in the multimedia marketplace and the dust has not yet settled to show what shape the new contracts will take. One of the reasons for this is that it is not clear what the economics of the new industry will be: eg, the source of the revenue streams; the most profitable distribution systems; the marketing costs and so on. However, it is possible to identify particular issues which will come up in most circumstances.

The first tasks are to identify:
- the product for which the rights are to be acquired;
- the prospective audience;
- the territories and/or languages and/or platforms required;
- the rights that need to be cleared, ie, the rights needed for all envisaged products;
- from whom the rights will come.

Conducting these exercises will enable the negotiator to decide what rights are *essential* and what might be *desirable*; and so to prioritise the requirements and ensure either that a suitable budget can be set or that the suit is cut to fit the existing cloth.

11.2 IDENTIFICATION OF RIGHTS AND RIGHTS HOLDERS

The issues in relation to multimedia works are in essence the same as those in relation to the acquisition of rights for film-making or publishing books or journals but the problems are multi-dimensional, in the sense that rights are not required simply for use in a film or for volume-form publication, but in a wider multimedia context. All the issues found in traditional media areas combine and regard must be had, for example, to: electronic use (ie copying a work on to an electronic platform and/or transmission over a network), film use, sound recording use, interactive use (manipulation), performance, production of printouts; and to the fact that not only is exploitation likely to be world-wide and multi-lingual, but delivery will be in a form that, in the absence of adequate controls, will enable the consumer relatively easily to make further use of it, whether or not he is specifically authorised to do so.

Accordingly, not only must more extensive rights for wider uses be on the acquirer's menu but, as a separate exercise, he must also spend more time and money on considering how to protect the resulting multimedia work. (For a consideration of protection issues *see* Chapter 7.)

It is important to decide at the earliest stage precisely what material, and what rights in that material, are or may be required for the particular use to which the producer intends to put the product. The material can be commissioned specifically for the project or bought outright (or licensed) on an exclusive or non-exclusive basis. The material can be cleared for all use or for limited uses with, perhaps, options for further use.

> **Example**
>
> The rights are required for one platform initially but the producer may, if the market receives the product enthusiastically, want to develop it for other platforms. Rather than go to the upfront expense of acquiring rights to all possible platforms, he may buy the rights for one platform first and at the same time buy an option for further platform(s) exercisable later.

11.3 SOURCE MATERIALS

Two different sources of material will be available:

(1) Specially commissioned work where the producer can, as a matter of contract, negotiate as part of the package the acquisition of the copyright or (failing that) of a licence, whether exclusive or non-exclusive, of all the rights (and waivers of rights) that he needs.
(2) Existing material which will be either licensed from picture or film libraries or from other third parties, or bought by way of assignment of, or licence under, copyright.

In the case of existing material, it may not be so easy to negotiate the necessary rights, particularly if there are conflicting prior grants. It may not necessarily even be easy to find out who are the relevant owners of the rights. It will be particularly important here to determine precisely what warranties the vendor or licensor is able to give and whether the vendor or licensor is worth 'powder and shot'.

Some think that the best way to deal with all the problems of rights clearance is to ignore all existing material and commission specifically for the intended product. This is probably not a realistic course for the majority of products.

WHERE WILL THE RIGHTS COME FROM? 11.4

> **Source materials**
> - Text
> - Musical scores
> - Still images
> - Fine Art
> - Performances
> - Motion pictures, including animation
> - Music
> - Libretti or lyrics
> - Audio
> - Computer software
> - Databases

11.4 WHERE WILL THE RIGHTS COME FROM?

At its simplest, a CD-ROM contains a number of works of different categories brought together and fixed in a 'single tangible medium of market expression'. These works maintain their original identity—the text is still the text and the video is still the video. With digitisation, however, everything is now ones and noughts mingled and mixed together (*see* Figure 11.1).

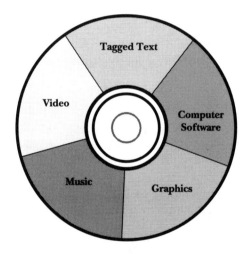

Figure 11.1 CD ROM: the contents

Where will the rights come from? *See* Figure 11.2. This figure shows all the people who are, in one sense or another, publishers of the works included on a CD-ROM. On top of them are the software developers, who provide the engine which drives the disk.

The producer of the CD-ROM will therefore approach publishers and distributors first to obtain their rights; but it is not self-evident that these people in the second circle are in a position to grant all of the rights needed to enable production of the CD-ROM. The contracts under which they themselves enjoy rights may be limited in scope, and/or geographically. When many contracts were written, the technology may not even have been invented and, in some cases, it will be a matter of accident whether or not the necessary rights were included in the grant to the publishers and distributors.

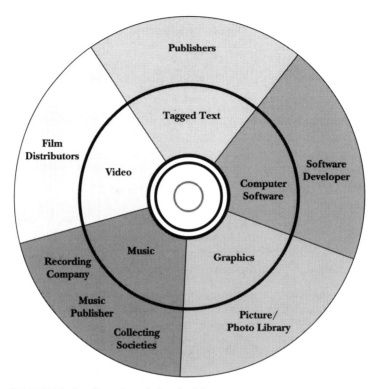

Figure 11.2 CD ROM: the first tier rights holders

In some cases the necessary rights will be included because language along the lines of 'all media now known or hereafter devised' will have been used; but the *Peggy Lee* case in America shows that, even in an Anglo-Saxon jurisdiction, such wording might not be adequate. In other countries, like France and Germany, that language is unlikely to be accepted by a court as being sufficient to pass rights unconditionally in the new media. At the least, there may be an obligation to pay further, equitable, remuneration for the rights.

> ### *Peggy Lee* case
>
> In 1952 Peggy Lee agreed to render her services to Disney as a singer and voice actor for the animated film *The Lady And The Tramp*. The letter of agreement withheld the right to 'phonograph recordings and/or transcriptions for sale to the public' and the court agreed with her that this included the video rights (see *Lee v Walt Disney* (above)).

The producer of the CD-ROM may therefore need to negotiate with the rights owners who lie beyond the publishers. *See* Figure 11.3. This shows a much larger number of people as being involved, including the people who created the original materials. Rights will need to be cleared back to this level unless the publishers on the middle ring can grant the rights and will offer adequate representations, warranties and indemnities.

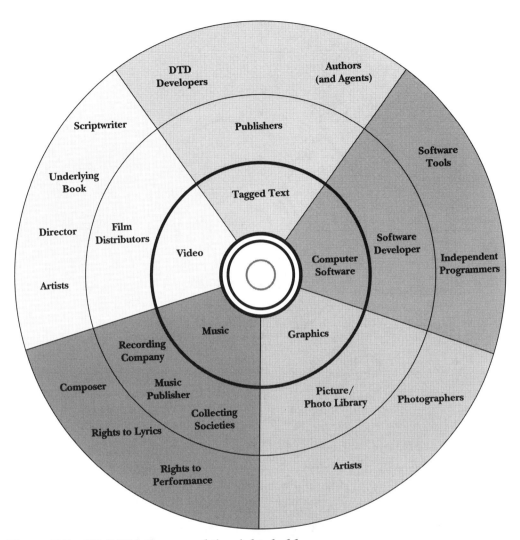

Figure 11.3 CD ROM: the second tier rights holders

Even though the copyright in pre-existing works may have been properly acquired for the purposes of the multimedia project, moral and other rights of authors and actors may in certain jurisdictions require clearance. *See* Figure 11.4.

The scale of rights clearance for CD-ROMs is larger, but not so much larger than that with which film producers and the producers of sound recordings have had to deal for many years. Nevertheless there are differences in terms of the acquisition of rights for CD-ROMs, and there are some new barriers to the flow of rights. Some of these barriers are obvious, such as limitations in rights. Some, such as territorial limitations, are commonplace but will become more significant as, with the investment required to make and promote a CD-ROM, publishers will probably wish to exploit it globally and, possibly, to include multiple soundtracks in different languages on the CD-ROM.

One of the barriers is uncertainty. Technology is moving very fast and the law is finding

11.4 ACQUISITION OF RIGHTS

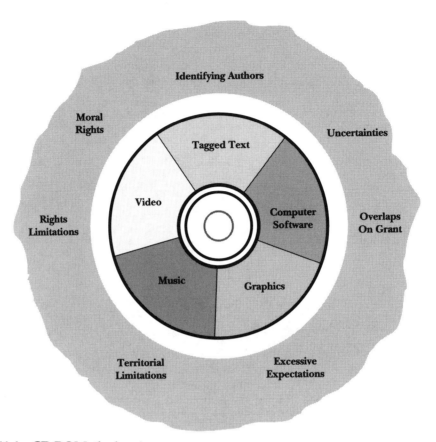

Figure 11.4 CD ROM: the barriers

it difficult to keep up; people are naturally cautious about the scope of licences and pricing and may be averse to the granting of sufficient rights to publishers.

> **Issues for consideration**
> - Who owns or controls the rights?
> - Are there any existing, non-competing grants?
> - Are there any existing, competing grants?
> - Are they exclusive or non-exclusive?
> - Are they territory specific or world-wide?
> - What languages are available?
> - What platforms are available?
> - What term of rights is available?
> - What price is negotiable?
> - Can moral rights be waived?
> - What about rights of publicity and privacy?
> - Are there any registers to search?

— • 12 • —

PRACTICAL ACQUISITION

Each industry has its own practices which range from the informal (more likely to be found at the publishing end) to the formal (more likely to be found at the film-production end). The variance is perhaps not surprising, since publishers traditionally deal in the main with intellectual property of a lesser financial value (in terms of the end product or the investment that goes into it) than the film industry where budgets can run into millions of pounds and where, if the underlying rights are not properly identified and acquired or cleared, there are enormous sums at risk.

With multimedia, all these separate practices, approaches and understandings will be stirred into one pot; there will be plenty of scope for misunderstanding and hence a much greater need for formal documentation.

Most of the material currently used by print publishers and film-makers is likely to be subject to copyright protection, whether in this country or abroad. Similarly, the material used in multimedia works will be subject to protection; accordingly, rights will have to be acquired or cleared. There is nothing particularly new in this. Multimedia exploitation is simply about taking existing techniques of exploitation and putting further dimensions on to it.[1]

12.1 PARTICULAR ACQUISITION PROBLEMS

12.1.1 LITERARY WORKS

Books, articles and other texts are all in great demand for multimedia products. Many publishers are very aware of the relevant issues in multimedia and electronic publishing. From a multimedia producer's perspective, the key issues are:

(1) Check that it is the publisher with whom you should be dealing. Authors and their agents are hanging on to their electronic rights, and there is currently a battle in the publishing world over whether it is the agent or the publisher who is the more appropriate person to be exploiting rights in the new media.

(2) Check the scope of the rights. 'Electronic rights' is the popular phrase in many circles and is practically meaningless in legal terms. A recent statement by the US Association of Authors' Representatives was prepared to admit that 'pure electronic publishing rights (non-dramatic, without audio or visual components, and without adaptation) resulting in a visible and readable text may in most instances have to be conveyed to the publisher'. However, this does not seem likely to be enough to drive the multimedia products of the future.

See the sample clause below which acquires the right to produce multimedia versions.

(3) Since it should be easier for the publisher to ensure that relevant clearances for multimedia use in a work have been carried out, a multimedia producer should ask for relevant warranties from the publisher. The main checks will be the usual employee, freelance, or third party copyright ownership issues with which we are all familiar. The multimedia market is currently dominated by the use of reference works. Indeed, it is quite obvious that if there is any element of publishing that is likely to be superseded by electronic versions in the next few years it is in this area. As a result, clearance difficulties for publishers have come less from text than from illustrations and photographs. Problems are more likely to arise in the use of newspapers, magazines and journals, subject to the licensing and syndicating of articles between publications—as has been shown by recent litigation in the US by journalists seeking to prevent on-line exploitation.

Sample clause: Multimedia rights
To prepare, reproduce, publish and sell, to distribute, transmit, download or otherwise transfer or make available and [with the Author's consent, which consent shall not unreasonably be withheld or delayed] to license others to do so, copies of the Work and any illustrations or photographs in multimedia versions. For the purposes of this Clause 'Multimedia Versions' shall mean versions that include the Work and any illustrations or photographs contained in the Work (in complete, condensed, adapted or abridged versions, and in compilations) for performance and display in any manner (whether sequentially or non-sequentially, and together with accompanying sounds and images, if any) by any electronic means, method or device including but not limited to, digital, optical and magnetic information storage and retrieval systems, on-line electronic or other transmission, and any other device or medium for electronic reproduction, publication, distribution or transmission, whether now or hereafter known or developed.

Requiring the author's consent, as this suggested clause does, is sensible but is also a possible material limitation on the rights.

> **Note**
> In acquiring rights to use a printed work there are at least two distinct copyrights, one in the text and the other in the typographical arrangement. There may well be additional copyrights if photographs or illustrations are involved.

12.1.2 PHOTOGRAPHS

Copyright in photographs made by employees, eg, a newspaper photographer or an employee of a corporation's communications department, are owned by the employer. Many photographers work as independent contractors. Copyright in photographs created by a photographer for a client are owned by the photographer unless:

- the client obtained an assignment of the copyright; or
- the photograph was made in the course of employment; or

PARTICULAR ACQUISITION PROBLEMS 12.1.3

- the photograph was taken before implementation of the CDPA 1988. Under the Copyright Act 1956, the owner of the film on which the photograph was taken was the copyright owner in the photograph

However, under the CDPA there exists a right of privacy in certain photographs and films (*see* 8.4) where they were commissioned for private or domestic purposes. Accordingly, permission to use such photographs would be needed (from the person who commissioned the photographs) as well as a copyright licence from the copyright owner.

Determining who owns the copyright in a photograph made by a freelance photographer can be difficult. If the photograph was created by a freelance photographer for a client and there is no written agreement between the two parties, the only way to determine who owns the copyright is to ask the photographer or the client. Either or both of these parties may have misconceptions about the rules of copyright ownership.

Many photographers are concerned that once their work has been digitised it can be copied, distributed and altered. They have therefore been reluctant to grant a licence to use their photographs in multimedia work. Alternatively, they have claimed prodigiously large sums for such use. If a producer plans to alter the image, he should make sure the licence wording is wide enough to give the right to do so, eg, that there are no specific restrictions and that there is a waiver or consent in respect of moral rights (*see* Chapter 8). Clearance may also be needed in respect of any copyright work included in a photograph. Use of a photograph, for example, of a piece of sculpture (unless in a public place), will require not just the authority of the photographer but also a licence from the owner of any copyright in the sculpture. Use of a photograph of a living person may require a release of publicity and privacy rights from that person if the work is to be distributed in countries where rights of publicity and privacy exist.

> **Example**
> If I am a photographer, can I object to the cropping of the photograph I supply to a magazine? Assuming that the photograph has been specially composed to balance the colour, light and placing of the subject-matter with the intention of creating a special composition, cropping by the editorial team *could* alter the whole balance. If moral rights applied (eg, the exceptions in the CDPA *did not* apply) and if my integrity was affected (the treatment was derogatory—*see* above) the answer is, yes, I could object even if the cropping was only of a few millimetres!

> **Note**
> People go to photo libraries for photographs, but picture or photo libraries only give a licence for the *use* of the photograph. It is up to the would-be user to clear any underlying *rights*.

12.1.3 WORKS OF FINE ART

With regard to works of fine art, there are also two ownerships: copyright in the image; and ownership of the physical work of art. These can, and usually will, be owned separately and permission may be needed from both owners—from the copyright owner to allow reproduction of the work and from the owner of the physical object if access to it is required.

There may also be severe moral rights problems. Moral rights exist in most countries, exercisable by the creator of the work rather than the copyright owner. They are often inalienable. Moral rights customarily include the right to object to derogatory treatment of the work; this could inhibit the exploitation of the work on a CD-ROM (*see* 8.2).

> **Example**
> If I am a composer can I, on the basis of my moral rights, object if someone takes extracts of a number of my works and combines them into one recording? The answer may be yes: *see* 8.2: *Bad Boys Megamix*, George Michael's case.

12.1.4 PERFORMANCES

The making of multimedia work directly from a live performance, or from a broadcast or cable transmission including a live performance, or from a recording of a performance, and the exploitation of such work, requires consent under the CDPA, Pt II. Consent is required from the performer in respect of the performance rights in his or her performance. Further, where a person has exclusive recording rights in a particular performance, consent is required either from the person having such rights *or* from the performer in question. However, in circumstances where a person has exclusive recording rights in a performance, care should be taken in relying on the performer's consent alone. Under the terms of the performer's agreement with the person having exclusive recording rights in his or her performance, the grant of consent by the performer may be in breach of such agreement. If the multimedia producer is aware of the existence of such agreement, he may be liable to the person having recording rights for the tort of inducing breach of contract by the performer. It should be noted that a performer's rights in a performance are non-assignable.

Since the coming into force of the CDPA, consent need no longer be in writing and may be implied from the circumstances of a particular situation. However, as a matter of good practice, it is still advisable always to secure consent in writing.

Live performance

In situations where the multimedia producer includes a live performance directly into a multimedia work or, more likely, makes a new recording of a live performance for inclusion in the multimedia work, the terms of the agreements under which the performers are engaged for such performance and/or recording must be checked carefully to ensure that the consents given under such agreements are sufficient for the intended exploitation of the multimedia work.

Sample clause: Warranty that performer's consents and waivers are granted

> The [Company] warrants that the [Artist] has granted to the [Company] all necessary consents and waivers under Part II of the Copyright, Designs and Patents Act 1988 and under any future legislation that may create rights in [the Artist's] performance to enable the [Company] to

make the fullest use of [the Artist's] services, whether in ways referred to or contemplated by this Agreement or in ways not yet invented or contemplated [provided they are not hereby expressly prohibited.]

This clause is to be used in conjunction with eg the moral rights warranty at 8.6.1.

Sample clause: Performer consents

You grant to the Company throughout the world: all necessary consents under Part II of the Copyright, Designs and Patents Act 1988 (or any statutory modifications or re-enactment) to enable the Company to make the fullest use of your services.

Existing recording

Where the multimedia producer is licensing an existing recording of a performance for inclusion in a multimedia work, the multimedia producer should ensure that in addition to securing the licences required in respect of the recording itself and any underlying copyright work(s) embodied in the recording, he also secures a warranty from the licensor that the licensor has secured all consents required from the performers whose performances are embodied in the recording to permit the inclusion of the recording in the multimedia work and the exploitation of the multimedia work in the manner now intended (*see* sample clause at 12.1.1). The licensor should also warrant that the consent by the performer extends not only to the licensor but to all successors in title, licensees and assigns of the licensor. The licensor should then assign the benefit of the performer's consent to the multimedia producer and provide an indemnity to the multimedia producer in support of the licensor's warranty.

In connection with relying solely on the licensor's warranty and indemnity it is worth repeating the warning that such warranty and indemnity are only of value to the extent that the licensor is likely still to be in existence at the time a claim under the warranty may be made and is of sufficient financial standing to honour the indemnity. If there is any doubt of this, the multimedia producer should undertake his own investigation of the licensor's rights documents in relation to the recording being licensed, to verify for himself whether the consents originally secured by the licensor are sufficient for the use it is now intended to make of the recording.

Many such rights documents and/or agreements with performers may have been entered into on standard terms of engagement agreed between producers and broadcasters and the performers' unions, Equity (actors) and the Musicians' Union (musicians) or on terms of engagement incorporating standard terms. These standard terms may not have envisaged exploitation of the performances in the manner now intended. However, they may have envisaged that they would be amended in the future as a result of further negotiation and agreement between the unions and the trade bodies of the producers and broadcasters. It remains debatable whether it would be accepted by the courts that the unions could act as agent of the performers and thereby grant consent by means of a subsequent agreement to a use that was not envisaged or permitted under the terms of the performer's original agreement. A list of the relevant unions is included in Appendix 5.

It is debatable whether the current ITC, BBC, Equity and Musicians' Union agreements permit multimedia exploitation under the additional uses clause. This allows the producer the right to exploit the work 'in any and all media' upon payment of an appropriate fee. The term 'all media' is defined widely as 'all means of distribution transmission exploitation now known or hereafter developed'.

There are further complications for music videos and musical performances included in multimedia works. This is because there may no longer remain, or it may not be possible to locate, documentary records relating to the recording of the musicians' performance. Administration of the recording may have been handled by a freelance 'fixer'. If need be, the Copyright Tribunal does have power to give consent on behalf of unidentifiable performers.

12.1.5 FILM AND TELEVISION BROADCASTS

The film and television industries have traditionally been more insistent than the print publishers in acquiring the copyright in the works they use. However, that does not necessarily mean that they will more easily be able to license the necessary rights to a multimedia producer.

There are many separate copyright works which go into the making of a film (*see* Figure 11.3 *above*):

- Is the film still in copyright?
- If it is not, will any of the underlying rights still be in copyright?
- If they are, do the film-makers enjoy sufficient rights in the underlying works to be able to grant the multimedia producer the rights he wants?

An examination of the title documents is unlikely to be a practical alternative to taking, if they can be obtained, warranties from the film producer that:

- he has the right to grant the licence;
- use in the multimedia product will not infringe third party rights; and
- he will indemnify the multimedia producer in respect of any claims.

In practice the film producer is likely to be willing only to offer a quit claim, effectively a licence of whatever rights the film producer has. This makes it important to review the film credits.

In the USA, there are reversionary copyrights—*see* the *Rear Window* decision, *James Stewart et al v Sheldon Abend*, 495 US, 109 L Ed 2d 184 (1990). This case, decided in the US Supreme Court, established that where an author died before he renewed the copyright, the author's heirs were able to regain the copyright at the end of the original term, thus bringing to an end all prior licences or assignments of copyright. This put them into a strong bargaining position to negotiate new fees. (In the USA the copyright period used to be an initial term of (generally) 28 years from publication followed by a second—the renewal—period of 28 years.) In the UK the reversionary provisions of the Copyright Act 1911 can still produce problems in relation to works created before the implementation of the Copyright Act 1956.

The film owner may not own world-wide rights. Many films are distributed by way of territorial distribution arrangements which may mean large clearance problems.

Copyright and other rights in traditionally organised industries are exploited on a country by country basis, so that the copyright owner may have licensed the rights to the work to others elsewhere in the world. This can make it very difficult to acquire all the necessary rights for international distribution of an electronic work and, in certain trade zones, particularly the EU, products lawfully put on sale in one country may lawfully be resold in another.

PARTICULAR ACQUISITION PROBLEMS 12.1.7

Lawful use of a film or television broadcast will usually require licences or releases to be obtained from a number of other parties:

- the owner of the copyright in the underlying work (novel, short story or play) on which the work is based;
- the owner of the copyright in the motion picture, television series or mini series, or documentary;
- the performers (and possibly other contributors).

Applicable union reuse fees may have to be paid. If the film clip contains music or choreography, separate licences may also have to be obtained for those.

> **Note**
> Watch out for logos and characters used in films and TV series or cartoon strips. The extent of merchandising rights and character rights are uncertain in the UK. They lie somewhere between copyright and trade-mark law.

12.1.6 GRAPHICS AND ILLUSTRATIONS

Graphics and illustrations created by employees (eg, a magazine cover created by an employee of a magazine publisher) are owned by the employer. If the graphics or illustrations were created by eg a freelancer, the right to reproduce them will need to be acquired by assignment or licence. Negotiations with a graphic artist or an illustrator for permission to use his or her work may involve a detailed discussion over the intended use, since many graphic designers are concerned about how their works will look when incorporated into live work. The rights to the artwork may not be at the disposal of the artist if, for instance, a prior licence is in existence or the work was created while the artist was an employee of someone else.

Still images

An image if it is capable of protection under copyright; the photographer may own the copyright if the work is or includes a photograph.

The multimedia producer will largely be working from photographs where it is often difficult to trace authorship and ownership. In these cases it will be sensible to source from a library and rely on its warranty. Note that few picture libraries will warrant clearance of the *subject-matter* of the picture.

Where the picture is of a recognisable individual, rights of publicity and privacy (*see* 10.5) may become relevant. There is no such separate right in the UK but other countries, such as the USA and France, have one or more of them.

12.1.7 CLIP ART AND MULTIMEDIA TOOLS

In multimedia projects, clip art and stock content for multimedia development tools can generally be used without obtaining licences. However, careful review should be made of the written material distributed with these works. In many cases, the material comes with express or implied licences that restrict the use of the collection.

12.1.8 MUSIC AND SOUND RECORDINGS

The first point to remember when dealing with music clearance is that the relevant rights will in most cases be owned by a number of different people and that, as with films, there are at least *two* copyrights involved: the copyright in the music and the copyright in the sound recording. This book cannot provide detailed instructions on music rights clearance but a brief guide to the position follows.

Performing Rights Society Ltd

In the UK, the Performing Rights Society Ltd (PRS) owns and administers the performing, broadcasting and cable programme rights ('the performing rights') in the music of its members. The interests of the PRS extend to both the music and the lyrics in musical compositions but not to the text of non-musical works, such as plays or sketches, and not to the performing right in ballets, operas, musical plays or other dramatico-musical works, when they are performed on the stage. The PRS does, however, administer these latter rights when they are performed by means of films made primarily for purposes of exhibition in cinemas. The PRS grants blanket licences authorising the holders to perform, broadcast, or include in cable programmes the works in the PRS repertoire. When the foreign repertoire of the PRS is taken into account, this licence includes virtually every piece of published copyright music.

The licence is normally granted to the proprietors of premises at which music is publicly performed, to broadcasters (*see* below) and to the promoters of musical entertainments not covered by the proprietors' or broadcasters' licences. Licences to perform music as part of live dramatic presentations, like musicals, are granted by music publishers directly.

Composers enter into contracts when they join the PRS, under which the performing rights in all their works, present and future (so long as they remain members of the PRS) automatically become vested in the PRS.

Mechanical Copyright Performance Society

In the UK, the Mechanical Copyright Performance Society (MCPS), owned by the Music Publishers' Association, grants 'mechanical rights' licences (the right to make and sell recordings of musical compositions in the MCPS repertoire) as agent for and on behalf of its publisher members. It also grants synchronisation licences (the right to synchronise musical compositions into a film soundtrack or a TV programme in synchronisation with the action) when authorised by its members to do so. Traditionally, mechanical licences have been granted mainly to record companies in respect of the pressing of records embodying recordings of musical works. In addition, the MCPS has granted individual synchronisation licences to film companies for the synchronisation of musical works into films and has entered into blanket licences with television and cable stations in connection with the synchronisation of library recordings of musical works into programmes produced or fully commissioned by the stations (*see* below). By analogy, a synchronisation licence would be required where music is synchronised into a multimedia work and a mechanical licence would be required where such multimedia work is to be exploited by means of the manufacture and sale of CD-ROMs.

With the repeal of the Copyright Act 1956, and with no provision for a statutory licence in the CDPA, record companies had to negotiate the licence fees for the right to record musical works and issue records of recordings. Following a reference to the Copyright Tribunal by the MCPS and the record companies' industry body, the British Phonographic

Industry (BPI)) as a result of disagreement over licence fee rates, there is once again a set scale for mechanical licences for the records of musical works and the issue of copies of such recordings by means of audio only records. However, such rates do not apply to multimedia works. At the time of going to press MCPS had yet to formulate suggested rates for the use of music in multimedia works; and any rates eventually suggested may need to be the subject of a further reference to the Copyright Tribunal.

Phonographic Performance Ltd

Phonographic Performance Ltd (PPL) is owned by the UK record companies. It licenses the separate right of copyright in sound recordings for the public performance, broadcasting (and, sometimes, the synchronisation) of the sound recording. PPL operates by taking an assignment of that part of the copyright in the records which enables it to authorise the public performance and broadcasting of the recordings belonging to members of PPL.

The fees charged by PPL for the licences issued to radio stations, television stations, dance halls, discothèques and the like depend on the size of the premises, the likely size of the audience, the type of audiences, etc.

Video Performance Ltd

Video Performance Ltd (VPL) is owned by the UK record companies, which in turn are the major producers of music promo videos (video clips of pop records). VPL licenses the use of promo videos by television and cable stations, programme providers for Direct Broadcasting from Satellite ('DBS') and cable television, clubs, discothèques and juke boxes. Its charges are negotiable. VPL issues blanket licences giving licensees access to its library. It only enjoys UK rights but has, in many cases in conjunction with the International Federation of the Phonographic Industry (IFP), cleared rights for Europe, thereby being able to grant pan-European licences for satellite television.

For an existing sound recording to be embodied in a multimedia work, licences would be required from the owners of copyright in both the sound recordings and the music and lyrics. For music composed especially for a multimedia work, the multimedia producer should if possible seek an assignment of the copyright in the music (and lyrics), subject to the rights of the PRS, and at the very least should secure a mechanical and synchronisation licence for use of the music in the multimedia work and exploitation of the music as part of the multimedia work in the manner intended. For recordings especially produced for a multimedia work there should be few instances where the multimedia producer should secure less than the copyright in the recording.

Blanket licences

Televsion stations in the UK enjoy blanket licences from the MCPS and the PRS in respect of recording and performing (including broadcasting) musical works (and incidentally, library sound recordings) as part of television programmes. These blanket licences do not envisage exploitation of television programmes and the musical works embodied in them in the form of multimedia works. Where music is to be used in a multimedia work, whether as part of a television programme or not, a separate licence will be required and a separate licence fee will be payable. The rates are currently being negotiated by the British Interactive Multimedia Association (BIMA) with MCPS. Web music service, Cerberus, negotiated a licence with the PRS to broadcast music over the Internet. Indeed, Cerberus was delayed in going on-line because the MCPS wanted some form of protection, and the appropriate encryption technology was not ready.

Sound recordings (which have a separate copyright to the musical work embodied in the recording) also need to be cleared for inclusion in the multimedia works and there is no universally easy way to obtain such clearance. The blanket licence that most UK television companies have with the PPL will not extend to multimedia. Once again, it should be remembered that a performing right in a sound recording may be triggered by the public showing of a multimedia work. When a sound recording is recorded into a multimedia work, the public performance of the multimedia work will also include performance of the sound recording. The underlying right must be cleared in the sound recording. Normally, the PPL is the clearing house for the performing right in sound recordings although the VPL acts as a clearing house for video exploitation.

Summary

As we have seen, a multiplicity of ownerships will frequently be involved. Music clearance is undoubtedly well left to experts. *See* Appendix 1 for details of the organisations mentioned above. Copies of the various standard forms can be obtained from them.

12.1.9 DATABASES

For a discussion of database rights, *see* 6.2.

12.1.10 SOFTWARE

All interactive products require software, and all products capable of being delivered over an on-line system must be stored on a server under software control. Software enjoys copyright protection, and rights to use the software incorporated into the multimedia product must be obtained. In some countries, particularly the USA, software may be protected as a trade secret or even patented; and additional clearance must be sought.

12.1.11 OTHER ISSUES

The Microsoft encyclopaedia, *Encarta*, contains 15,000 multimedia elements: sound, video or animation. It retails in the UK for £99 or less, often substantially less. Microsoft therefore cannot afford to pay very much for each clip it uses in *Encarta*. The same applies to other reference works and to CD-ROMs with content from a variety of sources. In many cases, the multimedia producer will want to pay a small permission fee for the non-exclusive use of a clip or a group of clips which are relatively unimportant in the context of the product as a whole. Indeed, they might never be accessed by the owner. It is only if large numbers of clips are used, or the entire product is substantially based on one work which is being licensed on an exclusive basis, that the producer will be willing to negotiate a larger fee or a share of the royalties.

Formalities

Neither the Berne Convention nor GATT/TRIPs requires 'formalities' for the existence of copyright. There are voluntary registers in Italy, Portugal and Spain for software owners to register their rights. In the USA, as a result of its adherence to the Berne Convention, the existence of copyright no longer depends on registration; nevertheless, registration at the Library of Congress does bring advantages and should be considered.

Searches

Copyright and title searches are available in certain countries, eg, the USA, but not in the UK. Searches are advisable and warranties should always be sought.

12.2 FEES AND ROYALTIES

12.2.1 KEY ISSUES

The key issues for fees and royalties are as follows:

(1) *Initial licence fee:* Whether the content provider should get an upfront fee or royalty advance to recognise the value of the production of the work in the first place will depend in part on the value of the brand name of the work, as a film, book, cartoon series or whatever.

(2) *Minimum royalties:* If the licence is exclusive for a particular format, should the content provider get minimum royalties to recognise the loss of opportunity to license elsewhere:?

(3) *Bundling:* If the licensee gets a deal to bundle a copy of the CD-ROM with hardware or some other software, should the royalty be reduced? The answer is usually yes, but not always. In addition, bundling has to be carefully defined and possibly limited, to avoid spoiling the market for the full-priced product.

(4) *On-line and rental income:* If the licence extends to use of the product on-line, or there is a rental market for the product, the licensor should consider obtaining a share of the revenue from this, possibly on a fixed fee per use basis.

Rights acquisition checklist

It will be necessary to identify:
  (a) all original authors and trace the subsequent chain of title;
  (b) the prior use made, or the scope and duration of licence, and holdbacks granted in respect of the material;
  (c) the use intended to be made of the material;
  (d) the nature of the rights to be acquired to enable proper licences to be drawn up incorporating all the appropriate rights;
  (e) the relevant warranties;
  (f) the product;
  (g) the prospective audience
  (h) the territories;
  (i) the languages.

It will be necessary to draw up (or agree) a budget, then to decide:
- whether you should acquire:
  — a copyright assignment or a licence;
  — exclusive or non-exclusive rights;
- whether you should seek:
  — all rights upfront;
  — only some rights, with either a bar on the exercise of the others or a right of first refusal (or an option).

It is important not to forget:
- synchronisation ⎫
                    ⎬ for music
- mechanical use   ⎭

(Cont'd)

- performer consents (note that these are *not* automatically acquired by an employer from his employee—(compare the position with regard to copyright))
- moral rights
- publicity and privacy rights (there are none recognised by English law but other jurisdictions do recognise them and multimedia rights will generally be acquired for world-wide use).

Checklist: authors' concerns

Authors will want to discuss the following questions:
(1) What languages will the work be published in?
(2) In what territories will it be published?
(3) What is the duration of the licence?
(4) Is there a minimum sales target?
(5) What is the price and will payment be on a royalty basis?
(6) Will the text be an unaltered version of the original and, if not, will abridgements be subject to the author's approval? If substantial changes are made so that the result becomes a derivative work, who will own the derivative version?
(7) In cases where a work is issued in electronic format, what physical and legal controls will be imposed on users?
(8) What safeguards (if any) will the product offer to render the text unalterable by the user?
(9) What is the liability where text can be edited by the user and then republished, and who will bear it?
(10) What percentage of the whole project does the text represent?
(11) Precisely what platform is being requested?
(12) What is the approval mechanism for transferring to another platform?

12.3 COMPULSORY LICENSING

Some think that the only way to deal with this tangle of rights is to have some kind of compulsory licensing system for use of copyright works in a multimedia product. Andrew White in his article, 'Multimedia and Copyright: Practical Options for Producers' (*Copyright World* (1993)) suggested that one of the options was the setting up of a rights clearance centre by creators' agents, libraries, collecting societies and other rights-holder groups. This centre would provide clearance facilities for bulk licensing of copyright materials for use in encyclopaedic-type works, for educational and cultural projects and possibly for reuse in traditional media. The clearance centre concept may work for limited areas of exploitation. One commentator has proposed an 'Accessright' under which the emphasis would be on controlling access to digital data rather than, as in copyright, on varying restricted acts and physical material.

By contrast, the Green Paper on Copyright and Related Rights in the Information Society issued by the EC in July 1995 (*see* Appendix 11) argues that while traditional notions of copyright and related rights, limited in their territorial application, might need review, and that digital technology may require multimedia works to have a separate status, nevertheless copyright is sound as a concept. This is a view with which the present authors have greater sympathy at this time.

12.4 COLLECTING SOCIETIES

Collecting societies currently offer a range of blanket licensing schemes although, in the case of the Copyright Licensing Agency (acting in the UK on behalf of publishers and authors in the reprographic field) this is currently not extended to electronic use. (*See* the list of UK collecting societies in Appendix 1.)

Collecting societies can be expected to develop new schemes for licensing rights for selected multimedia uses, and indeed need to do so as a matter of some urgency if unlicensed exploitation is to be held in check and calls for compulsory licensing systems resisted.

Collective licensing has its limitations and, as Jean François Verstrynge (then responsible at DG IV of the European Commission for copyright harmonisation) said, at a Congress hosted by VG Wort in 1992:

> If every time we can no longer enforce the exclusive nature of a right [and] if every time we act by creating a remuneration right only, we are gradually pushing copyright away from its nature of a fundamental right into a type of taxation system [and] if this continues without a reaction, copyright will be dead in 30 years.

There is also an inherent tension between collective licensing and competition law, since the former may lead to horizontal price fixing. A distinction therefore has to be drawn between collective licensing and collective administration of licensing.

However, collecting societies have worked well in the music field where, for example, the MCPS, the PRS and PP have been operating successfully for many years. There is no obvious inherent reason why they cannot evolve into multimedia collecting societies, using the attributes of computers to label the greater volume of works in use and to calculate royalties due. Because such a body would, like other collecting societies, enjoy a dominant position, it would have to be subject to the Copyright Tribunal which would have authority to revise and review tariffs and terms of trade. The enormous cost of taking issues to the Copyright Tribunal is said to curtail disputes and encourage realistic settlements. That being said, the enormous sums at stake, the position of the big battalions and the immaturity of the marketplace in the multimedia industry will probably lead quite early on to a number of Tribunal hearings as the parties jockey for position.

If collecting societies are to play a larger role, they will have to:

(a) ensure they get the 'electronic' rights from their members;
(b) broaden their base to include the large numbers of rights owners who are not currently members;
(c) be willing/able to give the necessary warranties and indemnity that a multimedia producer will want to have. The CDPA, s 136, implies into every scheme or licence for reprographic copying operated by eg a collecting society a limited indemnity against any liability incurred by reason of the licensee, acting within the limits of the licence, having infringed the right to make the reprographic copy; that is, that the collecting society did not have authority to make the grant. (The indemnity applies

only where the relevant works are not sufficiently identified in, and to enable licensees to decide whether the work falls within, the scheme or not.);
(d) be able to respond quickly, comprehensively and efficiently.

12.5 COPYRIGHT TRIBUNAL

The Copyright Tribunal was established by the CDPA to hear applications concerning licensing schemes for dealing with copyright material and relating to the appropriate 'reasonable' royalty; and to supervise certain copyright dispute areas. The increasing grants of rights to collecting societies gives them monopoly positions, and the Tribunal's jurisdiction is intended to counterbalance that.

One must consider the following when negotiating for rights.

12.6 FALLBACKS

The producer of a multimedia product should consider whether he will want to acquire (whether by way of assignment of, or licence under, copyright) *all* rights in a work, and certainly all 'electronic' rights.

It will be clear from this chapter that many authors, and more probably their agents, will resist wholesale acquisition. Accordingly, what are the fallbacks?

12.6.1 FULL GRANT

The first fallback is a *full grant* from the owner and an undertaking by the producer that there will be no exercise of certain of the rights without agreement between owner and producer as to the basis of exploitation, including the share of proceeds payable to the owner. The advantage of this for the producer of a CD-ROM is that he will *own* the rights, which means no one else can get them. The disadvantage for the owner is that he or she loses leverage in terms of the manner of exploitation and the negotiation of the price when the time comes.

12.6.2 RESERVATION OF RIGHTS

The second fallback is a *reservation* of the rights, with the producer acquiring an option over them exercisable within a specified period of time. Options sensibly require that the final price is settled at the time when they are granted. The advantage to the producer is that he has guaranteed access to the rights at an agreed price and on fixed terms and also that he does not have to pay that part of the purchase price upfront. The disadvantage to both parties is that they have to fix the price at a very early stage and cannot wait until the date on which the producer actually wants to use the rights.

12.6.3 RIGHT OF FIRST REFUSAL OVER RESERVED RIGHTS

The third fallback is a right of *first refusal* over the reserved rights. The advantage to the owner is flexibility: he or she can choose when, if at all, to exercise the rights and has more control over setting the level of the price. The disadvantage to the producer is a lack of control over the price and timing.

Sample clause: Right of first refusal for further rights

This clause is to be used if the publisher is unable to obtain a grant of multimedia version rights.

(a) The Author grants to the Publisher the first opportunity to acquire the sole and exclusive Multimedia Version Rights (as such term is defined below) in the Work with respect to each particular electronic means, method or device for publication, distribution or transmission of the Work in electronic form.

(b) The Author agrees to give notice to the Publisher offering the Publisher the first opportunity to acquire the Multimedia Version Rights before he offers them to any third party and to give the Publisher a period of [sixty] days thereafter within which to give notice to start negotiations. The said offer period shall not commence earlier than [sixty (60)] days after acceptance by the Publisher of the manuscript of the Work.

(c) If prior to expiry of the said offer period the Publisher shall give notice to the Author that it wishes to acquire the Multimedia Version Rights, the Author shall negotiate with the Publisher with respect to the terms of such rights acquisition.

(d) If within [   ] days after service by the Publisher of the notice that it wishes to start negotiations to acquire the said rights the parties are unable in good faith to arrive at a mutually satisfactory agreement, the Author shall be free to offer such rights elsewhere, PROVIDED THAT without following the procedure set out below the Author shall not enter into a contract with respect to any such rights with any third party in which the material terms are less favourable to the Author than those offered by the Publisher.

Any notice required to be given hereunder by one party to the other shall be in writing and shall be duly given:

(i) if delivered by hand to the address stated in this Agreement of the party to be served or such other address as may be notified in writing by that party to the other from time to time and shall be deemed to have been served at the time of delivery; or

(ii) if sent by pre-paid first-class post to the address referred to in (a) above the notice shall be deemed to have been served within two (2) working days following the date of posting;

(iii) if sent by facsimile (to the addressee's number notified to the sender by the addressee or recorded in any official index of facsimile numbers) four (4) business hours following transmission subject to proof by the sender that he holds an acknowledgment receipt of despatch of the transmitted notice.

12.6.4 MATCHING RIGHT

The fourth fallback is a *matching right*: once the owner has found another would-be purchaser, he or she must offer the rights to the producer on the same terms. The disadvantages to the owner include an effective 'encumbrance' on the rights, since it becomes difficult to find anyone who will negotiate for the rights knowing that all they are doing is setting themselves up to be trumped; the disadvantage to the producer again includes a lack of control over the timing and the cost.

Sample clause: Matching right

This clause is to be used if the publisher is unable to obtain a grant of Multimedia Version Rights.

(a) The Author agrees to give a third party sale notice to the Publisher once the Author has received from a third party a *bona fide* offer for the Multimedia Version Rights or any of them which the Author is minded to accept and in that notice to give full details of the offer. The Publisher shall have the right to acquire the rights mentioned in the third party sale notice by giving a matching notice within fourteen (14) days after service of the third party sale notice stating that the Publisher will match all of the material terms set out in the third party sale notice.

12.6.5 OPEN RIGHTS

A final alternative is simply to leave the rights 'open'. There are obvious advantages and disadvantages to this course of inaction.

In the last three alternatives, a further disadvantage to the producer is that the very success of his publishing of the initial material may put up the price which he has to pay in order to acquire the reserved rights.

---

[1] Some commentators argue that, because rights clearance is burdensome and because of greater technical and commercial possibilities of manipulation and reuse arising in particular from digitisation of data, the days of copyright are numbered and that works should become available as-of-right, subject to a payment. In the authors' view, rumours of the death of copyright are much exaggerated.

— • 13 • —

ACQUISITION AGREEMENTS

13.1 INTRODUCTION

The acquisition agreement, the document through which the producer acquires his rights, is the foundation for everything that follows. It is, and will remain, vitally important that formal agreements are entered into in respect of *all* contributions or potential contributions to the multimedia project. The film industry has long required everyone to enter into formal contracts and the multimedia industry requires the same attitude. It is no longer acceptable to take an informal attitude to contracting. In the first place there will be few, if any, trade practices to fall back on and secondly, too much money will be at stake.

We have already examined in Chapter 12 the issue of whether the rights should be assigned or simply licensed. Here, we look at the rights themselves and the strategies involved.

13.2 STRATEGIES FOR LICENSING: 'ACQUIRE BROADLY . . .'

13.2.1 EXISTING RIGHTS FRAMEWORK

The hierarchy of rights in respect of the acts of electronic publishing is still in its infancy. It is not clear whether the existing hierarchy of print-on-paper rights will hold sway, where publishers, certainly the trade publishers, acquire a prime right, being the exclusive right to publish the work in volume form (in other words, the right to publish in book or magazine formats) and a lesser right to negotiate the sale of the so-called subsidiary rights (a menu of rights which may include serialisation, anthology, dramatic, film and television, strip cartoon) and—in the recent past—certain more or less well-defined electronic rights.

The publisher's position in relation to these rights (some of which the industry would in any event regard as volume form, for example the serialisation rights) is often unclear under many existing standard form contracts. There will be pressure on publishers and authors to resolve these murky issues in the forthcoming new generation of agreements.

A tentative list of 'electronic' rights, drawn up by Charles Clark, general counsel at the International Publishers Copyright Council, follows the existing volume form or prime right and subsidiary framework format, is set out at Appendix 3.

It is not at all certain that the division between prime and subsidiary rights will be the approach finally used by the majority of rights acquirers. Book publishers, as they become part of much larger media groupings, may find that market forces require them to take a much broader view of rights acquisition.

13.2.2 NEW APPROACHES TO RIGHTS

One alternative approach is to think in terms of the following rights:

(1) *Initialisation/fixation right:* the right to input the work into electronic form.
(2) *Copying right:* the copying of the work previously subject to fixation; this right can be broken down into making copies for internal use only and making for distribution to the public on tangible platforms or uploading on to a server and permitting public display/downloading; it can also be divided in terms of particular platforms; but publishers should avoid defining rights by reference to particular technologies (remember Videodisc and DAT).
(3) *Public displays or on-line access:* this refers to making the work available on screen in public or to subscribers to an on-line transmission service.
(4) *Printout:* enabling viewers or subscribers also to print out the whole or extracts.
(5) *Communication/transmission.*

Another possibility is to start to think of volume rights as fundamentally a right to make the work available as a 'text stream' independent of whether or not it is in the form of print on paper. That extends the publisher's natural grant.

With multimedia, the shortcomings of current practices in literary publishing now come into sharp focus, opening up conventions on the literary work side to greater challenge.

> **Recommendation**
>
> Book publishers, with other publishers and distributors of copyright material, should be
> - revisiting the forms of contract that have been developed over the last few years; and
> - considering whether to renegotiate old contracts.

Where an author is willing to grant all rights he may want to provide for a reversion of some or all of them if they are not exploited within a reasonable period of time. There is an obvious difficulty in allowing partial reversion, which is the consequent possibility of competing electronic versions of the work (although that very possibility may mean that the reversion is worth little to the author).

Sample clause: Reversion

Notwithstanding the foregoing, the rights to publish or license Multimedia Versions shall be revocable by the Author upon giving written notice to the Publisher if the Publisher has not published or licensed publications, transmission or distribution of any Multimedia Version within [five (5)] years after [first publication by the Publisher of the Work in volume form] [the date hereof].

13.3 DRAFTING AND NEGOTIATING

Licence agreements should be reviewed in the light of the restricted acts under the CDPA (*see* Chapter 3). A licence should also include the right to license others to do the same.

13.3.1 KEY ISSUES

Rights acquirers must identify a number of major elements in order to give sufficient precision to the agreements they draw up.

Format

Defining a software platform (DOS, Macintosh or other operating system), a hardware platform, or both, is critical: 'software rights' could include anything existing or later invented. 'Personal computer' can mean IBM (DOS and OS/2), Macintosh, Apple, Next and other operating systems not yet in existence. 'CD-ROM' can mean CD-TV, CD-I, CD-ROM disks which are compatible with DOS or Macintosh, Sony Bookman and Discman and other systems not yet in existence.

Products

The same information can easily, through electronic manipulation, be used in a variety of products.

> **Example**
>
> If a publisher licenses a print almanac to a software publisher, does the software publisher have the right to create one product only? Could he break the almanac into subject matters or geographic areas and publish several different products using the same information organised in different ways?

What rights are needed and in what material?

Are illustrations required? If so, can the necessary rights be acquired?

Alterations and derivative works

Alterations may have to be made to the original work in order to adapt it to the new medium.

> **Example**
>
> Who owns the rights in the alteration (the 'derivative work')? Should the publisher be indemnified for liability arising out of the changes being made? Will portions of the works be combined with materials from other sources? What rights of review or approval are appropriate?

Use of names and trade marks

Is a licence to use the name of the original work and any trade marks associated with it needed? What credit lines acknowledging the source of the materials will be needed? What approvals are necessary or appropriate?

Payments

Are advances appropriate, and when? Should the payment be in the form of a one-time fee, or royalties based on sales? If royalties are used, how are they to be calculated? When do royalties accrue?

Sub-licensing
Obtain the right to sub-license.

Warranties and limitations of liability
What kinds of warranties, warranty disclaimers and/or limitations on liability should be included in the agreement?

The unconditional warranties should include:

(a) ownership of the work;
(b) the right to enter into the agreement;
(c) freedom from encumbrances, liens or other claims;
(d) non-infringement of third party rights.

There should also be an indemnity against all costs, expenses etc incurred as a result of a breach (or alleged breach) of any warranty.

Agreements granting the right to use materials in electronic formats have a great deal in common with other types of licensing and permission agreements, but they also present unique problems. Standard forms of permission, reprint and translation agreements are a starting-point, but are, for the reasons discussed above, generally inadequate to deal with these special issues.

13.4 CONTENTS OF THE AGREEMENT

The major issues to be incorporated in the acquisition agreement will include:

(1) *Definition of the 'work'*, including content and characteristics: note that adequate definitions are very important; as is a comprehensive specification.
(2) (a) Parameters of the rights to be acquired, including the right to mix the work with works by other authors; and to edit and adapt the work (moral rights questions);
    (b) Licence or assignment: is the owner willing to *assign* his or her rights or will he or she insist on a licence under copyright?
    (c) Ownership of derivative works: who will own works derived or spun off from the main work?
(3) *Delivery time:* complicated production schedules make agreement on, and adherence to, delivery dates very important.
(4) *Delivery medium:* if 'electronic' delivery is important, specify the software and the platform.
(5) *Exploitation use* (including market) and platform: it is important to define use and available platforms. *See* 1.2.
(6) *Ownership of rental rights:* to the extent that the product is a 'film', rental rights will be applicable.
(7) *Fees and royalties:* accounting.
(8) *Obligations and role* of author post-delivery and post-publication, eg, to update. To what extent is the author's continued involvement essential or useful?
(9) *Right of author* to be involved in eg transfer to a different system: if the grant is broad, to what extent should the author be entitled to be involved in an adaptation of the product from one language to another or on to new platforms?

CONTENTS OF THE AGREEMENT 13.4

(10) *Right to sub-contract* (by author); *right to sub-contract* (by publisher): these issues are no different from those of traditional publishing.

(11) *Right to assign:* this is also the same as that in traditional publishing.

(12) *Option on further work:* although further work will be as difficult to define and enforce as in traditional publishing contracts, it is necessary to consider what options there might be (if the original grant is limited) to acquire extended rights over the existing work.

(13) *Warranties and indemnity:* these are as important here, if not more so, as in a traditional contract.

(14) *(Non-) competition provisions:* care must be taken to ensure that restrictions do not fall foul of competition law rules.

(15) *Termination provisions*, and effect of termination on eg, pre-existing sub-licences. There are few new implications arising from multimedia; refer to traditional contracts for these.

(16) *Confidentiality:* refer to a traditional form of contract for this aspect.

(17) *Law and jurisdiction:* for this aspect, see the traditional form of contract.

Checklist: key issues for agreements

(1) Who is the owner?
(2) Is the author an employee or a freelancer?
(3) Does a written contract (assignment or licence) exist?
(4) What rights are granted under it expressly or by implication? Are these broad enough for the use contemplated?
(5) What rights are expressly reserved?
(6) Have moral rights been waived?
(7) Have performers' consents been obtained?
(8) Have personality and/or character rights been cleared?
(9) Are there any relevant trade marks? Does permission need to be obtained for their use or for the use of logos etc?
(10) Have music rights been obtained from eg composer (and author of lyrics), and recording company or PPL, VPL, MCPS, PRS?
(11) Has use of artwork been cleared?
(12) Are rights exclusive or non-exclusive?
(13) Have there been any prior sub-licences?
(14) If so, and if they were exclusive, can clearance be obtained from sub-licensees?
(15) Has there been any prior exercise?
(16) What is the extent of the available rights: period, territory, method of exploitation?
(17) What royalty or other payment obligations come with the rights (eg, for an existing work)?
(18) What are the credit obligations?
(19) Have warranties been obtained?
(20) Can rights be obtained through a collecting society?
(21) What is the term of the licence? Can it be terminated?
(22) Is manipulation of the text permitted?
(23) Is there a definition of the works covered?
(24) Bitmap or character encoded?

• PART 4 •

DEVELOPING AND DISTRIBUTING A MULTIMEDIA WORK

• 14 •

EXPLOITATION, DEVELOPMENT AND PRODUCTION

14.1 INTRODUCTION

For those familiar with the film industry and film contracts (particularly those for videos) multimedia product development and production contracts will hold few mysteries; the concepts are broadly the same, the end product is often similar even if the technology involved in it is new. There are, however, some crucial differences, particularly in respect of distribution.

The key to successful development and production is:

(a) a good concept, which may involve market research and a proper knowledge of the market;
(b) good product design and a tightly written specification;
(c) good initial costing;
(d) strict adherence to the concept and to the budget;
(e) control of the software source code and masters, gold discs or other material used in production.

14.2 EXPLOITATION

Any company wishing to produce a multimedia product has three basic choices: it can produce the product itself; it can enter into a joint-venture (or co-production) agreement with other parties to produce the product; or it can sub-license production and exploitation to a specialist producer. Each of these courses has its own advantages and disadvantages.

14.2.1 IN-HOUSE PRODUCTION/DIRECT SALE

There are at least two sub-choices here:

(1) To develop and produce the product in-house.
(2) To commission a specialist producer to do the work.

The common thread is that the company bears the whole cost itself. Development and production costs for multimedia products are high and, as the scope for interactivity or virtual reality increases, so the costs will get even higher. Accordingly, there is a need for very firm control of production methods and expense. This may appear to be easier when a production is done in-house but it is still remarkably difficult. Strict control is absolutely essential if a third party is contracted. Cost control is vital.

While control of the project will be completely in the company's hands, along with any revenue, the whole cost and risk will fall to the company as well. This will include all research and development, marketing, distribution and sales costs, although the responsibility for some of these latter tasks may be reduced by the appointment of agents.

The advantage is that the company will be able not only to keep absolute control of the intellectual property and associated technology but also to maximise its profit on sales of the product. In addition the company will be able to control dissemination, updating and the like.

Some protection for a parent company against disaster (such as an unsafe product or economic failure) can be provided through the use of a subsidiary company, a route that may be neccessary in some foreign countries for tax or regulatory reasons. However, the protection will be illusory if third parties dealing with the subsidiary insist on parent company guarantees.

Because of the risks, many choose to share the risks and the rewards by entering into a joint-venture or co-production arrangement.

An alternative to developing the product in-house or commissioning a specialist to develop it is to manufacture the product but to license sales of it through an independent distributor who will finance distribution, sales, advertising and after-sales functions in one or more specific markets. This method is often used to penetrate foreign markets, either by smaller companies which lack the resources to undertake those commitments themselves, or by larger ones which wish to capitalise on a local distributor's knowledge and experience in the market.

A local distributor may do more than sell the product; he may become involved in the product development and even in local manufacture or sub-assembly.

14.2.2 JOINT VENTURE OR CO-PRODUCTION

There are different types of joint venture: one is a contractual one; another involves the establishment of a separate joint-venture company which itself is owned jointly by the parties in the agreed proportions. In this latter case it is the joint-venture company which owns the rights and which enters into the contracts.

The advantage of a joint venture is that the very essence of the arrangement is that costs are likely to be shared. Each party brings its own (complementary) skills, resources and investment, whether in money or money's worth. This enables companies to enter a market or develop a product which otherwise would be impractical or too risky for either of them to do separately. Usually one party will contribute benefits such as cash, management, manufacturing and marketing facilities and the other the technology and ongoing technical and commercial advisory services. In such an arrangement each party would license to the other, or to the joint venture, any intellectual property owned by it.

It is essential in a joint venture to ensure that the hierarchy is agreed beforehand. Someone has to be in control even if certain decisions must be brought back to both parties for a joint decision. A frequent compromise is to give one party artistic control, subject to keeping within the design specification and the agreed budget, and only require joint decisions where it is necessary to step outside those parameters. The contract should contain a formula for breaking any deadlock.

Just as with a joint venture the costs are shared, the revenue is also shared. The parties will usually share the profits in the same ratio as the agreed value of their contribution.

> **Joint venture/co-production checklist**
> (1) Identify product and goals.
> (2) Allocate who does what: actual production work; rights clearance, creative work; physical manufacture; marketing etc.
> (3) Allocate research and development responsibilities.
> (4) Agree initial contributions: money; rights and the value attributable to them; properties; brand names etc; responsibility for overcost.
> (5) Production: agree budget; milestones for reporting; production schedule; delivery date.
> (6) Approvals: initial concept and structure; demo; individual components of product etc.
> (7) Marketing and distribution: territories; platform; general approach; specific responsibilities.
> (8) Credits: producer; intellectual property rights; moral rights; performers' rights, etc; placement and form of credits in product and packaging.
> (9) Ownership of rights in product: initially likely to be owned by the joint venture but will they then be split by country, language, platform or otherwise?
> (10) If a joint-venture company is used there are issues such as: who is on the board; who chairs it; who controls the board; and what is the dividend policy?
> (11) If a contractual joint venture is used, there will be similar issues, such as control of the joint venture.
> (12) Whichever type of joint venture is used there will be issues such as: who can commit to eg sales, termination etc.

Many companies will not have the capital to want to invest (or if they do have the capital, will feel they do not know enough about product development); if this is the case there is an alternative, to sub-license the rights to a specialist multimedia producer.

14.2.3 SUB-LICENSING

In sub-licensing the rights are licensed to a specialist multimedia producer who takes total responsibility for producing and then exploiting the product. The licensor's return may include:

- an upfront payment for the rights;
- a royalty based on the success of the product (either a per-unit royalty or perhaps a share of the net profits).

Apart from these payments, it has no other involvement, unless the deal includes, for instance, the right to exploit a particular part of the market.

Companies which choose not to manufacture their products at all (or only to do so in their own market) hand over to the sub-licensee (which should be better equipped or more knowledgeable in the local market(s)) the risk of exploiting the products.

The advantage of sub-licensing manufacture is that the licensor's capital investment can be minimised and the sub-licensee ought to be able to give the product a much quicker entry into the local markets. However, because the risk of failure is largely transferred to the sub-licensee, the licensor usually obtains a much lower profit than if it were to manufacture and sell the product itself.

A specific form of licensing is franchising, the essential element of which is the granting of permission to the franchisee to use the trade marks, logos, commercial and in some cases technical information which make up a particular business format.

There are of course many licensing permutations, with the dividing lines often being unclear. The broad principle, however, is that if a company shares the risks it will have to share the reward.

14.2.4 FACTORS INFLUENCING CHOICE OF METHOD

There is no one best way of exploiting IP rights and the method chosen will depend on a careful evaluation of all the relevant factors. The following guidelines should, however, be helpful in making the choice as to the best method of exploitation.

The IP owner

(1) *Resources available:* if the intellectual property owner is an individual or a small company, it may be impractical for it to be directly involved in all its potential markets. Some form of collaboration will therefore be more or less inevitable.

Furthermore, even larger companies will have taken strategic decisions as to which products and to which markets they will devote their resources. If a market for one of their products falls outside their agreed strategic direction, or if a product is developed which falls into this category, then a manufacturing licence or a joint venture may well be preferable.

(2) *Profit and rate of return desired:* a company is likely to earn the greatest profit on the exploitation of its rights if it carries out the exploitation itself. The financial targets of the IP owner may be so rigorous as to rule out any third party involvement. Alternatively the cost of exploitation of a product may be so prohibitively high that a joint venture or manufacturing licence is the only sensible method of exploitation.

(3) *Intended time scale for exploitation:* if, for instance, an IP owner is engaged in a race with a competitor to put a product on the market quickly, then direct sale may be the best way to achieve this. Alternatively, if the owner wishes to build up its presence in a market over time, then some other route might be attractive.

Type of product

The type of product under consideration is often one of the most important factors in deciding how to exploit it.

(1) *Product life cycle:* if this is very short, then the owner may have no option but to exploit the IP rights itself, especially if the product is easily copied. This is a common feature of the computer software industry. As software has a relatively short life cycle, it is customary for the software owner to keep tight control of manufacture of the software product itself, perhaps only appointing a local distributor.

(2) *Manufacturing costs and complexity:* for products with high manufacturing costs, or products which have to be produced in large quantities to be economically viable, the IP owner is more likely to want to share the risk of the enterprise with another business.
(3) *Strength of IP rights:* if the IP rights in the product are weak, then the owner is less likely to license the manufacture of the product, because he may well then have difficulty in controlling the exploitation of the product by licensees or joint venturers.
(4) *Distribution difficulties:* if the shipping costs of a product are high in relation to its value, or it is a perishable or fragile product, then local manufacture is quite often the only economic means of exploitation of the product.

Market conditions

(1) *Government regulations and restrictions:* exchange control regulation, controls on the foreign ownership of companies and import controls are common examples of government regulations and restrictions which may make local manufacture or a local joint venture inevitable.
(2) *Availability of local labour and raw materials:* in many under-developed countries the lack of these makes local manufacture difficult, if not impossible.
(3) *Competition:* the nature and extent of competition will determine the ease of penetrating the market and consequently the investment and financial risk involved.
(4) *Taxes:* The local tax regime and double tax treaties between the national market and the other countries in which the IP owner has operations may well be decisive in the method of exploitation chosen.
(5) *Tariffs:* tariffs in individual countries may affect the decision to manufacture locally. For example, many Japanese companies have, in the light of EC anti-dumping decisions, set up local manufacturing subsidiaries in Europe.
(6) *Strengths/weaknesses of local IP laws:* in many third world countries, the protection of IP is weak or non-existent. Although the position has improved in some countries in recent years, there are still many countries in which it would be very unwise to permit a local manufacturer to produce a product, as piracy is very likely to follow. In addition, some countries have technology transfer laws which require the transfer of technology to local entities. These factors could make a local manufacturing arrangement very unattractive to the IP owner.
(7) *Local laws:* these can influence the choice of method of exploitation in a wide variety of ways. For instance, local product liability laws may be so fierce as to make it highly desirable to introduce a local manufacturer or joint venturer who will have local knowledge and expertise and who might be used as a 'buffer'. Alternatively, local competition laws may restrict the form of arrangement into which an IP owner can enter and even his choice of partner in a local market.
(8) *Local custom:* in some markets, Japan being the legendary example, it is almost impossible for foreigners to market their own products successfully. A local distributor is essential in these cases.

14.3 DEVELOPMENT

Before investing in the production of a multimedia product, many companies conduct a feasibility study and enter into a development contract with a specialist multimedia producer.

This arrangement gives the company a chance to assess 'look and feel' and to get a clearer idea of what will be necessary to produce the finished product, to ascertain what rights, licences, clearances and permissions will be needed and to obtain a better idea of the costs involved.

It may also give an opportunity for initial market-testing to take place

14.3.1 DEVELOPMENT CONTRACT

If a development project is contracted out-house, the essential terms will include:

(1) *Confidentiality and exclusivity* (especially in relation to any proprietary user interface or where the product is part of a series) (*see* sample clause below).
(2) *The fee and payment schedule:* normally this would be a one-off relationship, with the developer agreeing to undertake and complete the development for a fixed fee and without any continuing financial or other interest in it. At what stages should the fee be paid? Often used stages are:
 (a) on signing of the contract;
 (b) on actual start of development;
 (c) at various agreed times during development as work is done;
 (d) on delivery of the product at the agreed stage of development.
(3) *The specification* for design, performance and functionality and how changes to the design will be incorporated.
(4) *Responsibility for clearance of rights.*
(5) *Preparation* of the multimedia work to the specification.
(6) *Copyright assignment:* delivery (or placing into escrow) of any source materials.
(7) *Warranties.*
(8) *Project management structure* (*see* sample clause below).
(9) *Approvals:* it would be sensible to agree a scheme for staged approvals through the life of the development process so that any deviations from expectation can be identified and dealt with early in the process; and so that quality control can be maintained. These may allow termination and/or withdrawal by the producer if development does not proceed as planned or if it is impossible or not feasible to change the design specifications; or if the feasibility study suggests there is no future for the product.
(10) *Changes to design specification* to take account of the foregoing.
(11) *Project timetable and delivery date.*
(12) *Product testing* prior to acceptance.
(13) *Engage the developer* to produce production copies: this is perhaps an option (but not a commitment) in favour of the commissioning party.

The essence of a development contract is that the developer is commissioned to develop the product and, on completion or delivery, has nothing further to do with it. Hence, the contract should provide that all rights pass from developer to producer and there is no need to specify a division of rights. Some contracts may, however, give the developer a right to participate in exploitation in some way; it will then be necessary to agree who shares what from which market and the percentages and per-unit royalties from sales.

Sample clause: Confidentiality obligation

1 The Supplier and the Publisher each undertake to the other to keep confidential all information, whether written or oral, concerning the business or affairs of the other

that it may receive or obtain in the performance of this Agreement or in any preliminary discussions, and shall not use the same without the prior written consent of the disclosing party for any purpose except as provided or permitted under this Agreement. These obligations of confidentiality shall not apply to information which is:
   (i) trivial or obvious;
   (ii) already in the possession of one party at the time of disclosure by the other, other than as a result of a breach of this Clause; or
   (iii) is or becomes in the public domain other than as result of a breach of this Clause.
2 The Supplier and the Publisher each undertake to the other to limit access to each other's confidential or proprietary information to those employees and permitted agents and sub-contractors who need access in order to perform their respective duties and to take all steps as shall from time to time be reasonably necessary to ensure that they comply with the provisions of Sub-Clause 1.

Sample clause: Acceptance tests

1 The purpose of the Acceptance Tests shall be to verify that the functionality, searchability, linkages, retrievability, user interface and required response time for the Work are satisfactory to the Publisher and conform to the Functional Specification.
2 Upon receipt of the Prototype, the Publisher shall not unreasonably withhold or delay the carrying out of the Acceptance Tests on the Prototype and shall, within [one week]:
   (a) notify the Supplier that the Acceptance Tests have succeeded;
   (b) notify the Supplier that the Acceptance Tests have failed, in which case the Publisher shall describe why this is the case; or
   (c) confirm in writing that the results of the Acceptance Tests are acceptable subject to certain minor changes being made to the Work before the Master is produced.
3 If the Acceptance Tests shall fail, the Supplier shall carry out any necessary modifications to the Work, redeliver the Prototype within one week and the Acceptance Tests shall be re-run as provided for above.
4 Where the failure to pass Acceptance Tests is attributable to the Supplier, costs incurred by the Supplier in making modifications to the Master and resubmitting the Master to Acceptance Testing shall be borne by the Supplier.
5 The Acceptance Tests shall be re-run on delivery of each Master before any commercial products are pressed or stamped. The Publisher shall again have the opportunity to indicate whether or not the Master has, in its reasonable opinion, passed the Acceptance Tests, and, in case of failure, the provisions of Sub-Clauses 3 and 4 shall apply again.
6 If any Prototype or Master for the Work fails three or more successive Acceptance Tests the Publisher may terminate this Agreement.

14.4 PRODUCTION

Once the feasibility study or development project has indicated that there is a market and that the final product can be made to a realistic budget, approvals can be given to move on to the production stage. In almost all cases, the actual production work will be sub-contracted. Again the primary objective of the production agreement, like a publisher's printing agreement, is to define what is to be produced, to set the cost parameters, and to specify quality.

In all cases, the deal should include a full assignment of all rights from the production company to the producer, except for software tools used in the work and for any navigation software incorporated in the work, in which only a licence is likely to be available. The responsibility for clearance of rights should be carefully defined. In addition to the terms contained in the development agreement, there should be provision for:

- testing: does the work meet the specifications?
- change control during production;
- delivery of the *tested* product;
- maintenance and support of the product, including provision of updates in some cases;
- appropriate warranties.

Payment stages should include instalments payable upon specific milestones, eg:

- on approval, after running of acceptance tests;
- following acceptance, say on expiry of the warranty period.

A number of people will be involved in the production: directors, designers, researchers, animators, actors, composers, scriptwriters, computer programmer consultants, photographers and cameramen. This line-up will more readily approximate to that for the production of a film than that for the production of a book. It is essential to require all those involved to assign or waive all their rights, and allow exceptions to this general rule on a carefully controlled basis only.

Warranties are essential.

14.4.1 PROJECT MANAGEMENT AND REPORTING STRUCTURES

With multimedia products, product specification is vital. Where a company is investing several hundreds of thousands of pounds in a project, it will want to ensure that the production company will not only stick to the production specifications, but keep to budget. Both the precise scope of the product and the production process necessary to develop it need to be detailed through production milestones and a strict consultation process for quality control. It might be necessary to keep development money separate through the use of specific bank accounts; to agree draw down dates; to adopt devices to control and penalise expenditure which goes over budget; and to reward any underspending. In the film industry the practice is to appoint a representative to:

- liaise with the production company;
- be the recipient of regular reports on progress; and (possibly)
- be a co-signatory on the bank account.

Sample clause: Project manager: appointment

1 The Supplier's Project Manager shall be the main point of contact for communication between the parties for the provision of information or approvals. The identity of the Supplier's Project Manager shall be changed only in circumstances outside the reasonable control of the Supplier and the appointment of a new Project Manager by the Supplier shall be subject to the reasonable approval of the Publisher.
2 The Publisher shall appoint a project manager to act as the main point of contact with the Supplier.
3 The Supplier shall provide regular written progress reports on work in progress and, in the event of any delays or other difficulties which may have an impact on costs or the production timetable, the Supplier shall brief the Publisher fully on the issues.
4 The parties shall also liaise regularly by telephone, fax or personal meeting in order to

schedule production work and to address any problems arising during development and acceptance testing, all with a view to the smoothing of work flows and the early addressing of potential problems.

14.4.2 INSURANCE

Insurance is an important element. If the insurance is taken out by the production company, the company should require that its interest is noted on the policy. In film financing, the financier will often require that the producer takes out a completion bond with one of the specialist bond companies. In return for a fee, usually calculated as a percentage of budget, the completion guarantor guarantees either that the product will be completed and delivered as contractually required or that the investment will be returned. Some of the higher priced projects may well justify such an investment.

The insurance should include errors and omissions (E&O) insurance. This is another name for professional idemnity (PI) insurance and differs only in that it does not apply just to the professions. The policy will customarily provide an indemnity (subject to excess and aggregate limit) to the insured for loss arising from a claim resulting from any breaches of duty including negligent acts, errors, omissions, breaches of warranties or breaches of trust. 'Bolt-ons' to E&O cover are available, such as fidelity cover and libel and slander. Directors and officers insurance (D&O) is similar to E&O, differing only in that its purpose is to cover loss arising from claims against directors and officers.

Agreement will be needed on how under- or over-spending is dealt with. Sometimes the producer may qualify for a share in any saving. If the project runs over budget, the company will want to take the necessary decisions to bring the project back under control again. If all else fails, the company will want the right to take over production; indeed, if a completion guarantor is involved, it will insist on this right.

14.4.3 Source materials

The source materials are the key to a multimedia product. They could include:

- software source code;
- computer-coded text (enabling hypertext links);
- film or audio material.

Without access to the source materials, one cannot amend or correct the product. Developers are often reluctant to hand over the source materials because with them go any control they have over the product. The producer needs source materials because without them he cannot service the product.

A frequently used compromise is to use an escrow holder, with whom a copy of the source materials is deposited on terms that enable the producer to obtain access to it if the developer:

- becomes insolvent;
- fails to support the product;
- falls into breach of the development or production agreements.

Sample clause: Source code: supply or security deposit of escrow

X.1 The Licensor shall, at the request of the Licensee and on terms to be agreed, provide to the Licensee a copy of the source code for the Programme [together with any associated documentation] for the purpose of maintaining [and enhancing] the Software.

14.4.3   EXPLOITATION, DEVELOPMENT AND PRODUCTION

OR

X.1 If the Licensor terminates the maintenance service provided for in this Agreement the Licensor shall provide to the Licensee [at no additional charge] a copy of the source code for the Programme [together with all necessary associated documentation] for the sole purpose of enabling the Licensee to undertake such maintenance [either itself or using sub-contractors approved in writing for this purpose by the Licensor.]

X.2 Notwithstanding the provisions of Clause X.1, in the event that the Licensor shall become bankrupt or go into liquidation, other than a voluntary liquidation for the purpose of reconstruction or amalgamation, the Licensor shall, insofar as it is permitted in law to do, provide to the Licensee at no additional charge a copy of the source code for the Programme [together with all necessary associated documentation] for the sole purpose of enabling the Licensee to maintain the Programme.

or use Escrow

X.1 The Licensor has arranged a source code deposit ('escrow') agreement covering the source code and any associated documentation for the Software with an escrow custodian. During the term of this Agreement the Licensee will be entitled to the benefit of such escrow agreement providing that it shall enter into a separate written escrow agreement with the Licensor and the escrow custodian.

Multimedia production agreement: Checklist

(1)   (a) • Content, eg text, artwork, animation, soundtrack;
- design of user interface;
- functions;
- user searching functionality;
- overall product design;

(b) choice of software.

(2) Documentation (eg user manuals) to be supplied by the producer with the product.

(3) Development of:
(a) functional specifications;
(b) user interface;
(c) design specifications;
(d) overall multimedia product.

(4) Project management:
(a) reporting procedure;
(b) liaison officers;
(c) meetings.

(5) Trials.

(6) Revision of design and specification.

(7) Final testing and delivery:
(a) scope of testing;
(b) delivery date(s).

(8) Acceptance/Rejection.

(9) (a) Product ownership, copyright and ownership of customised features;
(b) ownership of other physical materials, eg:
- network;
- photographs;
- masters;

(Cont'd)

> - film;
> - disks, eg of manuals.
> (c) source materials.
> (10) (a) Warranties, eg:
>   - entitled to enter into the agreement;
>   - work original and all rights in it owned or controlled;
>   - use of work will not infringe the rights of any third party;
> (b) indemnity
> (c) limitation of liability (so far as law will allow. Consider the effect of the Unfair Contract Terms in Consumer Contracts Regulations).
> (11) Payment:
>   (a) fixed fee;
>   (b) hourly fee (for additional labour);
>   (c) percentage.
> (12) Confidentiality.
> (13) Default.
> (14) Termination, eg for material breach or insolvency.
> (15) Law and jurisdiction (and consider whether provision for arbitration may be useful).

14.5 SOFTWARE

Software licensing issues can fill a book of their own and the following is only an outline of some factors which relate to multimedia products.

Software clearly plays a key role in any multimedia product. Specific programs will be required to prepare the content of the product for use. These will include programs:

- for sampling sound;
- for capturing and digitising images etc;
- to render computer-generated content such as screen displays and other graphics;
- to allow other multimedia technology to work with the content—eg storing and compressing; and
- to drive the product—allowing the user to access, search and retrieve the content and thus navigate around and interact with the product.

Clearly to form the user interface strong product concepts and content are ineffective without suitable software. The design, ownership and control of the user interface is particularly important. The question of who is to provide the software often determines the structure of multimedia deals and joint ventures.

A multimedia producer can decide:

(a) to create the necessary software and related technology specially for his/her own product; or
(b) use software and technology already used and developed by others.

In most cases some third party software will be used, particularly for development tools.

Producers who may create successful multimedia application software are then able to license that to others for use with their products subject to any limitations in licences for other software products or tools incorporated or used in the newly created software. Where software is being developed in-house the standard IP ownership issues will arise. If outside consultants are being used there must be:

- a clear assignment of rights;
- warranties that there is no infringement of third party rights (as explained above *see* 12.1.10, the parameters of copyright and patent protection for multimedia software are unclear, so a producer must be very careful that the consultant is not borrowing from elsewhere); and
- confidentiality provisions restricting their use of the company's product information with other clients.

Alternatively a producer may ask a software house to develop software which will then be assigned to it, in which case a development agreement specifically for the software will be required: this will need to take in the points raised above and other development agreement issues regarding control and use (*see* below).

Many software producers may, however, simply license in software, particularly for software engines to multimedia CD-ROMs.

Where the multimedia product being designed is intended for an on-line service provided by another party, it will be necessary to test the product with the service provider's own operating system software to ensure that the two can work together. Given the importance of this the producer will normally take a licence of the operating system and associated development tools from the service provider to use in the development of the product.

The standard issues to consider when taking a licence are:

(a) warranties:
  - of title,
  - that if the program is used as directed, it will perform as described in the specification;
  - that if the licensee has taken the program after the licensor has examined the licensee's requirements, the program is reasonably fit for its purpose;
(b) that the licensee can copy or adapt the program:
  - for the particular multimedia product being developed;
  - in order to correct errors;
  - in order to meet changing product requirements and so that the statutory rights to decompile and make backup copies are not undermined;
(c) that, after any change is made to the program or improvements and associated applications are developed, ownership is retained in the new elements and a copy of the outdated version can be retained for use when a reconstruction of the software is needed;
(d) that satisfactory maintenance arrangements are available: these must cover both the licensee when developing the product and the end user. For instance when calling up a help-line is the licensee able to offer support or is the licensor required to do so?
(e) that access to the source code is granted to all or part of the software (or whether escrow arrangements are necessary);
(f) that the licensee has a right to receive, or to be offered a licence in respect of, any

improvements to the program developed by the licensor or which the licensor has the right to license;

(g) that the licence allows for the onward licensing of the completed multimedia product to the end user and whether an agreed form of shrinkwrap licence is to be used.

• 15 •

LICENSING AND DISTRIBUTION

15.1 ... 'AND LICENSE NARROWLY'

Multimedia licensing is most commonly used for CD-ROM. We deal with on-line distribution and interactive supply via the network separately.

The first task is to identify the distribution goals:

- maximise distribution;
- minimise piracy;
- limit liability;
- achieve flexibility in arrangements.

The second task is to identify the distribution route. Good distribution is an important element in the profitability of a project. At the same time it is necessary to agree a marketing and distribution plan: these two should go hand in hand with the concept development.

15.1.1 CONSIDERATIONS BEFORE ENTERING INTO NEGOTIATIONS

It is desirable for a company to be as fully prepared as possible before approaching any potential licensees: this will add to its credibility with the licensee and give it a stronger negotiating position. The various specific points to consider when dealing with an IP licence will be dealt with in detail in 15.2.1. There are, however, five preliminary questions which should be addressed before deciding on the appropriate course of action:

(1) What rights are to be licensed? Although the licence may relate to the manufacture of one product there may be several different IP rights involved. In addition to any patent or patent applications there will be related know-how and there might be registered or unregistered designs and copyright in drawings and documentation relating to the product. If the licensor's trade mark is to be used or a new trade mark has been created then these will also have to be dealt with.

(2) In order to target the licensees who have the appropriate manufacturing, marketing and other skills, the licensor must first work out who will actually want to buy and use the product.

(3) The licensor must decide when the licence will be given: individual circumstances will determine this. A licensor will want to have the manufacturing arrangements set out if it is making considerable investment in further development and obtaining necessary regulatory approvals. The licensee may be keen to obtain exclusive

rights at an early stage or may not want to have to wait while the idea is developed.
(4) As part of the general strategy the licensor must decide whether to give exclusive, sole or non-exclusive licences (*see* 15.2.1).
(5) The licensor has to work out the price required.

15.1.2 APPROACH TO POTENTIAL LICENSEES

In the excitement of exploiting a new idea it is surprising how often IP owners forget to maintain confidentiality. If the approach is by letter, consider writing a short initial letter asking for a confidentiality letter to be signed before disclosing details. This is important not only to protect un-patentable know-how which can only be protected by confidence but also, if any inventive step is involved, any future patent application will be jeopardised if there has been publication other than subject to confidence. Although confidentiality obligations arise under common law in certain circumstances, the extent of these is often unclear, so a written confidentiality agreement should be entered into as a matter of course. However, large organisations are often reluctant to sign such an agreement, in case one part of the organisation has something similar in course of development already and sometimes quite a complex agreement becomes necessary. In other cases reaching agreement is impracticable but the IP owner then proceeds at his own risk and abuse is not unknown.

15.1.3 FORM OF LICENCE

Once the commercial basis for a licence has been worked out this has to be put into a workable form of agreement. In practice, several types of IP rights are often being licensed together. This may cause problems. If, for example, a patent licensed together with other rights is void the whole licence may fail and it is worth considering having separate licences for each type of right. However, this too has drawbacks because of the quantity of paperwork and danger of inconsistency. In practice, it may be a good idea to have one key document with various short form licences for publicity or registration.

15.1.4 HEADS OF AGREEMENT

It is quite common for a summary or heads of the key commercial terms of an agreement to be drawn up and signed by both parties as an initial stage in the negotiation process. These can be helpful, provided they are clearly expressed as being non-binding (except for any confidentiality provisions). However, they can also cause very considerable problems if it is unclear whether or not they have legal effect or if, as is often the case, an attempt to summarise has led to misunderstandings; the standard example is an agreement to pay an X per cent royalty—X per cent of what? Consider instead agreeing a summary at each stage of negotiations rather than, when negotiating a licence, becoming involved in arguments as to what was meant when negotiating the heads of agreement.

15.1.5 SELECTING A DISTRIBUTOR

The points to consider when selecting a distributor are:
- objective (*see* 14.2);
- IP rights involved;

- territorial coverage; language;
- quality of other products handled; are the other products complementary or competitive?
- skill of sales force and/or penetration of market;
- financial strength; track record;
- known management or reputation;
- size of fee or commission.

Market specialists

Distributors who specialise in the market are an obvious first choice. They should bring a specialised knowledge of the product-type and of the marketplace. Engagement of such a distributor dispenses with the need for an in-house sales and marketing force. They charge fees for their work, which may be a flat fee or linked to success.

Options not involving a distributor

If no distributor is involved, the producer has the choice of:

- direct sales to the public, through newspaper or direct mail channels or over the net. The advantages include: the producer keeps all the revenues less the marketing and sales costs; a mailing list will be built up; and there will be direct feedback. The disadvantages may include: an unsophisticated approach to selling; customer resistance to direct sales; the cost of in-house staff;
- direct sales to retailers: although this route will bypass the middleman and develop the mailing list/direct customer contact benefit, it suffers from the same disadvantage as the first option;
- 'packaging' the product for a publisher, who agrees for a fee to put his logo on to the product and give it the benefit of his own sales and marketing force. Multimedia, originally thought of in the same category as, and therefore sold with, computer software, is now as likely to be found with video products.

Control over rights licensed out

A producer must ensure that he does not license out more than the rights he has acquired. This is a simple message, but is one that is often overlooked. Under the new Database Directive (96/9/EC), (*see* 4.5) it will be necessary to license *very carefully* the right to include the work on any database which is to be subject to physical distribution. It is proposed that the exhaustion of rights principle will apply to physical sales but not to supply on-line.

Accordingly, a producer must consider whether it is appropriate to supply physical database material *by rental only*.

Who will manufacture the product?

A producer needs also to decide whether to manufacture the product or license the distributor, or someone else, to do so. He should license only the right to sell (or rent), not the right to adapt, unless that is part of the distribution deal.

15.2 PHYSICAL DISTRIBUTION

15.2.1 PARTICULAR TERMS IN LICENCES

Competition law restrictions

It is important to recognise that freedom of contract is considerably restricted by both UK and EC competition law. It is often possible to draft around UK law because of its form-based nature, although there are proposals for a radical change in the law which could stop this. EC law, however, looks at the effect of an agreement; offending clauses are void and unenforceable. For competition law *see* the standard textbooks. Chapter 16 provides a summary of the competition principles applying to multimedia products.

Both UK and EC competition law should be considered when the form and content of a licence are being settled. To avoid being deluged by individual notifications of licence agreements, the EC has enacted a number of 'block exemptions' from the operation of art 85 of the EC Treaty for certain types of licences, including those dealing with:

- patents (and know-how where it is secret and permits a better exploitation of the licensed patents);
- pure know-how (which exemption also covers mixed patent and know-how related licences); and
- franchises.

Broadly speaking, if the licence terms comply with the 'blue prints' in a block exemption the licence is automatically exempted from art 85. Usually, however, one is faced with a choice as to whether to modify the commercial agreement between the parties to get it to fit within the terms of the relevant block exemption or to notify the agreement to the EC.

The block exemptions that apply to patents and pure know-how overlap to a considerable extent so that if a licensee is acquiring both know-how and a patent licence it is often possible to structure the licence to fit one block exemption rather than the other. For example, the know-how licence block exemption is more favourable to the licensor than the patent block exemption if the licensor's patent portfolio across the EC is weak or incomplete.

Formal Provisions

We will deal with each provision in turn:

Parties It is necessary to ensure that the correct parties are identified. As regards the licensor, the proprietors of all relevant IP rights must be named. It may in some cases be necessary to include eg both the holding company and its subsidiary.

As regards the licensee, particularly if a group of companies is involved (dealing with different aspects of manufacture, distribution etc), the correct licence must be granted to the right member of the group. For example, it is useless to license the holding company to manufacture and then prohibit any sub-contracting to the subsidiary which is actually to carry out the manufacture. Where groups of companies are involved, there should always be a termination provision which is triggered if the relevant company leaves the group.

There may be third parties who hold relevant IP rights, especially non-registrable rights such as copyright in computer software which must be licensed separately.

Recitals It is useful to set out the history and purposes of the licence but, while recitals are not in the operative part of a licence, it must be remembered that a statement that a licensor holds a patent or trade mark could be taken as a warranty. This could be extremely inconvenient if the same patent or trade mark had in fact lapsed or is subsequently invalid for some reason and could form the basis of a court action.

Definitions As in any form of legal document, it is vital to define key terms. Once this is done, make sure that the definitions are not circular. Particular definitions required are:

(1) *The rights being licensed:*
   (a) registrable rights (ie, patents, trade marks and registered designs) should be listed in a schedule with full details (if there are applications then the application number, date and details should be listed). The definition can cover any future applications or rights if required, and also any improvements (subject to what is said below). Particularly with trade-mark licences, it is important to describe the goods to which the mark may be applied because if the mark is misused, it may be lost;
   (b) with copyright or an unregistered design right, it is worth referring to or annexing the relevant document or drawings, eg a manual produced by a graphic design company for a new corporate image. With copyright and unregistered design rights, it is quite normal and lawful to license future work but in that case, the work must be defined;
   (c) know-how, confidential information and technical information can be very difficult to define and definitions can be extremely wide or very narrow. The key question is to consider what information is necessary for the licensee to carry out his obligations under the licence and which the licensor needs to be sure is kept confidential. The best way of dealing with this in practice is for both sides to discuss what should be covered, whether just technical data and drawings or expertise and practical experience; and indeed whether marketing and sales methods should be covered. In franchising, where the licensor licenses a large number of licensees, it is customary for there to be a franchising manual detailing production, sales and marketing techniques.

(2) *The product:* once the rights to be licensed have been defined, the product should be defined by reference to those rights. There are various traps for the unwary and the agreement must state clearly what is covered. For example a definition of the product as being 'equipment based on a patent' is in fact much narrower than the definition of the product as 'equipment incorporating an invention' which could cover machinery in which the patented part was only very small.

(3) *Net invoice value, or other measure of royalties:* the financial arrangements for licences can be complex and it is usual to have some form of royalties based on a percentage of sales. This begs the question as to what exactly is meant by sales. For royalties, *see* 12.2.

Other terms may well need to be defined, such as the 'licensed process'; subdivisions of technical information, confidential information and know-how; terms such as 'associated company' and other standard terms.

Grant of licence There are various ways in which the scope of a licence can be limited. These divide into three areas: use, exclusivity and territory.

(1) *Use:* it is possible to license the manufacture, use, hire or sale of products either separately or together. For example, a producer of a CD-ROM might license a dis-

tributor to make distribution copies from a master disk, rather than providing the copies himself. The scope may be further limited by specifying the end use of the product so that eg a trade mark may be used only on certain goods within a class for which it is registered. In practice, licensors often attempt to specify end users but this is extremely difficult to monitor and often falls foul of EC competition law. If a producer is drafting a patent or know-how licence, he must remember that a use restriction which tracks the block exemption, will be valid but he should beware of going further.

For limits on use to be enforceable, the product concerned must be wholly covered by the IP rights licensed.

(2) *Exclusivity:* with a non-exclusive licence, the licensor is free to exploit the licence himself and to grant further similar licences to other licensees. In a sole licence the licensor may not grant other similar licences, but is free to exploit the IP rights himself. In an exclusive licence, the licensor agrees not to grant other similar licences and not to exploit the IP rights himself.

Because some may be uncertain as to the meaning of these expressions, there are advantages in spelling out what is meant:

(a) should exclusivity be given? This is a commercial decision. A licensee may not be prepared to commit itself unless it has exclusivity because of the necessary outlay. It is possible to have a licence which is exclusive for some applications of a protected technology and non-exclusive for others. Generally, if an exclusive licence is to be given, it is sensible to ensure that the licensee has the capacity to reach the potential market; and to consider building in safeguards, such as minimum sales provisions or minimum royalties with a provision for the licence to become non-exclusive if the targets are not met;

(b) with trade-mark and know-how licences, it is in the licensor's interest to have few licensees: for trade marks, this is because the registration must be protected (or else the trade mark may be lost if products of different quality or a wide variety of products all bear the same mark). So far as know-how is concerned, because it is indefinable and difficult to protect, it should only be made available on a need-to-know basis to those who have given specific undertakings as regards confidentiality.

(3) *Territory:* as regards registrable rights, unregistered design and copyright, the licensor is restricted to countries where protection is available. For patents, registered designs and trade marks or applications made at an early stage, it is open to a licensor to consider in which further territories to register. This will often be a question of balancing licensing requirements with costs of registration. Otherwise, subject to any competition law problems, it is a commercial question as to which territories should be covered. When dealing with the registration of rights, it should be remembered that copyright is registrable in some countries.

Once the producer has decided in detail what rights to grant, the actual grant can be dealt with in an express licence clause. Patent, trade-mark and registered design licences should then be registered.

In the case of patents, an exclusive licensee can sue an infringer but registration is in any case necessary to give third parties notice of the licence and to ensure that any transferee of the patent takes subject to the licence. If the licence is not registered within six months it is not possible for the licensee to claim damages or account of profits on any infringement between entitlement and registration. This also applies to registered designs.

The 1994 Trade Mark Act deregulated the licensing of trade marks. The 'trafficking' prohibition of the old 1938 Act was dropped, as were the strict requirements for registered user agreements and quality control. It is now left to the self-interest of trade-mark proprietors to ensure licensing does not damage their marks by ensuring that the terms of any licence provide sufficient control over the licensee's use of the mark. However a licence is still a 'registered transaction' under the 1994 Act and details of the licence must be supplied to the Trade Mark Registry.

Sample clause: Grant of rights by producer

1. In consideration of the payment of the Remuneration by the Publisher the Producer as beneficial owner assigns to the Publisher (and where the subject matter of such assignment is copyright, by way of present assignment of future copyright):
   (a) all rights of copyright which may subsist in the work and in any works created or acquired in the course of the work; and
   (b) all of the Producer's other right, title and interest in and to the Work and all products of the Producer's Services which may have been or may subsequently be created pursuant to the Agreement,
   for the Publisher's use and benefit absolutely for the full period of copyright throughout the world including all reversions, renewals and extensions created, or provided, by the law of any country. The Producer undertakes to execute all such documents and take all such steps as may be necessary to secure to the Publisher the rights assigned or intended to be assigned by this clause.
2. The Producer as beneficial owner further sells and transfers title to the Publisher to all physical materials created, acquired or produced by the Producer in connection with the Work to the intent that the Publisher shall be the sole legal and beneficial owner of all such physical materials.

Sample clause: Exploitation of rights

Without prejudice to the generality of the Rights assigned by Clause [ ], the Publisher shall have the right to make, produce, sell, publicly exhibit, lease, license, hire, market, publicise, distribute, diffuse, transmit, broadcast, adapt and reproduce mechanically, graphically, electronically, digitally or otherwise howsoever by any manner and means (whether now known or hereafter devised) and otherwise exploit all works created in the course of the Work and all products of the Producer's Services in whole or in part with or without adaptation throughout the World.

Restrictions on licensee It is normal, where exclusive rights are granted, for provisions to be included to ensure that the licensee:

- devotes appropriate resources to the development and distribution of the product;
- uses its best or reasonable endeavours to promote the product and imposes minimum royalties.

In addition the licensee is often restricted from:

- manufacturing or selling competing products;
- marketing the product outside the territory; or
- using the licensed technology other than for the licensed use.

Any restrictions of this type will, however, have to be carefully drafted in the light of competition law.

Term Each aspect of the licence can be limited in time. The term does not have to be the same for all rights. The term of the agreement itself can be different again. There are various points to bear in mind for each type of IP right when considering how long the agreement should be for.

(1) *Patents:* as long as it is valid, the licence may be for any length and, if it is for several patents, it can be until the last of these expires. But producers should remember that if a licence is for life of a further improved patent, it will be invalid in the USA and could be void under UK patent law, with the result that the contract would be terminable after the initial patent has expired. In addition, it is important to ensure that the provisions are within the patent block exemption under EC competition law.

If the patent licence is combined with know-how, it is possible to go beyond the end of the term of the patent but royalties must be adjusted and the licence should be brought within the know-how block exemption. In the UK, there is a statutory right for three months' notice of termination to be given for patent licences once all British patents have expired.

(2) *Copyright:* there are no statutory rules for copyright and the term is merely a commercial question, ie, should the licence be for the term of the copyright, or a shorter period?

(3) *Trade-mark licence:* this can be indefinite as trade marks, if renewed and properly maintained, have an indefinite life. In practice, licences are often for a fixed term and renewable.

(4) *Know-how:* once know-how comes into the public domain, it is of no further use, but it is possible for payments still to be due under the licence. Again, it is important to ensure that the licence comes within the know-how block exemption. Subject to this, the length of term is a commercial question.

Validity of ownership A licensee will want to ensure that the IP rights are valid and that it will not be sued for infringement. A licensor will want to protect its rights. There are various types of provisions that are commonly used. The key ones are:

(1) A licensor may give a warranty that he owns the IP rights, but should be very wary of warranting validity: a patent may always be open to challenge. Because of the problem in warranting the validity of patents, a clause is often included stating that the licensor cannot guarantee that the licence is valid. The most that a properly advised licensor would give is that, so far as the licensor is aware, the patent is valid and the licensor has not dealt with it so as to affect its validity.

(2) In order to prevent a challenge by the licensee of its ownership of IP rights, licensors sometimes require licensees to agree not to challenge the licensor's ownership of those rights. These 'no-challenge' clauses are void under EC competition law and the most that can be done is for there to be an automatic termination of the licence if the licensee mounts a challenge.

(3) The licensee will want the licensor to make applications for and maintain valid and subsisting registrations, where possible. The licensor will want the licensee to join and assist in such applications and not do or neglect to do anything which would lead to, for example, the trade mark being invalidated.

(4) A general information provision requiring the licensee to give the licensor information of anything affecting validity can be useful.

Infringement The rights being licensed may be extremely valuable and both parties will want to ensure that they are protected. It is possible to go into great length detailing arrangements as to who will conduct litigation and bear the costs. In brief, the key points are:

(1) If the licensor will not carry out litigation at his own cost, the licensee should be able to conduct litigation in the licensor's name at the licensee's cost.
(2) The licensor and licensee should assist each other with litigation as appropriate.
(3) The position as to recovery of damages and costs should be considered.

Confidentiality It is particularly important to protect know-how. The starting-point is to identify which information is confidential and make sure that those under an obligation of confidentiality are aware of what is confidential information. If the net is cast too wide, the obligation may be of no effect. Employees, sub-contractors and sub-licensees must be brought under an obligation of confidence, but again it must be made absolutely clear to them exactly what information is confidential. In drafting, it is necessary to work out whether the obligation is to be mutual. It is standard for the obligation to continue beyond the end of the term of the agreement.

To make this clear, there should be an express provision dealing with confidentiality.

Sub-licence It is a commercial question as to whether the licensee can successfully exploit the market on its own or whether others should be licensed as well. It might be better to allow sub-licences, rather than to give several non-exclusive licences. If sub-licences are allowed, however, it is important to control the terms, especially to ensure that trade marks and confidential information are protected. This can be done either by specifying the terms and making the licensee responsible or by having a direct agreement between the licensor and sub-licensee dealing with the key rights. If there is no consideration this should be under seal. At the same time, the draft should deal with what would happen if the head licence terminates. The options are essentially either for a direct licence between licensor and sub-licensee or for termination.

Sub-contract It may be necessary for the licensee to contract out part of the manufacture. Confidentiality should in such circumstances be protected expressly and quality control should be ensured.

Financial provisions There are various standard points to consider when working out provisions for payment. The type of payment may be any or all of:

- fixed sums;
- annual fees;
- expenses;
- share of profits; or
- royalties.

In drafting, the time of payment should be specified and, where royalties on sales are used, it must be made clear whether the figure on which royalties are calculated is inclusive or exclusive of packing, transport, taxes, tariffs, trade discounts, any defective goods returned and bad debts. In order to monitor this, there should be reporting provisions and possibly audits. Currency of payment should also be dealt with as this could make a very considerable difference to the amount of money actually received.

Sample clause: Accounting

1. The Distributor shall make up accounts for the Work twice yearly to 30 June and 31 December following publication and each such account shall be delivered to the Publisher by 31 July and 31 January respectively and settled by the Distributor within two months thereafter.
2. For the duration of this Agreement and for the period of six months thereafter the Distributor and the Publisher shall each have the right at any time upon written request and upon reasonable notice to examine the records of account of the other insofar as those records relate to the royalties payable under this Agreement. The costs of any such examination shall be borne by the party requesting the examination, except where errors to the disadvantage of the party requesting the examination exceed [ten] per cent of the value of the royalties in the immediately preceding accounting period in which case the cost shall be borne by the party who prepared the erroneous accounts. Any over payment by either party may be deducted from any sums subsequently due to the other party in respect of the Work.
3. In the event of any dispute as to the accuracy of accounts prepared under this clause the parties shall:
   (a) refer the dispute to an independent chartered accountant to be nominated by the parties or, failing such agreed nomination within seven days, to an independent chartered accountant as is appointed on the application of either party by the President of the Institute of Chartered Accountants in England and Wales; and
   (b) on request, promptly supply to the independent chartered accountant such assistance, documentation and information as he may require for the purposes of his appointment; and the parties shall use all reasonable endeavours to procure the prompt determination of this issue.

   The independent chartered accountant shall be deemed to act as an expert and not as an arbitrator, his determination shall (in the absence of manifest error) be conclusive and binding upon the parties and the cost of any such determination shall be borne as the independent chartered accountant shall determine and, in the absence of such a determination shall be borne equally between the Distributor and the Publisher.

15.2.2 COMMERCIAL CLAUSES

In addition to the formal provisions common to most contracts, other issues in a licence need to be considered. These 'commercial clauses' are the ones that businessmen usually pay most attention to. They vary widely from licence to licence.

Transfer of technical knowledge

For the protection of both parties, the amount of technical knowledge to be supplied, whether in the form of copies of documentation or demonstration and training, should be set out. The licensee will need to be sure that sufficient backup is available. The licensor will not want to give an unlimited commitment to providing support for the whole term of the agreement.

Production and quality control

Quality control is vital in the cause of maintaining the reputation of the mark. Provisions can be made for:

PHYSICAL DISTRIBUTION 15.2.2

- adherence to codes of practice;
- no changes to the product without the licensor's approval;
- inspection by the licensor; and
- samples from the licensee.

The foregoing is useful comfort for a licensor who is supplying materials to a licensee and may therefore be liable for damage caused by defective products.

Marketing

There is usually some obligation on the licensee to market the product produced. The licensee may in turn require a commitment from the licensor for marketing support. This may be dealt with by imposing targets on the licensee and requiring the licensor to provide information and advice with supplies of such things as advertising materials, packaging, training manuals; and a commitment to provide training and technical assistance.

Sample clause: TV clip licence

X.1 In consideration of the Licence and permission hereby granted by the Licensor to the Licensee, the Licensee shall pay to the Licensor the sum of £   [forthwith upon signature hereof] [not later than the earlier of the first use by the Licensee of any of the Multimedia CD-ROM Chip Material or the   day of   19].

X.2 In consideration of the payment by the Licensee, the Licensor grants to the Licensee the non-exclusive right to use the Multimedia CD Clip Material in the TV Programme and to broadcast it and to authorise third parties to broadcast it as part of the TV Programme in the United Kingdom [and to grant to third parties the right to broadcast it in any other part of the World], but subject to the terms hereafter contained.

X.3 The Licensee's rights are to be subject to the following limitations:

(a) the Multimedia CD Clip Materials shall not be used for any purpose other than inclusion in the TV Programme and shall not be used for promotional, advertising or publicity purposes [whether related to the TV Programme or otherwise] [unless related exclusively to the TV Programme];

(b) the TV Programme containing the Multimedia CD Clip Material shall not be broadcast except on the following occasions:
  (i) on 1/2/3 occasions in the United Kingdom during the period from the   day of   199   to the   day of   199 ;
  (ii) [in any territory of the world outside the United Kingdom on not more than 1/2/3 occasions in each such territory between the   day of   199   to the   day of   199   ;]

(c) [not more than an aggregate of   minutes   seconds of the Multimedia CD Clip Material shall be used in the TV Programme;]

(d) any soundtrack synchronised with each excerpt comprised in the Multimedia CD Clip Materials shall be as synchronised in the Multimedia CD and in particular no voices shall be dubbed provided that the Licensee shall be entitled to improve a 'voice-over' commentary;

(e) neither the Multimedia CD Clip Material nor any part thereof shall be used except in the form supplied by the Licensor to the Licensee or obtained by the Licensee with the Licensor's permission including any copyright notice appearing thereon;

(f) the Multimedia CD Clip Material shall only be broadcast over the television channel referred to above or such other channels [including any overseas channels] to which the Licensor may consent in writing;

(g) all recordings whether in eye or machine readable form of the Multimedia CD Clip Material shall be destroyed within   days after the last broadcast permitted hereunder and the Licensee shall notify the Licensor in writing of each such destruction promptly thereafter;

(h) neither the Multimedia CD Clip Material nor any part thereof shall be used in any manner which could be defamatory of the Licensor or any person connected therewith nor in any manner which might diminish the value of the Multimedia CD [by more than the payment to the Licensor hereunder];

(i) neither the Multimedia CD Clip Material nor any part thereof shall be used for commercial advertising of any goods, product or services [other than of the TV Programme itself].

Improvements

Either or both of the licensor or licensee may develop the ideas being licensed and each will want access to the new ideas. Some contracts will provide for a royalty for exchange; an assignment to one party; or indeed a non-exclusive licence. The terms will depend partly on bargaining power, but any relevant block exemptions must be borne in mind where relevant.

Supply of goods

The licensor may be supplying materials as well as a licence of rights. The terms of supply need to be dealt with. It is important to note that an attempt to force the licensee to take non-essential materials will fall foul of EC competition law.

Information

The licensor will want information regarding sales and the market. Licences usually deal with provision by the licensee of regular reviews and reports of financial and marketing information, including information relating to competitors.

Government approvals

If these are needed, it should be made clear who should obtain, maintain and monitor them.

Warranties

Particularly if goods are being supplied, express warranties and related exclusions of liabilities and possibly indemnities should be considered. It is best to seek to agree in advance what will happen if product liability or other claims arise and what will happen if know-how or patents are used incorrectly—bearing in mind the provisions of the Unfair Contract Terms Act 1977 and the new Regulations (*see* 15.2.3) and the Consumer Protection Act 1985 if the end product is sold in the UK, and local consumer protection law if sold elsewhere.

Termination

Potential licensors and licensees are generally reluctant to think about termination, but they should consider whether there will be mutual rights to terminate on notice, for breach of key terms, failure to achieve sales or financial targets, insolvency or change of control etc. Many countries have legislated to protect agents, distributors and, to some extent, licensees against termination and the impact of such legislation on the effectiveness of termination clauses must be considered. The UK has implemented the EC Commercial Agents Directive (*see* 15.2.4).

Consequences of termination

The parties should think through what would happen in the event of termination and deal with such matters as existing manufacture, royalties on sales, fulfilment of existing orders, the return of know-how, the licensee ceasing to use any trade mark, the return or destroying of materials or masters, together with the provision to the licensor of a certificate of destruction.

Many companies will devote substantial resources to researching, developing and commercialising a product, but then give very little thought to what method of exploitation is actually in their best interests; and give even less thought to the detailed provisions of a licensing agreement. That is a short road to potential disaster.

Law and jurisdiction

Finally where the parties are from different jurisdictions a choice of law clause is essential and provision should also be made for dispute resolution.

Sample clause: Governing law and arbitration

1. This Agreement shall be governed by and construed in all respects in accordance with [English] Law.
2. Any dispute or difference of any kind whatsoever arising between [any of] the parties hereto in connection with this Agreement shall be referred to arbitration [in London] before a single arbitrator.
3. If the parties are unable to agree as to the appointment of such arbitrator within [30] days of one party serving notice on the other calling for the appointment of an arbitrator then the arbitrator shall be appointed on the application of either party to the President for the time being of [the Law Society of England and Wales/the Chairman of the Bar Council].
4. [The award of the arbitrator shall be final and binding on the parties and judgment upon the award rendered may be entered in any Court having jurisdiction or application may be made to such Court for judicial acceptance of the award and any order of enforcement as the case may be.]
[NB: Applies to non-domestic arbitration agreements only.]
5. [In accordance with s 3 of the Arbitration Act 1979 the right of appeal by either party to the High Court under s 1 of that Act shall be excluded in relation to an award of the arbitrator and neither party shall have the right to apply to the High Court under s 2(1)(*a*) of that Act for the determination of any question of law arising in the course of the reference to arbitration.]
[NB: Applies to non-domestic arbitration agreements only.]

15.2.3 UNFAIR TERMS IN CONSUMER CONTRACTS REGULATIONS

Bear in mind the provisions of the Unfair Terms in Consumer Contracts Regulations 1994 (SI No 3159) which were introduced into UK law pursuant to the EC Directive of the same name. These extend consumer protection further than ever before. They apply to all contracts for the supply of goods or services where the supplier is a business and the recipient an individual who is not acting in the course of a business and where the terms are not individually negotiated. There are exceptions (see the Regulations).

Where a contract will not work without a term which is unfair, the *contract* will not bind the consumer. Where an unfair term can simply be struck out, it will be, and the contract will then continue without it.

'Unfair' means:

- anything not expressed in plain, intelligible language; or
- anything not included in 'good faith' where it causes 'significant imbalance' to the consumer's detriment, in the parties' rights.

The whole contract has to be examined, together with the surrounding circumstances. In deciding, the judge has also to look at:

- the parties' bargaining power;
- any inducements given;
- whether goods were made to special order; and
- whether the consumer has been treated fairly and equitably.

15.2.4 COMMERCIAL AGENTS DIRECTIVE

The EC law on the 'co-ordination of the laws of Member States relating to self-employed commercial agents' has now been implemented in the UK.

The definition of commercial agent excludes:

- an employee, a partner or a receiver of the principal; and
- an agent selling services rather than goods.

Each of the EC Member States will have its own regulations implementing the Directive though in some territories, such as Germany, there are already much stricter terms for the protection of agents.

The new provisions will be superimposed upon existing contracts between principal and agent so as to give the agent additional rights, eg to receive information from the principal. The agent will now be automatically entitled to commission in respect of introductions resulting in transactions concluded after the termination of the agency contract. The agent may also be entitled to compensation on termination to the extent that the agent is deprived of commission and prevented from recouping the costs of establishing the Agency. This compensation has to be specifically claimed within a year of the termination of the agency. It is not recoverable if termination is due to the agent's default or the fact that he has voluntarily brought the contract to an end.

Points to include in a distribution agreement

- the licensed media or platform; and the language: have all rights been cleared for this?
- holdbacks;
- distribution channels;
- territory;
- exclusive or non-exclusive;
- period;
- marketing effort/minimum return/reversion;
- use to which product can be put;
- quality;
- credit;
- control of publicity;
- speed of production/commitment to launch; *(Cont'd)*

- payment/accounting:
  — fee per unit;
  — royalty on retail price;
  — share of net profits;
- warranties;
- responsibility for pursuing infringers;
- sub-licensing rights (if any);
- trade marks;
- limit of liability; it is usual to limit liability to the greatest extent permitted by law, both by restricting the actual warranties made but also by seeking to apply a 'cap' or upper limit to the amount that can be recovered in the event of a breach;
- termination and effect of termination.
- proper law and dispute resolution

Distribution checklist

(1) (a) Are all rights in material incorporated into the product cleared for the distribution routes chosen, eg:
- platform;
- site-based;
- on-line;
- television;
- rental;

(b) marketing: channels, sales force, advertising and direct marketing, etc.

(2) What will the distributor's involvement be?
  (a) straightforward sales/marketing;
  (b) manufacturing;
  (c) exclusive or non-exclusive;
  (d) which territory;
  (e) who is responsible for advertising;
  (f) end-user licences; *see* below for issues. Licensor to have the right to approve terms;
  (g) limit activities eg, rental, on-line distribution.

(3) (a) Pricing: remaindering, low prices;
  (b) bundling: hardware and software, limits: eg time, quantities etc.

(4) (a) Distributor's financial position: fees, commission, accounting;
  (b) exclusive/non-exclusive;
  (c) sales performance: targets, minimum payments, etc;
  (d) collecting societies and royalties: calculation and payment.

(5) Period, termination.

(6) Holdbacks: license narrowly, reserve all rights not granted, with the right to exploit.

(7) Assignability.

15.3 ON-LINE DISTRIBUTION

15.3.1 INTRODUCTION

Rights owners in content (be that financial data, a literary work, or a film or music) are keen to find additional avenues for exploiting works; distributors of products and services of every description (from banking to potted plants) are looking for new ways of making connections with, and selling to, customers. On-line services and, in due course the Information Superhighway, may provide a new avenue or even a boulevard. There is growing interest already in testing the water by establishing a presence on-line, ie distributing content or promoting goods or services over a network, be it the Internet, a home shopping channel or a simpler supply or promotion over a dedicated or dial-up cable or telephone network.

The Internet is ideal for promotional material, imaginatively presented, providing the opportunity for a trader to establish a direct relationship with a remote user, and is becoming increasingly popular as a means of disseminating information on-line. However, at the moment it remains primarily a free service, for reasons we have explained in Chapter 1.

This is likely to change in the transition from Internet to the fully-fledged Superhighway and, to the distress of some of the 'net community', signs of the commercialisation of the Internet, and particularly the World Wide Web, are already becoming evident. Digital television will hugely increase the number of broadcast channels using compression technology, but the Superhighway requires a back channel or return path, for example a telephone line, to provide true interactivity (*see* Chapter 1).

15.3.2 LOCAL AREA NETWORKS

The simplest form of network, perhaps, is a closed network of a type which might be found in an office. Most likely, this will be a PC-LAN (Local Area Network). Distributors are already facing the same types of issues which distributors of software have had to face for some years:

- does the licence permit use only on a single PC?
- may the material, by contrast, be loaded on to a server and accessed and used by a number of concurrent users (and if so, how many)?
- does the licence allow the network to extend into other buildings owned by the same company, or indeed group of companies?
- does the licence allow access and use by employees of the company working at home or from remote locations who dial from laptops into the company's computer system?

Software distributors have developed a number of models for site or company-wide licences, which address these points.

Publishers of CD-ROMs face difficulties in finding an appropriate pricing policy for their product when loaded on to a LAN. Does the licence fee take account of the fact that *anyone* in the office may access the CD-ROM over a network? Do you distinguish between those employees who are more likely to access it than others? Indeed, should one take the ultimate customer's line and argue that there should be no difference in price for network use, on the same basis that a large firm of lawyers will pay exactly the same price for a conventional legal text book as a sole practitioner? Publishers' problems may be compounded by the terms of any licence under which they reproduce the software engine incorporated into the CD-ROM, which may require additional licence fees where the CD-ROM is made available over a network.

15.3.3 COMMERCIAL ON-LINE SERVICES

As you move upwards from a CD-ROM on a PC-LAN, to a wide-area network with many subscribers, the issues begin to get more complex. The principal players in on-line services are:

- the information provider (or content provider), who provides content or the service;
- the service provider who packages that material and other material licensed in from a variety of other information providers; and
- the network provider, who might be a public telephone operator or a local cable company, over whose network the information is made available to end users.

(The suppliers of the terminal equipment used in the user's home or place of business also have a key role, especially if the information is encrypted or they control the standards necessary for home delivery, but we will ignore them here.)

It is important to understand the relationships between and among the players:

Network operator and user

The contract between these parties will primarily cover installation and servicing of the network connection and equipment necessary, eg the set top box. It will be similar to the current agreements offered by cable companies and by BT to consumers, and will deal with rental charges, on-line charges and billing. The network operator will also need to state the extent of its liability for information conveyed over the network, or to disclaim liability, and to limit liability for network failures. If information over the network is partially or wholly encrypted, the contract may need to set out the means by which it may be decrypted and the contractual basis for this. Alternatively, decryption may be a matter between the service provider and the user. The user must also agree not to misuse the network.

Service provider and user

The user is likely to contract with one or more service providers, or network providers, who will make available one or more packages of services.

The contract should:

- specify the information and services on offer;
- provide for variation of the services;
- impose a base subscription fee;
- provide the basis of payment for use of particular services or access to information;
- specify the extent to which the service provider is responsible for information or services made available by independent information providers;
- impose limitations on use or reuse of information or services provided by the service provider (*see* below).

Depending on its own arrangements with the relevant service provider, the information provider may, or may not, need to enter into a direct contractual relationship with users. In our estimation, normally he will, for a number of good reasons:

(1) Direct access to customers is facilitated by electronic systems, and enables the information provider to be put into a closer relationship with its own customers, which is better for the development of goodwill and in terms of quality management.

(2) Payment can perhaps be made direct by users to the information provider, which reduces risk and the need to pay the middleman.
(3) The information provider can form a direct contractual relationship with the user, which is useful for warranties, limitations of liability and, importantly, for imposing contractual limitations on reuse of copyright material.

Where the information provider contracts direct with the user, it will be necessary to make it clear, probably by means of screen messages prompted by actions taken by the user, exactly when the contract is formed and, if the user is in a different country, where and subject to whose laws it is made. Prior to formation of the contract, the user may need to be made aware of the express terms of the contract, and the information provider may wish (if he is legally able to do so) to modify or oust terms that otherwise would be implied by law. These areas are regulated by numerous UK laws and, increasingly, by EC measures, some of which are discussed elsewhere.

Information provider and service provider

If information providers contract direct with users, the contract between an information provider and a service provider may be quite limited in scope and provide only for:

- capacity to be made available on a server;
- conversion services (if required);
- provision of the information over the network;
- third party monitoring of use of that information;
- audit trails in respect of enquiries received; and
- payments, which may flow either way and be fixed, variable according to use, or royalty based.
- guarantees of network integrity and security.

The information provider will then agree to observe a set of rules regarding the nature of information that he may load into the server.

If service providers undertake a greater role in the supply of goods or services of an information provider, and particularly if they receive and redeliver copyright works, the arrangements necessarily become more complex and will need to include elements of distribution, contract and licence (*see* Chapter 14). In this case, the user is likely to pay the service provider for the services or information and the service provider must then account for the sales, after deduction of whatever margin or commission he is entitled to receive. The contract would also set out the respective responsibilities of the parties for taking action against any person who infringes copyright or otherwise misuses the service, and how the costs and recoveries will be shared.

Network operator and service provider

This agreement is likely to take the form of a traditional agreement between a telecommunications operator and a supplier of value-added services, such as a BT Callstream contract. The agreement will cover issues such as:

- attachment of terminal equipment and its maintenance;
- technical quality of network provision;
- assurance of network capacity available to the information packager, particularly with regard to the flexibility of capacity required by an on-demand service;

- quality of the service provider's services, eg that it will not bring the network into any disrepute;
- payments which may be fixed, variable according to use or royalty based;
- liability for any misuse of the network by the service provider; and
- confidentiality of technical information.

The three separate roles of information provider, service provider and network provider can be said to exist even if, in some cases, they are merged. For certain on-line services addressing specialist vertical markets (like Reuters for financial information and Profile for property information) the roles of information provider and service provider are merged. In the BT experiment, referred to in Chapter 1, BT appears to act as both service provider and network provider. Nonetheless the role and numbers of independent service providers, such as CompuServe or Cityscape will grow; service providers will take on the role of department stores or shopping mall owners.

15.3.4 LICENSING COPYRIGHT WORKS FOR AN ON-LINE SERVICE

The owner of the content, the information provider, will be concerned with:

- the terms of his licence to the service provider; and
- the terms of the licence from the service provider to the users.

Making copyright works available to users by an on-line service requires the service provider or information provider to load the work concerned on to a server, perhaps to modify it (in the sense of abridging or editing it, or merging it with other material); to transmit the material and present it to users over the network and perhaps also to authorise users to copy the work on the users' own storage device and/or reuse it for limited purposes.

Many of the issues relevant to the licence from the information provider to the service provider are similar to those which apply to the licensing of any other copyright work, which have been canvassed in Chapter 3. However, in the case of on-line distribution, the information provider is also concerned to know the capabilities of the on-line system and the manner in which the material is to be made available to users, the technical controls embedded in the system and the contractual restrictions imposed by the service provider on users, and indeed how those terms might be enforced.

Licensing issues particular to business on-line services

(1) Controls on reuse
   (a) the user may call up information for display; but should he also be able to print out information, and *all* of it or *extracts* only?
   (b) may the information be retransmitted or posted to a bulletin board?
   (c) may the user resell all or extracts of the information?
   (d) may the user incorporate extracts in, eg, a broker's briefing document?
   (e) should credit be given?

(Cont'd)

> (2) Controls on alteration
>   (a) should the user be restricted from adapting the information, expecially if it is of a technical nature? (Some refer to this as a *droit d'authenticité*);
>   (b) should information be downloaded only in the form of bit-mapped images, or in editable text?
> (3) Controls on merger
>   (a) may the user merge the information with other material if the sources remain distinguishable?
>   (b) may he, if they do not?
>   (c) do the controls on reuse apply equally to merged or altered information?

Where the information provider retains copyright ownership as he should always try to do, unlic-ensed reuse of material (with or without change) is likely to be an infringement of copyright if it is on a sufficiently substantial scale (*see* Chapter 3). Nonetheless, an information provider should always support copyright by ensuring that any network over which information will be carried provides adequate technical security and that the materials are used for limited and strictly defined purposes only. Controlling copying is the most important issue here. If copying is handled correctly, it may be possible to find lucrative opportunities for additional revenue generation while at the same time protecting the information provider's copyright on technical controls in the system and by contract terms, such as are listed above (*see* also 15.4.1 below).

Revenue stream (on-line fees)
There are a number of alternative strategies for managing the revenue stream for use of copyright works which flow upwards from user; and it is still too early to say which will be adopted. Flexibility and creativity of approach will probably be required of information providers as the on-line market matures. We list below some of the alternatives (which could of course be combined):

(1) Per access/use. This is the more traditional approach, where the information provider receives a percentage of revenue paid by the user on a per-access or per-use basis, which might be fixed at a level irrespective of the price of the service to the end user.
(2) Lump sum. This is an upfront licence fee paid by the service provider for the rights, irrespective of use. This has the advantage of security, but may be inflexible, and it is difficult to assess a fair fee.
(3) Time. A charge may be based upon the proportion of time during which the material is in use on the network.

The need for meticulous attention to detail in crafting the licence framework and detailed terms is brought into sharp focus by the inherent properties of digitisation, which facilitates reproduction of the material in first-generation quality, and its reformulation, redistribution and reuse. Where users receive copies of first-generation quality they clearly gain a greater potential to become resellers or reusers. Information providers are vulnerable to a potential loss of central control and service providers and information providers must agree upon which controls and contract terms should be in place to reduce the risk.

ON-LINE DISTRIBUTION

All of this requires, in our view, the forming of an intelligent partnership between lawyers and engineers. As detailed above at 7.4, engineers may be able to build in technical controls to restrain what the average user may or may not do in relation to information (in its widest sense) transmitted over the network. Lawyers must then try to control the risk areas. To adopt again the phrase of Charles Clark, General Counsel to the International Publishers Copyright Council, the answer to the machine lies in the machine: it may be possible to encode information with usage tracking elements. Any copy made would include these elements, and they would, perhaps, prevent use on hardware that did not recognise them. Software could also record usage time, and copies made, and periodically convey this information to the service provider who would debit the user and account to the information provider. The information provider may lose control, in the sense of regulating whether or not copies are made at all, but could gain market share and an income stream. It may also be possible to introduce protection against serial copying (as with Digital Audio Tape 'DAT' or with the Macrovision encoding on pre-recorded video tapes). Alternatively, it may be possible to encrypt some or all of the data and to control the supply and use of decryption devices.

15.3.5 SECURITY, ENCRYPTION AND CONTROLS

Digital signatures

As discussed at 7.4 above, cases of unauthorised reuse, hacking and financial loss arising from use of on-line services have already been reported. The need for greater security, particularly where financial transactions are involved, is leading to the development of new techniques for encrypting information, including, at the most sophisticated level, that of electronic dealing systems, methods for attaching 'digital signatures' to messages to confirm their origin and authenticity. The encryption means could be within the software used in the system or even in a microchip built into term-inal equipment. The ownership of encryption means, and the right to use those means, will become important factors in the evolution of on-line services.

C-Dilla

A number of other encryption technologies have been developed: C-Dilla, in the UK, has developed a system which works by encrypting data loaded on to a CD and using a special decryption program to read it. But before unlocking the encrypted data, the decryption software looks for an electronic signature buried on the CD. The system is designed so that, while users can record the data files on to a blank CD, they cannot copy the signature. As a result, the data remains encrypted and the copied disk cannot be read.

Laserlok

MLS of Greece and Diskxpress of the UK have launched Laserlok, a system designed to stop copying on three levels. The first system allows users to download data from a CD-ROM on to a computer hard disk (eg a computer game) but the data can be retrieved only when the original CD-ROM disk is in the computer's CD-ROM drive. This stops users from copying data on to a floppy disk and distributing it. The other two systems are designed to stop CD-ROMs from being copied on a CD recorder or professional CD pressing system. Use of these systems can be harmonised with commercial strategies in order to introduce metering, 'try and buy' and time-sensitive releases, which permit use only for a limited period and will then 'lock' unless payment is made and a key made available.

15.3.6 LIABILITY

The information provider will retain a responsibility for the accuracy of information made available on-line; and the service provider and network operator will require warranties and indemnities against that information being inaccurate (particularly in the case of business data), obscene or defamatory, or breaching any third party right of privacy or copyright. *See* discussion of these topics in Chapter 10.

15.3.7 REGULATION

In the UK, a licence is required for the running of a 'telecommunications system' and for the provision of a 'prescribed diffusion service' or a 'local delivery service' in this country. These requirements are briefly discussed below.

Telecommunications systems licence

It is an offence under the Telecommunications Act 1984, s 5 ('the 1984 Act') to run a telecommunications system without a licence, subject to certain exemptions in favour of:

- broadcasts by wireless telegraphy for general reception;
- specialist systems, and systems within individual buildings, which are unconnected to the public systems.

It is also an offence under that section to connect a telecommunications system with another, if the licence does not permit that interconnection.

Licences may be granted under the 1984 Act, s 7. Most systems in a single building which are connected to public systems are covered by a class licence (the TSL) but there is a restriction on the provision of entertainment services (not video-on-demand) and equipment must be type-approved. Obtaining individual licences for networks outside buildings will be the responsibility of the network operator, but the other parties will need to satisfy themselves, perhaps by means of warranties, of the network operator's compliance. Since 1991, holders of individual licences under the 1984 Act who are also PDS licensees (*see* below) may provide all forms of telecommunications services in their own right. Certain companies which enjoyed a PTO licence under the 1984 Act at that time, including BT, remain restricted from offering entertainment services under their licences (*see* Chapter 2) but video-on-demand appears to be outside that restriction and so is permitted even to BT.

Transmission of a television programme through a telecommunications system is licensable under the Broadcasting Act of 1990. Conceivably, advances in compression technologies could lead to services equivalent to television programmes being provided on the Internet, to which the present regulation might arguably extend. The practical difficulties of regulating individuals using the anarchic, global Internet are such, however, as to make application of the Broadcasting Act extraordinarily problematic. There is no doubt however that as near-video-on-demand and video-on-demand services move from a trial to a commercial basis they will need to be licensed under the Broadcasting Act, as the law stands at the moment (*see* below).

Entertainment services licences

The provision of entertainment services over a network requires an additional licence under the Cable and Broadcasting Act 1984 ('the C&B Act') and/or the Broadcasting Act 1990 ('the 1990 Act'). Under the C&B Act, which has now been replaced by the 1990 Act, the now-defunct Cable Authority granted prescribed diffusion services licences (PDS licences) to a number of cable operators. PDS licences were granted for 15 years but might be extended for up to eight years more if the operator concerned had a licence under the 1984 Act for the longer period. A franchise granted under the C&B Act continues in force notwithstanding that the regime has now been replaced, under the 1990 Act, by a system of local delivery licences granted by the ITC.

PDS licence   These licences are subject to numerous conditions, including controls on transferability and cross-media ownership restrictions: thus the holder of a Channel 3 licence or a local radio licence and the proprietors of local and national newspapers are limited as to the shareholdings they may have in the holder of a PDS or local delivery licence. (These limitations are currently under review both at the national and European level.)

LPS licence   A licence will also be required under the 1990 Act to run a 'Licensable Programme Service' ('LPS licence'), defined in the 1990 Act, s 46 as:

(1) A service consisting in the provision by any person of relevant programmes with a view to their being conveyed by means of a telecommunications system:
   (a) for reception in two or more dwelling houses in the United Kingdom otherwise than for the purpose of being received there by persons who have a business interest in receiving them, or
   (b) for reception at any place, or for simultaneous reception at two or more places, in the United Kingdom for the purpose of being presented there either to members of the public or to a group or groups of persons some or all of whom do not have a business interest in receiving them,
whether the other telecommunications system is run by the person so providing the programmes or by some other person, and whether the programmes are to be conveyed as mentioned in paragraph (a) for simultaneous reception or for reception at different times in response to requests made by different users of the service.

'Relevant programme' is defined in the 1990 Act as a television programme other than one consisting wholly or mainly of non-representational images, and a person has a 'business interest' in receiving programmes if he has an interest in receiving them for the purposes of his business, trade, profession or employment.

The 1990 Act goes on to provide that this requirement does not apply to:
(2)(b) a service where the running of a telecommunication system does not require to be licensed under Part II of the C&B Act; or
   (c) a two-way service, that is to say a service on which it is an essential feature, that while visual images or sounds (or both) are being conveyed by the person providing the service there will or may be sent from each place of reception, by means of the same telecommunication system or (as the case may be) the part of it by means of which they are conveyed, visual images or sounds (or both) for reception by the person providing the service or other persons receiving (other than signals sent for the operation or control of the service).

By virtue of paragraph (c), certain forms of two-way service may be exempted from licensing, but most forms of consumer service over a Superhighway are likely to require an LPS licence.

Sub-section 46(3) of the 1990 Act specifically declares that anyone who

uses their telecommunication system for conveying relevant programmes . . . or runs a telecommunication system which is so used, is not to be regarded as providing a licensable programme service in respect of any such programmes except to the extent that they are provided by that person with a view to their being so conveyed by means of that system.

This language appears to exempt a network provider, acting simply as such, from the need to acquire an LPS licence, while leaving the service provider with the need to obtain the licence. How this works in practice will depend on the precise role of each.

Other controls

Regulation comes in at other levels too: A large number of bodies in the United Kingdom already exercise regulatory control over the content of different forms of media (*see* Chapter 10). It is probable that the roles, if any, of these organisations, and others, will need to be reviewed in the context of the Information Superhighway and the growth of on-line services. Moreover, there are moves, since the presentation of the Bangemann Report, for an as yet unformed European authority to assign aspects of the regulation of Information Superhighways to a single European body. New initiatives in this area may be expected. In the meantime, network operators and service providers will be regulated under the 1984 Act and 1990 Act, and the respective licences granted under that legislation. They must also be aware of their responsibilities under copyright law and laws relating to sale of goods (*see* 15.3.8 below).

15.3.8 HOME SHOPPING AND CONSUMER PROTECTION

The evidence so far indicates that consumers like home shopping so interactive, on-line catalogues are likely to be substituted for their traditional mail order counterparts thus increasing home shopping's share of the overall retail market. Goldman Sachs International have gone on record with their opinion that electronic retailing is a 'killer' application.

A variety of laws and codes of practice regulate the sale of goods and provision of services in the UK and provide consumer protection. None, so far, is specifically directed to the sale of goods and services over Superhighways, although some do or will apply more generically to so-called 'distance selling' and part of the ICSTIS code (*see* 10.1.1) applies to sales over the premium-rate telephone call service. It is essential to be clear from whom the user, or consumer, is buying the product or service. *Prima facie* it is that person who is responsible if goods are not delivered, not of satisfactory quality, or not fit for the purpose.

The principal laws in this area include:

- the Sale of Goods Act 1979, which generally regulates the sale of goods and implies warranties and conditions;
- the Supply of Goods and Services Act 1982, which incorporates implied conditions in contracts for the 'transfer of goods' (other than contracts of sale and hire-purchase already covered by statute) and in contracts for the supply of services;
- the Unfair Contract Terms Act 1977, which excludes or restricts the operation of certain provisions in sales contracts (*see* also below);
- the Consumer Protection Act 1985, which provides that all products must reach a reasonable level of safety;
- the Trade Descriptions Act 1968, which makes it an offence to apply a false trade description;
- the Consumer Credit Act 1974, which regulates certain consumer credit transactions and may apply to home shopping: if the Consumer Credit Act applies then the buyer is likely to gain an automatic cooling-off period.

ON-LINE DISTRIBUTION 15.3.8

There are also codes of practice issued by the ASA, the ITC and the Direct Marketing Association and other rules for mail-order services.

In addition, there is increasing intervention by the EU in this area. For example, the Unfair Contract Directive 93/13/EC was implemented in the UK by the Unfair Terms in Consumer Contracts Regulations 1994 (SI No 3159) and the EC Directive on Distance Selling was adopted in July 1995. Its main provisions are set out below.

Distance Selling Directive

- There is to be a seven-day cooling-off period from receipt of the product or, in the case of a service, from receipt of documentation informing the consumer that the contract had been concluded, in which the consumer may cancel a contract without penalty. Associated credit agreements must also be cancelled, including a transaction made at a distance by payment card.
- At the time of solicitation the consumer is to be provided with information at least as to the identity of the supplier, the main characteristics of the product or service, the cost of transport charges and payment for delivery. He must also have a right of withdrawal and know the period of validity of the solicitation. The consumer must receive the same information in writing no later than the time of delivery, together with the address of the supplier's most appropriate place of business for the consumer, details of payment arrangements and guarantees, and arrangements for exercising the right of withdrawal.
- In respect of television selling, the full contents of a contract solicitation must be sent in writing at the consumer's request if they are not displayed on screen.

The introduction of a general seven-day cooling-off period is a significant change for UK law. At present, if the Consumer Credit Act 1974 applies, a five-day cancellation period is available for regulated agreements which are cancellable. Moreover, the proposed right of withdrawal would arise even if there is no defect in the goods. Where a product or service is purchased on credit, the Directive would provide for the cancellation of any credit agreement with the supplier when the right of return is exercised where the credit:

(a) has been supplied directly by the supplier; or
(b) has been provided by a lender on the basis of prior agreement with the supplier of the product or service.

It remains true, however, that even with digital compression technology, goods that are ordered over the Superhighway will need to be physically delivered. Partnerships between retailers on the Superhighway and distribution infrastructures such as the Post Office and its competitors will be the key to the provision of a reliable, competitive, speedy, secure and convenient end-to-end home shopping service. Branding will be of paramount importance to success, as consumers are likely to trust the major retail players to be able to navigate the new shopping environment. Advertising may need to develop a new, more personal, customer-retailer relationship in tune with the greater intimacy of business dealings over the Superhighway.

15.4 USER LICENCE

It is important to consider how to control use and re-use of the product. Issues to be considered include:

- copying;
- downloading;
- transmission;
- manipulation;
- on-line or bureau service/rental rights.

There will continue to be problems in this area so long as technical methods of control are inadequate. In terms of the legal techniques, however, it is important to have sufficient familiarity with the technology to appreciate the ways in which the product can be misused so as to build appropriate safeguards into the product licence. Some of the issues to consider are:

(1) *Networks:* should usage on a network be banned, or limited to a particular site or node or group of companies or to a stated number of concurrent uses?
(2) *On-line services:* should posting of material from the product on a bulletin board or making it available for access via an on-line service be prohibited?
(3) *Manipulation of material:* should the editing, recolouring or other digital manipulation of the material in the product be prohibited, or only allowed in limited circumstances?

15.4.1 CONTROL OF COPYING

The control of copying is probably the most important issue here. If handled correctly it can provide lucrative opportunities for additional revenue generation. But in addition to basic product protection steps consider whether it is possible to build technical limits into the product to control copying and to support them by provisions in the licence, such as:

(1) *Printing copies:* for example, in a CD-ROM product the number of copies made can be controlled by using a 'dongle', so that the user has to contact the licensor to get a code to print further copies, in exchange for a fee.
(2) *Number or type of enquiry:* for an on-line service, it may be possible to limit the user's enquiries either by number of searches, number of search results accessed or downloaded or any combination of these; to maximise revenue, additional facilities can be made available in exchange for a fee.
(3) *Copy quality:* if the user has a right to take copies of photographs or graphics, it is possible to limit the copies to a relatively poor quality format or resolution to make their reuse value limited. This should be supported in the licence by a prohibition on trying to avoid copy protect devices and a grant of permission only to copy in the stipulated format.

15.4.2 DATABASE PROTECTION

The Database Directive (*see* 4.5) specifically provides at art 7.2(b) that 'the sale of a copy of a database within the EU' by or with the owner's consent 'shall exhaust the right to control resale within the EU of that copy'.

On-line services are specified to be 'an act which will have to be subject to authorisation where the copyright so provides'. It is also provided that exhaustion of rights does *not* apply to a material copy made from an on-line database service.

It is essential that licences restrict very tightly the user's rights. If, for instance, redistribution rights of physical materials are not limited, protection of the database may be substantially weakened.

15.4.3 SHRINKWRAP LICENCES

English courts[1] have not yet had the chance to decide on the legality of shrinkwrap licences and a number of different methods are currently used to ensure that a licence is binding upon the purchaser. There is strong authority in English contract law to suggest that all that is required is for the purchaser to have had brought to his attention before he buys the product the fact that it is subject to a licence the terms of which are readily available from the publisher (and/or manufacturer). In practice, this can be achieved by a clearly visible sticker on the outside of the product box. Although in most cases the purchaser will not bother to obtain the licence details, he should buy subject to its terms. A copy of the licence will in any case normally be included inside the box.

> **WARNING!! READ THIS END USER LICENCE CAREFULLY. IT CONTAINS DETAILS OF YOUR RIGHTS AND OBLIGATIONS.**

This option only applies to high street sales. Mail order will of course not allow the purchaser to see any sticker before he buys but wording could be included in the mail order catalogue or spoken by telephone sales personnel and in any case a return system might well operate.

Another approach puts a shrinkwrap around the disk inside the product box and states, on the copy of the licence inserted between the inner and outer wrappers, that if the purchaser, having bought the product and taken it home, now reads the licence terms and does not agree with them he can send the product back to the publisher, the inner shrinkwrap unopened, for a refund. Few purchasers will take such action but this may be seen as something of a more consumer-friendly gesture.

> **WARNING!! READ THIS END USER LICENCE CAREFULLY BEFORE YOU BREAK THE SEE-THROUGH PLASTIC PACKAGING AROUND THIS PRODUCT. THIS END USER LICENCE CONTAINS DETAILS OF YOUR RIGHTS AND OBLIGATIONS. ONCE YOU BREAK THE PACKAGING YOU ARE DEEMED TO HAVE ACCEPTED THE TERMS OF THE END USER LICENCE. IF YOU DO NOT AGREE WITH THESE TERMS AND CONDITIONS, YOU SHOULD RETURN THE UNOPENED DISK PACKAGE AND ALL ACCOMPANYING ITEMS TO YOUR SUPPLIER WITH PROOF OF PURCHASE FOR A FULL REFUND.**

The difficulty, from the legal viewpoint, is that by the time the purchaser sees this warning, the product has been purchased, and the contract made. This is more apparent with mail-order purchases where, unless the purchaser has had the licence terms drawn to his attention at the time of ordering, preferably backed up by a signature on the order form, nothing is seen until the package has been delivered (long after the time when the contract was entered into).

> THIS PRODUCT WILL ONLY BE SUPPLIED TO YOU ON THE BASIS THAT THE SALE IS CONDITIONAL ON YOUR ACCEPTANCE OF THE TERMS AND CONDITIONS SUPPLIED WITH THE PRODUCT. YOU MAY NOT USE THE PRODUCT UNTIL YOU HAVE AGREED TO BE BOUND BY THOSE TERMS AND CONDITIONS. YOU MAY OBTAIN A COPY OF THE TERMS AND CONDITIONS BEFORE YOU ORDER THE PRODUCT BY WRITING/TELEPHONING/FAXING TO (   ) QUOTING THE PRODUCT REFERENCE. IF YOU ORDER THE PRODUCT IT IS ON THE UNDERSTANDING THAT YOU ACCEPT THE FOREGOING.

Choosing which approach to adopt is thus more of a commercial decision based upon marketing strategy and packaging designs rather than a purely legal point.

15.4.4 LIMITATION OF LIABILITY

Most shrinkwrap licences go on severely to restrict the publisher's liability to the purchaser and to offer only very limited warranties. The difficulty is that, although rarely tested, some of these purported restrictions on a consumer's rights could be held to be unenforceable by an English court under existing legislation. Further, with the implementation of the EU Unfair Contract Terms Directive in this country, there is an additional requirement for terms not to be 'unfair', ie, contrary to a requirement of good faith or causing a significant imbalance in rights to the purchaser's detriment. It remains to be seen how the courts in this country will apply this in practice. However these terms may remain effective in discouraging some purchasers from demanding refunds or replacements.

Many of the remaining elements of a shrinkwrap licence are straightforward; usually all that the vendor allows the purchaser to do with the software is the minimum laid down by statute in this country following the EC Software Directive (*see* 4.2).

With multimedia products such as CD-ROMs, the software engine that enables navigation of the rest of the contents is merely part of the product. However, although the issues are slightly different from those arising on the sale of standalone software, licence terms in respect of the incorporated software remain important.

Sample clause: Terms and conditions of use

X.1 The Licensor grants to you a non-exclusive non-transferable licence for the life of the copyright in the Product to make use of the Product solely in the manner described in the User Manual. Title to the Product (including the Software) is not transferred to the User. Ownership of the enclosed copy of the Software and of any copies made by the User is vested in the Licensor subject to the rights granted to the User in this Agreement.

X.2 The User is entitled to use this Product on a single computer in a single location (subject to Clause X.4 below) and on only one terminal at any given time. Any further use is prohibited.

X.3 The User may make one back-up copy of the Software. Any copies made will be subject to the terms and conditions of this Agreement in all respects.

X.4 The User may not loan, copy, lease, distribute or transfer the Product or the Software of any copies thereof. The user may not decompile, disassemble or reverse engineer the Software or permit any third party to do so for any purpose. If the User wishes to achieve interoperability of the Software with any other program the information required to achieve this will be available from the Licensor.

[NOTE difference between Software and Product]

15.5 TAXATION

This section deals with certain tax and VAT issues which are particularly relevant to multimedia transactions, in particular those issues that need to be considered in the negotiation and drafting of specific documentation. It is not a general survey of taxation issues, which can be found in specialist text books. All parties engaged in multimedia transactions will need to take their own tax advice on the tax consequences for them of the particular arrangements being made.

15.5.1 WITHHOLDING TAX

Withholding tax is not a specific tax and is not specific to any jurisdiction but is the convenient name given to any tax required to be deducted from payments by the payer. Many jurisdictions require the payer of certain types of income, eg interest or royalties, in certain circumstances to deduct tax from the payment and account for it to the tax authorities. This is referred to generally as withholding tax.

Both the payer and the recipient will want to know whether any particular payments under multimedia agreements are going to be subject to the withholding of any tax. They will need to establish in every case what exactly the payments are and what they are for.

Different countries have different rules about payments from which withholding should be made. There are some common features. The UK rules as they are likely to apply to multimedia are set out here. Where the payer is in the UK tax at the basic rate (currently 25 per cent but 24 per cent from 6 April 1996) should be deducted from:

(a) royalties or other sums paid for the use of a patent;
(b) royalties or other sums paid for the use of copyright where the copyright owner is outside the UK;
(c) certain other regular payments where the recipient holds the rights for which they are paid as an investment and the payments represent 'pure income profit'.

Copyright for the purposes of (b) above does not include film copyright. Accordingly film royalties paid to a person outside the UK can be paid without any withholding.

There is not normally any obligation to deduct tax from a payment of capital, eg, where an amount is paid for the purchase of rights rather than the use of them. An exception to this is where a non-UK resident sells UK patent rights for a capital sum. In that case the purchaser should deduct UK tax at the basic rate from the capital sum.

There is no obligation to deduct tax from payments for the provision of services (unless the payment is to an employee) (and *see* also 15.5.2. below). It is a question of fact whether payments are made for the performance of services or for the use of particular rights. Where, however, payments are genuine compensation for services performed, there is no withholding in the UK.

Many other countries impose a withholding tax on the payment of royalties or at least royalties paid to a person outside the jurisdiction. Few countries will impose a withholding tax on payments for the genuine performance of services or on payments of capital sums for the purchase of rights. The definition of royalties varies from jurisdiction to jurisdiction and the rates of withholding tax may also vary according to the exact rights for which the royalty is paid.

Where a payer is obliged to deduct tax from payments, this obligation may be overridden if there is an appropriate double tax treaty between the country of residence of the payer and the country of residence of the recipient. The treaty may provide that the royalties are to be taxed only in the country of residence of the recipient, in which case the payer should not make any deduction, or perhaps that tax is to be deducted at a reduced rate. The double tax treaty between the USA and the UK, for example, provides that royalties are to be taxed only in the country of residence of the recipient. This means they can be paid without deduction by a US payer to a UK resident recipient or vice versa even if the normal US or UK law would require deduction to be made from those payments.

The double tax treaty will not apply automatically. It is necessary for the recipient to apply for the benefit of the treaty and the tax authorities to confirm to the payer that payment can be made gross or at a reduced rate of withholding.

The possible incidence of withholding tax should be addressed in licensing and other agreements. The licensor receiving payments under an agreement will normally want to ensure that payments are received without any withholding and that if any withholding is required by law, the payer will provide appropriate certificates of withholding and do whatever is necessary to assist the recipient in an application for exemption or reduction if appropriate under any relevant double tax treaty. In some cases the recipient may want to require the payer to gross up for any withholding, ie to increase the payment so that after withholding of tax it is equal to the payment which would have been due if no withholding were imposed. The payer will obviously not want to agree a grossing up provision and should normally resist it. The payer will also want to ensure that it is entitled to withhold tax if required to do so by law. A reasonable payer will normally be happy to agree to co-operate in any necessary application for treaty exemption.

15.5.2 PAYMENTS TO PERFORMERS

Payments to employees and other workers are often subject to the deduction of tax. In the UK an employer making payments of remuneration to an employee is required to deduct UK tax at source under the Pay As You Earn (PAYE) system.

Where payments are made for services to a person who is not an employee, there is not normally any obligation to deduct tax. Some countries, however, have special rules for payments to performers.

In the UK, a person such as a producer who makes payments to an entertainer who is non-resident in the UK for performances carried out in the UK is obliged to deduct basic rate tax. The tax must be accounted for to the Foreign Entertainers Unit of the Inland Revenue. The Foreign Entertainers Unit is also able to make agreements with the producer or other payer as to the precise amounts to be deducted where for example there are allowable expenses.

15.5.3 VALUE ADDED TAX

Value Added Tax (VAT) is a tax on the supply of goods or services. It applies in each country of the EU, within the framework set out in European directives. The following sets out the UK position, but the same principles should apply in other EU countries.

It is for the supplier to charge VAT as appropriate on supplies and account for it to the tax authorities (HM Customs & Excise). A person making supplies in the UK should normally account for VAT at the standard rate (currently 17.5 per cent). This is the supplier's output tax, ie, tax on his output. If an agreement is silent as to VAT, the consideration stated in the agreement is taken to be inclusive of any applicable VAT and the supplier must account to Customs for the VAT out of that consideration.

A person who incurs VAT on the purchase of goods or services is entitled to reclaim that VAT provided it is incurred in the course of a business involving his own taxable supplies of goods or services. The VAT incurred is input tax, ie, tax on supplies in to the business.

The grant of a licence of rights and the sale of rights are supplies of services. The licensor/vendor should normally charge VAT on the consideration, whether this is a lump sum or periodical royalties or other payments.

Certain supplies are treated as made where the recipient is. These include transfers and assignments of copyright, licences, etc. Where the licensor/vendor is in the UK but the licensee/purchaser is outside the EU, the supply is treated as taking place where the recipient is and therefore is outside the scope of UK VAT. No VAT will therefore be chargeable by the UK licensor/vendor.

Where the licensor/vendor is in the UK and the licensee/purchaser is in another state of the EU, the supply will be outside the scope of UK VAT provided that the licensee/purchaser is carrying on business in that other state and is registered for VAT there. This means that there is no UK VAT chargeable but the licensee/purchaser must account for VAT in his own country on the 'import'.

Equally a UK licensee/purchaser receiving rights from a person in another EU state or from a person outside the EU should account for UK VAT under the so-called 'reverse charge' procedure. This VAT is input tax which the UK licensee/purchaser can recover if it is itself making taxable supplies in the course of a business for VAT purposes.

Documentation of multimedia licensing and contracts should normally provide that the consideration is exclusive of any applicable VAT. This is principally a point for the licensor/vendor who will be receiving the consideration and who is responsible for accounting to the tax authorities for applicable VAT.

15.5.4 STAMP DUTY

In many countries there is a stamp duty or transfer tax charged on documents of transfer.

In the UK stamp duty at the rate of 1 per cent of the consideration is payable on a transfer of certain forms of property including an assignment of IP.

It is also chargeable on an agreement to transfer property except to the extent that the consideration is attributable to moveable property which passes by delivery.

Stamp duty is a duty on documents and not a liability on persons. The sanction for failure to stamp a document is that a document which is not properly stamped cannot be produced in evidence in proceedings in the UK. Where a transfer needs to be registered, eg a transfer of land or of trade marks, the appropriate registrar will require the document of transfer to be duly stamped before registration. Penalties and interest are due if a document is stamped more than 30 days after execution. Where, however, the document is executed outside the UK, penalties and interest do not start to run until 30 days after it is brought into the UK.

15.5.4

The grant of a licence is not subject to stamp duty unless it is essentially a transfer of the property licensed. For example, an exclusive irrevocable licence for a long period and for all territories will effectively be a transfer of the rights 'licensed'. It will therefore be stampable as a transfer of property.

---

[1] But see (Scottish Case) *Beta Computers (Europe) Ltd v Adobe Systems (Europe) Ltd*, December 1995.

• 16 •

APPLICATION OF COMPETITION LAW TO MULTIMEDIA PRODUCTS

16.1 INTRODUCTION

Both the licensing of the underlying rights necessary to create multimedia products and the subsequent supply of the products can raise competition issues. The following is an outline of the competition principles which may apply to such products.

16.2 APPLICABLE LAW

The applicable UK law is as follows:

- The Restrictive Trade Practices Act 1976;
- The Fair Trading Act 1973;
- The Competition Act 1980;
- The Resale Prices Act 1976.

The applicable EC law is as follows:

- EC Treaty, arts 22, 30–36;
- EC Treaty, arts 59–66;
- EC Treaty, art 85;
- EC Treaty, art 86;
- various block exemption regulations.

16.3 UK LAW

16.3.1 UK COMPETITION AUTHORITIES

The main UK competition authorities are:

- the Secretary of State for Trade and Industry ('the Secretary of State'), who has overall responsibility for UK competition policy;
- the Office of Fair Trading ('OFT'), which monitors monopolies, mergers, restrictive agreements and anti-competitive practices generally and takes action if required;
- the Director General of Fair Trading ('DGFT') who, as the head of the OFT, advises the

Secretary of State, may seek undertakings from firms and may take direct action in relation to particular practices;
- the Monopolies and Mergers Commission ('MMC'), which investigates and reports on matters referred to it by the Secretary of State or the DGFT, including mergers, monopoly situations, and anti-competitive practices.

16.3.2 THE COMMON LAW RESTRAINT OF TRADE DOCTRINE

This doctrine states that:

- at common law, contracts in restraint of trade are on the face of it void and unenforceable;
- parties to an agreement must show that the restraint in question is fair between them and fair to the world at large for the agreement to be enforceable;
- legislation supplements the common law position.

16.3.3 FAIR TRADING ACT 1973

Under the Fair Trading Act 1973 ('FTA') the Secretary of State and the DGFT can refer suspected monopoly situations to the MMC for investigation. The Secretary of State may also refer qualifying mergers to the MMC for investigation.

Monopolies

The FTA 1973 covers two types of monopoly situation:

(1) *Scale monopolies*: where at least 25 per cent of goods and services of any description are supplied by or to one and the same person.

> **Example**
>
> The MMC found that Sega held a scale monopoly position for hardware and software for the year ending June 1994 (*MMC Report on the Supply of Video Games in the UK* (1995)).

(2) *Behavioural/complex monopolies*: these occur where at least 25 per cent of the relevant goods or services are supplied by a 'group' of two or more persons who behave or have behaved in such a way as to restrict and/or distort competition. Thus the parallel behaviour of firms, where there is no actual agreement, may be investigated.

> **Example**
>
> The MMC found that Sega and Nintendo were in a complex monopoly situation. Together they supply more than one-quarter of video games sold in the UK, and, according to the MMC, they behave in such a way as to prevent, restrict or distort competition, in particular by their software licensing arrangements, pricing of software relative to hardware and rental practices (*MMC Report on the Supply of Video Games in the UK* (1995)).

UK LAW

Qualifying mergers

Under the FTA 1973 there is a merger if two or more enterprises have ceased to be distinct enterprises. A merger will qualify for investigation if it will result in the creation or strengthening of a 25 per cent market share in relation to goods or services in all or a substantial part of the UK or if there is a take-over of assets with a balance sheet value of £70 million or more. The MMC will consider whether a monopoly and/or qualifying merger situation exists and if so whether it may be expected to operate against the public interest.

Consequences

The practical consequences of a finding by the MMC that the monopoly and/or merger may be expected to operate against the public interest are that:

(1) The MMC has power to recommend that the firm(s) in question take action to overcome the adverse effects of the monopoly/merger situation.
(2) The Secretary of State may then, on the basis of the MMC's recommendations, advise the DGFT to seek undertakings from the companies concerned as to future conduct.
(3) Alternatively the Secretary of State may make orders by way of statutory instrument.

> **Example**
> The MMC found that a number of Sega and Nintendo's activities were against the public interest, including:
> (1) their discriminatory price structure for software and hardware;
> (2) the imposition of restrictive conditions in licensing arrangements with competing software publishers, such as:
>   (a) restrictions on the quantity of games which may be published;
>   (b) requiring approval of games, programs and concepts before publication;
>   (c) controlling packaging and presentation;
>   (d) controlling the manufacture of games and cartridges and charging excessive prices for these cartridges;
> (3) the imposition of restrictions on video game rental.
>
> The MMC recommended that the licensing arrangements of Sega and Nintendo should be modified to include the removal of a number of licence conditions, in particular the requirement that Sega and Nintendo control the manufacture of games cartridges (*MMC Report on the Supply of Video Games in the UK* (1995)).

16.3.4 COMPETITION ACT 1980

Under the Competition Act 1980 the DGFT can investigate 'anti-competitive' practices of a single firm and may refer such practices to the MMC, provided the firm has at least 25 per cent of the relevant market and has a turnover of at least £10 million. If the firm is a member of a group of interconnected bodies corporate, the market share and turnover of other members of that group will be taken into account. The MMC determines whether the practices operate or may be expected to operate against the public interest. If the MMC

16.3.5 RESTRICTIVE TRADE PRACTICES ACT 1976

The RTPA 1976 applies to:

- restrictive trading agreements;
- between two or more undertakings;
- carrying on business in the supply of goods or services;
- under which relevant restrictions are accepted by two or more parties.

If the RTPA applies, parties must supply details of the agreement to the DGFT within specified time limits. Details of the agreement will be placed on the Register of Restrictive Trading Agreements, which is open to public inspection unless confidentiality concerns in relation to particular provisions can be justified.

Often intellectual property licensing agreements will not be covered by the RTPA 1976 because:

- there is not considered to be a supply of goods or services within the meaning of the RTPA 1976;
- the licence may not be viewed as restrictive, on the grounds that without the licence, the licensee would have no right to exploit the licensed rights and therefore the restriction may simply amount to a limitation of the grant;
- the restrictions are often only imposed on one party;
- the licence may be exempted under Sched 3 to the RTPA 1976.

The consequences of failing to register a registrable agreement are:

- restrictions in the agreement are automatically void and unenforceable;
- a possible action for breach of statutory duty.

The DGFT's duty in relation to registered agreements

The DGFT has a *prima facie* duty to refer any restrictions in the agreement to the Restrictive Practices Court to determine if they are contrary to the public interest, or can be justified on one of the grounds set out in the Act. In practice the DGFT usually decides that the restrictions are not sufficiently significant to justify referral to the Restrictive Practices Court. Alternatively the parties may agree to modify the offending parts of the agreement.

Points to consider when drafting an agreement include:

- does the proposed agreement contain any relevant restrictions?
- are the tests for registration met?
- if so, furnish details to the DGFT in time or amend the agreement to fall outside the Act.

16.3.6 RESALE PRICES ACT 1976

The RPA 1976 prohibits producers from attempting to fix the minimum price at which their products may be resold. This prohibition applies at both the vertical level (eg, between supplier and distributor) and the horizontal level (eg, between suppliers) of trading.

16.4 EC LAW

The UK as a member of the EU is subject to EC law. EC law prevails over conflicting national law. EC legislation may be directly applicable, being automatically part of national law. EC law may also have direct effect in that individuals can rely on provisions of EC law in actions before the national courts. EC law may be enforced against non-EC parties. The EEA Agreement applies equivalent provisions on competition to those in the EC Treaty to those EFTA countries, excluding Switzerland, which are not already part of the EC.

16.4.1 EC COMPETITION AUTHORITIES

Directorate General IV of the EC Commission has overall responsibility for EC competition law. The Surveillance Authority applies competition law to those EFTA countries subject to the EEA which are not EC members. The EC applies the competition rules:

(1) It may act on its own initiative or on a complaint from a third party which feels it may be affected by the anti-competitive practice in question.
(2) It has extensive powers to investigate any alleged breaches of the EC Treaty, arts 85 or 86.
(3) The Commission can require information to be supplied.
(4) The Commission can enter a firm's premises and search for documents if there is a suspected breach of EC law.
(5) The Commission issues regulations, directives, decisions and comfort letters.

> **Example**
> The world's second-largest PC software company complained that Microsoft prevented competitors entering the market for PC operating system software by anti-competitive practices, including Microsoft's standard licensing agreements to PC manufacturers. The Commission subsequently investigated the complaint and Microsoft following the investigation undertook to amend some of its licensing practices.

The Court of First Instance ('CFI') at Luxembourg may review the EC's decision. Appeals can be made from the CFI to the European Court of Justice ('ECJ') on questions of law.

16.4.2 THE RELEVANT EC TREATY PROVISIONS

The relevant treaty provisions and the areas to which they apply are as follows:

- EC Treaty, arts 22, 30–36, 59–66, 85 and 86: may affect the licensing of intellectual property rights;
- EC Treaty, arts 85 and 86: the principal rules on competition in the Treaty;
- EC Treaty, art 222: provides that the rules of the Treaty do not prejudice the rules of the Member States governing the system of property ownership;
- EC Treaty, arts 30–35: provide for the free movement of goods between Member States of the EC;

- EC Treaty, arts 30 and 34: (respectively) prohibit quantitative restrictions on imports and exports and all measures having equivalent effect;
- EC Treaty, arts 30–35: these are subject to art 36, which permits restrictions for the protection of industrial and commercial property provided that the restriction does not constitute a means of arbitrary discrimination or a disguised restriction on trade between Member States;
- EC Treaty, arts 59–66: similar to arts 30–36 in relation to the provision of services between Member States;
- EC Treaty, 36: applies by analogy to arts 59–66 of the Treaty (*Coditel v Cine Vog* [1980] ECR 881).

The licensing of IP rights (such as copyright, trade marks, patent and design rights) raises difficult issues for competition law. IP rights represent a legal monopoly granted by national legislation to encourage innovation and to safeguard the skill and investment of those responsible for the creation of works. However, the object of the competition rules is to ensure free competition. In particular the EC rules on competition are intended to establish an internal market without frontiers in which the free movement of goods and services is ensured. The very existence of national rights, which permit the exclusion of owners from using IP rights and which permit the licensing of those rights on a territorial basis, conflicts with these aims. In order to resolve this conflict three principles have emerged:

(1) While the existence of an IP right is not affected by the Treaty, the manner of its exercise within the Common Market (and now the EEA) can be regulated.
(2) Within the EC (and now the EEA) the extent to which a right can be exercised depends on the essence of the right, or its so-called specific subject-matter.
(3) Once an IP right has been exercised by the owner, or with his consent, by placing goods on the market in a Member State, the right is exhausted and cannot be relied on subsequently to prevent the goods being imported into another Member State.

These three principles are considered below.

The existence and exercise distinction
The competition and free movement rules of the Treaty cannot affect the existence of an IP right but they can regulate the exercise of the right. In particular an IP right may not be exercised so that it artificially partitions the market. In order to ascertain whether particular conduct relates to the existence rather than the exercise of an IP right, the notion of the 'specific subject-matter' of an IP right has been developed. Conduct which is necessary to preserve the specific subject-matter of the right can be exercised without being limited by the Treaty rules on free movement or competition.

The specific subject-matter concept
The specific subject-matter varies according to the right in question. For example:

(1) For patents, it has been held to be 'the exclusive right to use an invention with a view to manufacturing industrial products and putting them into circulation for the first time, either directly or by the grant of licences to third parties, as well as the right to oppose infringements' (Case 16/74 *Centrafarm BV and Adriann De Pejper v Winthrop BV* [1974] ECR 1147, [1974] 2 CMLR 480).
(2) For trade marks, it has been held to be 'the guarantee that the owner of the trade mark has the exclusive right to use that trade mark for the purpose of putting prod-

ucts protected by the mark into circulation for the first time, and is therefore intended to protect him against competitors wishing to take advantage of the status and reputation of the trade mark by selling products illegally bearing that trade mark' (Case 16/74, *see* above).

(3) For copyright, it has been held to be 'the exclusive right to reproduce the protected work to ensure a reward for the creative effort (Case T-69/89 *Radio Telefis Eireann v Commission* [1991] II ECR 485, [1991] 4 CMLR 586).

In relation to any particular clause in a licensing agreement the crucial question, therefore, is whether it can be shown that the particular clause is necessary to protect the specific subject-matter of the right.

The exhaustion of rights principle

The owner or licensee of an IP right cannot rely on that right to prevent the import of goods from another Member State if he has previously marketed the goods (or given his consent to their marketing) in a Member State outside the country to which the goods are being imported. The right is said to have been exhausted on first marketing. The Member State of first marketing can include, but is not limited to, the country from which the goods are to be imported. This principle generally applies to patents, trade marks, non-performance copyright (such as books, videos and sound recordings) and design rights. The principle of exhaustion does not apply to performance copyrights, ie the exhibition of films or TV and radio broadcasts.

> **Examples**
> - The holder of rights under German copyright law in sound recordings could not rely on the rights to prevent goods being reimported into Germany which had been previously marketed in another Member State by that copyright owner's French subsidiary (Case 78/70 *Deutsche Grammophon v Metro* (1971) ECR 487, (1971) CMLR 631).
> - The Belgian owner of copyright in the film *Le Boucher* was able to prevent the transmission of the film by cable television companies in Belgium, which had picked up the film from a German television broadcasting company. The rights were not exhausted in this instance by the granting of a licence to broadcast in Germany (Case 62/79 *Coditel v Cine Vog Films (No 1)* (1980) ECR 881, (1981) 2 CMLR 362).

16.4.3 ARTICLE 85

Article 85 applies to agreements between undertakings, decisions by associations of undertakings and concerted practices:

- which may affect trade between Member States (this test is interpreted broadly);
- and which have as their object or effect the prevention, restriction or distortion of competition within the Common Market.

Agreements without an appreciable impact on competition or trade between Member States will not breach art 85. In general this means agreements involving undertakings with an aggregate annual turnover of no more than ECU300 million and a market share of no more than 5 per cent (Commission, *Notice on Agreements of Minor Importance*).

Examples of possible infringements of art 85 are:
- price fixing;
- controlling production, markets, technical development, or investment;
- sharing markets or sources of supply;
- applying dissimilar conditions to equivalent transactions;
- making conclusion of the agreement conditional on the other party accepting supplementary obligations not usually connected with such contracts.

Consequences of a breach of art 85(1)
(1) Any agreement or decision in breach of art 85 is automatically void and unenforceable by virtue of art 85(2). The whole agreement may therefore be invalid if the offending terms are fundamental to, and cannot, therefore, be severed from that agreement.
(2) The Commission may investigate the infringement and may make an order terminating the infringement and fining the offending party up to 10 per cent of its total annual world-wide turnover (including that of its parent or subsidiaries).
(3) A person suffering loss as a result of the breach of art 85 may be able to sue the participants for damages or injunctive relief in the national court.

Obtaining an exemption from art 85(1) under art 85(3)
Article 85(3) provides that art 85(1) may not apply if the agreement, decision or concerted practice contributes to improving the production or distribution of goods or to promoting technical or economic progress, while allowing consumers a fair share of the resulting benefit, provided that it does not:

- impose restrictions which are not indispensable to these objectives; or
- give the companies concerned the opportunity of eliminating competition in relation to the products in question in a substantial part of the Common Market.

Obtaining an exemption from art 85(1) can be obtained either by:

- applying to the Commission for an individual exemption in respect of the agreement under art 85(3); or
- drafting the agreement to fall within one of the block exemptions.

Applying for an individual exemption To make such an application the parties must notify the agreement, decision or concerted practice to the Commission. If the agreement is notified and subsequently found to be within art 85(1), the parties are exempt from fines in respect of the agreement, decision or concerted practice from the date of notification, even if fully implemented in that period, unless there is blatant disregard for the Treaty provisions.

Awaiting a Commission decision may be a lengthy process. The parties may instead decide to accept a comfort letter, but this is not binding as it does not formally exempt the agreement from the prohibition of art 85(1). Many cases are in practice settled by means of a comfort letter.

Block exemptions The following block exemptions may be relevant in a multimedia context:

- Regulation 1983/83 on exclusive distribution agreements;
- Regulation 1984/83 on exclusive purchasing agreements;
- Regulation 2349/84 in patent licensing agreements;[1]
- Regulation 556/89 on know-how licensing agreements;[2]
- Regulation 417/85 on specialisation agreements; and
- Regulation 418/85 on research and development agreements.

If the agreement falls within the terms of a block exemption it does not need to be notified to the Commission for an individual exemption. It is automatically exempted. All the terms of the agreement must, however, fall within the block exemption. Otherwise the parties cannot rely on the block exemption.

Licensing agreements relating to trade marks and copyright (including software licences) are not covered by any block exemption although the patent and know-how block exemptions can be used as guidance to the attitude of the Commission on the application of art 85(1) and 85(3) to particular terms of a copyright or trade-mark licence.

General structure of block exemptions These tend to follow a pattern. Each has a Black List, a White List and a Grey List.

(1) The White List specifies clauses which usually fall outside art 85(1), but which are exempted if they do fall within art 85(1), ie, if all the terms of the block exemption are satisfied.
(2) The Grey List specifies clauses within art 85(1) but which are exempted if all the terms of the block exemption are satisfied.
(3) The Black List specifies clauses within art 85(1) which are not exempted; if these are included in an agreement, the agreement will not benefit from the block exemption.

> **Article 85 checklist**
> (1) Is there an agreement, decision or concerted practice between undertakings?
> (2) Is the agreement, decision or concerted practice such that it may affect trade between Member States?
> (3) Does the agreement have the object or effect of distorting competition within the EC?
> (4) Is there a relevant block exemption?
> (5) If so, make sure all the terms of the agreement fit within the block exemption.
> (6) If not consider seeking an individual exemption from the Commission or the Surveillance Authority where relevant.
> (7) Are the tests for obtaining an individual exemption likely to be met?

16.4.4 ARTICLE 86

Article 86 applies to an abuse by one or more undertakings of a dominant position within the EC or a substantial part of the EC which may affect trade between Member States.

Dominance is considered to exist where a company has the ability to act independently of competitors, customers and consumers. It is not assessed purely in terms of market share, although market shares of 30 per cent and over *may* be indicative of dominance. It largely depends on how the remaining market share is divided among competitors. To assess market share it is necessary to define the relevant product market. Regard should be had when assessing the size of the market to other products which are substantially interchangeable with the relevant product. It is the *abuse* of the dominant position, not the dominant position itself, which is prohibited by art 86.

Even though an undertaking has an exemption under art 85, it may still be in breach of art 86.

> **Example**
>
> In the *Tetra Pak* case, the acquisition of rights under an exclusive licence of patent rights was held to amount to an infringement of art 86 as Tetra Pak held a dominant position in the relevant market, notwithstanding that the patent licence itself was exempt from art 85(1) by the patent licensing block exemption (Case T-51/89 *Tetra Pak Rausing v Commission* (1990) II ECR 309, (1991) 4 CMLR 334).

Examples of possible abuse are:

- imposing unfair prices (eg, excessive, predatory or discriminatory prices);
- imposing unfair trading conditions;
- discriminatory treatment of equivalent transactions and/or persons;
- refusal to supply;
- bundling of goods.

> **Example**
>
> The TV companies, BBC, ITP and RTE, were held to be in a dominant position under art 86, because they had a *de facto* monopoly over the information used to compile listings for television programmes received in most households in Ireland. They were able to prevent effective competition in the secondary market of weekly television guides. By refusing to grant licences to third parties to reproduce their copyright television programme lists in a comprehensive weekly television guide they had committed an abuse of their dominant position (Cases C-241 and 242/91P *Radio Telefis Eireann v Commission* (ECJ Judgment, 6 April 1995)).

There is no power for the Commission to exempt conduct falling under art 86.

Consequences of a breach of art 86

(1) The Commission has the power to order the company to terminate the abusive conduct.
(2) The Commission may fine the offending party up to 10 per cent of total annual world-wide turnover (including the turnover of the party's parents or subsidiaries).

EC LAW 16.4.4

(3) A person suffering loss as a result of breach of art 86 may be able to sue for damages and/or injunctive relief in the national court.

The following are examples of particular terms which may raise competition issues.

Checklist of terms likely to raise competition issues if included in a licence

- exclusivity provisions;
- export bans;
- territorial restrictions;
- excessive royalties or royalty provisions not related to the product itself;
- tying a product to the supply of another product;
- obligations not to compete;
- no-challenge clauses;
- lengthy contract duration;
- limiting the customers the licensee or purchaser may supply;
- refusal to supply;
- specifying conditions of supply not related to the product being supplied;
- refusing access to essential facilities, eg access to a network where there is no available alternative.

---

[1] The Commission has proposed that the block exemptions relating to patent and know-how licensing will be replaced by a combined block exemption regulation for technology transfer agreements OJ No C178, 30.6.94, p 3.

[2] See footnote 1 above.

Appendix 1

COLLECTING SOCIETIES

UK BODIES

Authors Licensing and Collecting Society (ALCS)
(Exploitation of literary and dramatic works)
74 New Oxford Street
London   WC1A 1ES
Tel: 0171–255 2034

Copyright Licensing Agency Ltd (CLA)
Includes **CLA Rapid Clearance Service** (CLARCS)
(Reprography of literary and dramatic works)
90 Tottenham Court Road
London   W1P 0LP
Tel: 0171–436 5931

Design and Artists Copyright Society Ltd (DACS)
(Exploitation of artistic works)
Parchment House
13 Northburgh Street
London   EC1V 0AH
Tel: 0171–336 8811

Educational Recording Agency (ERA)
(Educational establishments' off-air recording of broadcasts and cable programmer)
74 New Oxford Street
London   WC1A 1ES
Tel: 0171–436 4883

Mechanical Copyright Protection Society Ltd (MCPS)
(Exploitation of recording rights in musical works)
41 Streatham High Road
London   SW16 1ER
Tel: 0181–769 4400

Performing Rights Society Ltd (PRS)
(Licensing public performance and broadcasting of musical works)
(Head Office) 29 Berners Street
London   W1P 4AA
Tel: 0171–580 5544

Phonographic Performance Ltd (PPL)
(Public performance and broadcasting of sound recordings)
14 Ganton Street
London   W1V 1LB
Tel: 0171–437 0311

Publishers Licensing Society (PLS)
(Licensing of secondary use of published texts)
90 Tottenham Court Road
London   W1P 9HE
Tel: 0171–436 5931

Videogram Performance Ltd (VPL)
(Public performance and broadcasting of members' videograms)
Ganton House
14–22 Ganton Street
London   W1V 1LB
Tel: 0171–437 0311

OVERSEAS BODIES

International Federation of Reproduction Rights Organisations (IFRRO)
(The representative body for national reprographic societies)
Goethestrasse 49
D-80336 München
Germany
Tel: †49 89 51 41 20

Individual overseas collecting agencies can be found in Appendix 9 where they are identified by an *.

Appendix 2

COPYRIGHT MANAGEMENT INITIATIVES FOR ELECTRONIC RIGHTS

The spread of digital communication has brought with it a 'Pandora's Box' of disputes over electronic rights for textual, photographic, sound and video works. The following describes some programmes recently started by artists and collective agencies in the US to monitor and control access to copyrighted works electronically.

(1) *The Copyright Clearance Centre* (CCC): offers a system for the licensing of digital materials, for local area networks and for the Internet.
(Danvers, Massachusetts. Tel: 508-750-8400.)

(2) *ASCAP Clearance Express* (ACE): an electronic depository, accessible by modem. Offers information about the ASCAP repertory in four search fields: title; title and recording artist; writer/arranger, and publisher of a title.
(New York City. Tel: 212-621-6521.)

(3) *The Authors Registry*: the Authors Guild, the American Society of Journalists and Authors, other writers' groups and the Association of Authors' Representatives (the agents' trade association) recently established the Authors Registry. Accounting and royalty payment procedures for UK outline and CD-ROMs.
(New York City. Tel: 212-563-6920.)

(4) *NWU/CARL*: the National Writers Union (NWU) and the CARL Corporation have set up a programme to clear copyrights and distribute royalties to writers for magazine and journal articles faxed, upon request, from CARL's UnCover database of citations to cover 17,000 periodicals. A new publications rights clearing house, set up by the NWU, will handle rights clearances and royalty disbursements.
(New York City. Tel: 212-254-0279.)

(5) *MP©A*: the American Society of Media Photographers has established the MP©A, on behalf of ASMP members, to address the complex marketing, licensing, delivery and enforcement issues raised by the distribution of images in the electronic environment.
(Princeton Junction, New Jersey. Tel: 609-799-2233.)

(6) *Copyright Office Registration and Deposit System (CORDS)*: proposes regulation for digital copyrights, particularly digital identifiers and tracking technology.
(Library of Congress Copyright Office.)

(7) *Confédération Internationale des Sociétés d'Auteurs et Compositeurs (CISAC)*: International organisation representing the musical, literary, dramatic and visual arts collecting societies.
Paris. Fax: +33 7 47 23 02 66.)

(8) *IMPRIMATUR*: intends to devise processes to protect and trade all types of IP so that rights are respected while the needs of users are met.
(London. Tel: 0171-255-2034.)
(9) *SESAM*: a new society set up to manage the rights of writers wherever their works are used in a multimedia product.
(Paris. Tel: +33 1 47 15 49 06.)

Appendix 3

CHARLES CLARK'S CLASSIFICATION OF ELECTRONIC RIGHTS

PRIME RIGHTS

TO ISSUE A COPYRIGHT WORK ON ELECTRONIC MEDIA

Publication in on-line form (eg the Lexis legal service) and in distributed form (eg, Oxford University Press CD dictionaries)

TO AUTHORISE THE STORAGE OF A COPYRIGHT WORK IN ANY MEDIUM BY ELECTRONIC MEANS

For example, the authorisation of storage by a document supply centre to enable it to deliver copies to its customers (as to whether these copies are print-on-paper copies or electronic copies will depend on what subsidiary rights are granted).

SUBSIDIARY RIGHTS

INCLUSION INTO ANOTHER PUBLISHER'S/PRODUCER'S ELECTRONIC PRODUCT OR SERVICE

The materials appropriate to different products or services will range from learned articles and chapters of books for educational electronic study packs, to portions of novels and poems for language learning, to tourist guides and maps for hand-held CD-ROMs, often called 'electronic books'.

SCREEN DISPLAY

An essential feature of most electronic products and services, it is itself an act of reproduction in some copyright laws, or an act of display in others. The act is restricted by the copyright in the work being displayed, and should be licensed as such. However, some would argue (eg, Laddie Vitoria & Prescott, in *The Modern Law of Copyright and Designs*, 2nd edn, p 104) that the CDPA must be construed as a whole and that therefore it cannot be that s 17(6) prohibits displaying a work on the screen of a television receiver).

PERFORMANCES

Display on screen may take place in circumstances, eg in a lawyer's office in the presence of clients or in a pub in front of customers, which could suggest that an act of public performance takes place.

DOWNLOADING/DISTRIBUTION

This activity follows the act of storage and must itself be licensed.

NETWORKING

Downloading may take place to an identifiable number of terminals on a known and licensable site (eg a university), or it may take place to an indeterminable number of terminals (eg across many university sites, as in the UK's SuperJanet project). Networking is a complex issue and the experience and schemes of software publishers are highly relevant to site licences for eg laptops, extension to associated sites or to companies, etc.

PRINTING OUT OF HARD COPIES

Hard copies may be printed out for individual use by a user working at home; for class preparation by a teacher; or in multiple quantities for training purposes in industry. They may be printed out from a network on one site or at many sites.

EDITING

This difficult issue affects artistic as well as literary copyright works. In education, many teachers wish to edit texts electronically in order to present relevant materials for their particular students; pictures can be re-engineered; and in scholarly and scientific research, researchers may want to extract and amend the texts written by others as part of the process of their own research. It may be possible to license editing on the explicit understanding that no moral rights of the relevant authors have been waived, so that any non-attribution of authorship or any derogatory editing of text or artwork are at the risk of infringement of the author's moral rights.

INCLUSION IN MULTIMEDIA WORKS

How to license and how to gain reward for the inclusion of literary works in multimedia works is a major task for the community rights holders.

Appendix 4

REGULATORY BODIES THAT EXERCISE CONTROL OVER MEDIA CONTENT

Advertising Standards Authority (ASA)
2 Torrington Place
London   WC1E 7HW
Tel: 0171—580 5555

British Board of Film Classification
(BBFC)
3 Soho Square
London   W1V 5DE
Tel: 0171—439 7961

Broadcasting Complaints Commission
(BCC)
35–37 Grosvenor Gardens
London   SW1 0BS
Tel: 0171—630 1966

Broadcasting Standards Council (BSC)
5–8 The Sanctuary
London   SW1P 3JS
Tel: 0171—233 0544

The Data Protection Registrar
Wycliffe House
Water Lane
Wilmslow
Cheshire SK9 1PF
Tel: 01625—545700

European Leisure Software Producers Association (ELSPA)
Suite 1, Haddonsacre
Station Road
Offenham
Nr. Evesham
Worcestershire   WR1 5LW

Independent Committee for the Supervision of Standards for Telephone Information Services (ICSTIS)
229–231 High Holborn
London WC1V 7DA
Tel: 0800—500212

Independent Television Commission
(ITC)
33 Foley Street
London   W1P 7LB
Tel: 0171—255 3000

Office of Telecommunications (Oftel)
50 Ludgate Hill
London   EC4M 7JJ
Tel: 0171—822 1600

Video Standards Council (VSC)
Research House
Fraser Road
Perivale
Middlesex   UB6 7AQ
Tel: 0181—566 8272

Appendix 5

UNIONS

British Actors Equity Association
Guild House
Upper St Martins Lane
London   WC2H 9EG
Tel: 0171–379 6000

Musicians Union
60 Clapham Road
London   SW9 0JJ
Tel: 0171–582 5566

Writers Guild of Great Britain
430 Edgware Road
London   W2 1EG
Tel: 0171–723 8074

Directors Guild of Great Britain
15–19 Great Titchfield Street
London   W1P 7SF
Tel: 0171–436 8626

Society of Authors
84 Drayton Gardens
London   SW10 9SD
Tel: 0171–373 6642

Appendix 6

PERFORMER'S RIGHTS

The authors are not aware of the existence of an exhaustive list of the countries that possess performer's rights legislation. The Performances (Reciprocal Protection) (Convention Countries) Order 1994 (SI No 264) has been extended to the following countries, which are designated as enjoying reciprocal protection under Part II of the 1988 Act:

Argentina	Guatemala
Australia	Honduras
Austria	Ireland
Barbados	Italy
Bolivia	Japan
Brazil	Lesotho
Burkina Faso	Luxembourg
Chile	Mexico
Colombia	Monaco
Congo	Netherlands
Costa Rica	Niger
Czech Republic	Nigeria
Denmark (including Greenland and the Faroe Islands)	Norway
	Panama
Dominican Republic	Paraguay
Ecuador	Peru
El Salvador	Philippines
Fiji	Spain
Finland	Slovak Republic
France (including all Overseas Departments and Territories)	Sweden
	Switzerland
Germany	Uruguay
Greece	

The authors have confirmed with the Institute of Advanced Legal Studies that the best way (indeed the only way that the librarians there could suggest) to confirm and update this list would be to go through the WIPO publication *Industrial Property and Copyright*, which publishes updates to *Copyright Laws and Treaties of the World*. The Institute has a complete set of this journal.

Appendix 7

MORAL RIGHTS

The following countries are signatories to the Paris Act 1971 of the Berne Convention. (This contains certain moral rights.)

Albania	Germany
Argentina	Ghana
Australia	Greece
Austria	Guinea
Bahamas	Guinea-Bissau
Bahrain	Holy See
Bangladesh	Honduras
Barbados	Hungary
Benin	Iceland
Bolivia	India
Bosnia & Herzegovina	Italy
Brazil	Jamaica
Bulgaria	Jordan
Burkina Faso	Kenya
Cameroon	Lesotho
Central African Republic	Liberia
Chile	Libya
China	Luxembourg
Colombia	Macedonia (former Yugoslav Republic of)
Congo	Malawi
Costa Rica	Malaysia
Croatia	Mali
Cyprus	Malta
Czech Republic	Mauritania
Denmark	Mauritius
Ecuador	Mexico
Egypt	Monaco
El Salvador	Morocco
Finland	Namibia
France	Netherlands
Gabon	Niger
Gambia	Nigeria

Norway	Surinam
Paraguay	Sweden
Peru	Switzerland
Philippines	Thailand
Poland	Trinidad & Tobago
Portugal	Tunisa
Rwanda	Turkey
Saint Lucia	United States of America
Senegal	United Arab Emirates
Slovakia	United Kingdom
Slovenia	Yugoslavia
South Africa	Zaire
Spain	Zambia
Sri Lanka	Zimbabwe

This list can only represent a starting-point, for a number of reasons:

(1) Some countries are not signatories to the entire Paris Act.
(2) The list is not necessarily up to date.
(3) The authors have no confirmation that those countries which are signatories do in fact have the corresponding national legislation; also some countries such as Belgium, which the authors would expect to have moral rights legislation, are not signatories to the Paris Act and so do not appear on the above list.

Appendix 8

NATIONAL COPYRIGHT AGENCIES

*ABDR—Associaçâo Brasileira de Direitos Reprográficos
Avenida Ipiranga, 1267–9° andar
BR—01039–907 Sâo Paulo-SP
Brazil
Phone: +55 11 227 2539
Fax: +55 11 227 2539
Key representative: Raul Wassermann

ADAGP—Société des auteurs dans les arts graphiques et plastiques
11, rue Berryer
F=75008 Paris
France
Phone: +33 1 45 61 03 87
Fax: +33 1 45 63 44 89
Key representative: Jean-Marc Gutton

Association of American Publishers (AAP)
1718 Connecticut Avenue, N.W. Suite 700
Washington DC 20009
USA
Phone: +1 202 232 3335
Fax: +1 202 745 0694
Key representative: Nicholas A. Veliotes

*Associazione Italiana per i Diritti di Riproduzione delle Opere a Stampa (AIDROS)
Via delle Erbe, 2
I–20121 Milano
Italy
Phone: +39 2 809506
Fax: +39 2 809506
Key representative: Giancarla Mursia

Authors' Guild Inc
330 West 43rd Street
New York NY 10036
USA
Phone: +1 212 563 5904
Fax: +1 212 564 8363
Key representative: Helen Stephenson

Authors' Licensing & Collecting Society (ALCS)
Isis House
74 New Oxford Street
London WC1A 1EF
United Kingdom
Phone: +44 171 255 2034
Fax: +44 171 323 0486
Key representative: Janet Hurrell

Bildkonst Upphovsrätt i Sverige (BUS)
Dalagatan 7
S-11123 Stockholm
Sweden
Phone: +46 8 10 70 90
Fax: +46 8 10 64 88
Key representative: Mats Lindberg

Book Publishers Association of Israel
29 Carlebach Street
Tel-Aviv 67132
Israel
Phone: +972 3 5614 1214
Fax: +972 3 5611 996
Key representative: Amnon Ben-Shmuel

APPENDIX 8

Börsenverein des Deutschen Buchhandels e. V
Grosser Hirschgraben 17–21
D-60311 Frankfurt/Main
Germany
Phone: +49 69 13 06 313
Fax: +49 69 13 06 300
Key representative: Harald Heker

Canadian Book Publishers' Council (CBPC)
250 Merton Street, Suite 203
Toronto, Ontario M4S 1B1
Canada
Phone: +1 416 322 7011
Fax: +1 416 322 6999
Key representative: Jacqueline Hushion—Executive Director

*Canadian Copyright Licensing Agency (CANCOPY)
6 Adelaide Street East, Suite 900
Toronto, Ontario M5C 1H6
Canada
Phone: +1 416 868 1620
Fax: +1 416 868 1621
Internet: http://www.cancopy.com
Email: amartin@cancopy.com
Key representative: Andrew Martin

*Centre Français d'exploitation du droit de Copie (CFC)
3 rue Hautefeuille
F–75006 Paris
France
Phone: +33 1 43 26 95 35
Fax: +33 1 46 34 67 19
Key representatives: Patrick Join-Lambert and Anne Riviere

*Centro Espanol de Derechos Reprográficos (CEDRO)
Jos Maranón, 10–3°
E–28010 Madrid
Spain
Phone: +34 1 594 1575
Fax: +34 1 445 3567
Key representative: Juan Jaenicke

*Christian Copyright Licensing Inc (CCLI)
6130 N.E. 78th Ct., Suite C-11
Portland, OR 97218
USA
Phone: +1 800 234 2446
Fax: +1 503 257 2244
Key representative: Howard Rachinski

*Copy-Dan
Ryesgade 53B
DK–2100 København Ø
Denmark
Phone: +45 31 39 35 11
Fax: +45 31 39 82 82
Key representatives: Litten Hansen (Press copies) and Grethe Erskov (Copy-sector)

*Copyright Agency Limited (CAL)
Level 19
157 Liverpool Street
Sydney NSW 2000
Australia
Phone: 61 2 394 7600
Fax: 61 2 394 7601
Key representatives: Michael Fraser and Caroline Morgan

*Copyright Clearance Center
222 Rosewood Drive
Danvers, Massachusetts 01923
USA
Phone: +1 508 750 8400
Fax: +1 508 750 4343
Key representative: Joseph S. Alen

*Copyright Collecting Agency (Ireland) Ltd (CCAI)
8th Floor, Liberty Hall
Dublin 1
Ireland
Phone: +353 18 748694
Fax: +353 18 749250
Key representative: James J. Eadie

*Copyright Licensing Agency Ltd (CLA)
90 Tottenham Court Road
London   W1P 0LP

NATIONAL COPYRIGHT AGENCIES

United Kingdom
Phone: +44 171 436 5931
Fax: +44 171 436 3986
Key representatives: Colin P. Hadley and Dinah Woodward

*Copyright Licensing Ltd (CLL)
P.O. Box 101 271
North Shore Mail Center
Auckland
New Zealand
Phone: +64 9 444 4300
Fax: +64 9 444 2030
Key representative: Jack Sprosen—Executive Officer

Design and Artists Copyright Society Ltd (DACS)
Parchment House
13 Northburgh Street
London EC1V 0AH
United Kingdom
Phone: +44 171 336 8811
Fax: +44 171 336 8822
Key representatives: Rachel Duffield and Janet Ibbotson

Deutscher Journalisten-Verband e.V
Bennauerstrasse 60
D-53115 Bonn
Germany
Phone: +49 228 22 29 71–78
Fax: +49 228 21 49 17
Key representatives: Dr Hermann Meyn and Benno H. Pöppelmann

*Dramatic, Artistic and Literary Rights Organisation (Pty) Limited (DALRO)
P.O. Box 31627
Braamfontein 2017
South Africa
Phone: +27 11 403–6635
Fax: +27 11 403–1934
Key representatives: Paul Roos and Gérard Robinson

European Writers' Congress (EWC)
The Federation of European Writers Organisations
Konradstrasse 16
D-80801 München
Germany
Phone: +49 89 345 581
Fax: +49 89 392 094
Key representative: Lore Schultz-Wild

Federacion de Gremios de Editores de España
c/o Juan Ramón Jiménez 45-9.A
E-28036 Madrid
Spain
Phone: +34 1 350 91 05
Fax: +34 1 563 92 76
Key representative: Fermin Vargas

Federation of European Publishers (FEP)
204, avenue de Tervuren
B-1150 Brussels
Belgium
Phone: +32 2 770 11 10
Fax: +32 2 771 20 71
Key representative: Volker Schwarz

*Fjölis
Borgartun 24
PO Box 399
121 Reykjavik
Iceland
Phone: +354 562 7611
Fax: +354 562 7186
Key representative: Ragnar Adalsteinsson

Gewerkschaft Kunst, Medien, freie Berufe
(The Austrian Labour Union of Journalists)
Bahnhofstrasse 16
A-4600 Wels
Austria
Phone: +43 7242 47374–225
Fax: +43 7242 29348
Key representative: Alexander F. Baratsits-Altempergen

Industriegewerkschaft Medien
Postfach 10 24 51
D-70200 Stuttgart
Germany
Phone: +49 711 20180
+49 711 929 2410
Fax: +49 711 2018–199
+49 711 929–3579
Key representative: Lutz Franke

International Association of Scientific Technical & Medical Publishers (STM)
Muurhuizen 165
NL—3811 EG Amersfoort
The Netherlands
Phone: +31 33 65 60 60
Fax: +31 33 65 65 38
Key representative: Lex Lefebvre—Secretary General

International Council of Graphic Design Associations (ICOGRADA)
P.O. Box 398
London W11 4UG
United Kingdom
Phone: +44 171 603 8494
Fax: +44 171 371 6040
Key representative: Mary Mullin (Secretary General)

International Federation of Journalists (IFJ)
rue Royale, 266
B-1210 Brussels
Belgium
Phone: +32 2 223 22 65
Fax: +32 2 219 29 76
E-mail: APCIFJSAFENET@GN
Key representative: Aidan White

International Federation of the Periodical Press (FIPP)
Imperial House
15–19 Kingsway
London WC2 6UN
United Kingdom
Phone: +44 171 379 3822
Fax: +44 171 379 3866
E-mail: Flipp.Nemo@Nemo.Geis.Com@Internet#

Key representative: Per R. Mortensen—President and COO

International Publishers Association (IPA)
Avenue Miremont 3
CH—1206 Geneva
Switzerland
Phone: +41 22 346 30 18
Fax: +41 22 347 57 17
Key representative: J. A. Koutchoumow

*Irish Copyright Licensing Agency (ICLA)
Irish Writers' Centre
19 Parnell Square
Dublin 1
Ireland
Phone: +353 1 872 9090
Fax: +353 1 872 2035
Key representative: Orla O'Sullivan

Japan Book Publishers Association (JBPA)
6, Fukuro-machi, Shinjuku-ku
Tokyo 162
Japan
Phone: +81 33 268 1301
Fax: +81 33 268 1196
Key representative: Toshikazu Gomi

*Japan Reprographic Rights Center (JRRC)
Daiichi Aoyama Bldg. 3F, 3-3-7
Kita-Aoyama
Minato-ku
Tokyo 107
Japan
Phone: +81 3 3401 2382
Fax: +81 3 3401 2386
Key representatives: Kiyoshi Obayashi (President) and Kunio Yamashita (Secretary)

*KOPIKEN
PO Box 31191
Nairobi
Kenya
Phone: +254 2 245146
Fax: +254 2 336771
Key representative: Stanley Irura

NATIONAL COPYRIGHT AGENCIES

*KOPINOR
Stenersgate 1A
N-0050 Oslo
Norway
Phone: +47 22 17 07 80
Fax: +47 22 17 01 60
Internet: kopinor.post@ccmail.telemax.no
X.400:G=kopinor; S=post; P=ccmail;
A=telemax; C=no URL:
http://www.oslonett.no/home/kopinor
Key representatives: John-Willy Rudolph and Olav Stokkmo

*KOPIOSTO R. Y
Hietaniemenkatu 2
SF-00100 Helsinki
Finland
Phone: +358 0 406 197
Fax: +358 0 493 579
Key representatives: Tarja Koskinen-Olsson and Jukka-Pekka Timonen

*KOPJAMALT
Villa Yvonne
36 Ta'Xbiex Terrace
Ta'Xbiex MSD 11
Malta
Phone: +356 338525
Fax: +356 485950
Key representative: Joseph John Meli

*Literar-Mechana
Linke Wienzeile 18
A-1060 Wien
Austria
Phone: +43 1 587 21 61
Fax: +43 1 587 21 619
Key representative: Franz-Leo Popp

Media Entertainment and Arts Alliance
245 Chalmers Street
Redfern, NSW 2016
Australia
Phone: +61 2 333 0999
Fax: +61 2 333 0933
Key representative: Christopher Warren

*MUSIKEDITION
Gesellschaft zur Wahrnehmung von Rechten und Ansprüchen aus Musikeditionen
Registrierte Genossenschaft mit beschränkter Haftung
Postfach 334/348
Baumannstrasse 8–10
A-1031 Wien
Austria
Phone: +43 1 5058695
Fax: +43 1 5052720
Key representative: Marion von Hartlieb

National Union of Journalists of Great Britain and Ireland (NUJ)
314 Gray's Inn Road
London   WC1X 8DP
United Kingdom
Phone: +44 171 278 7916
Fax: +44 171 837 8143
Key representative: Jacob Ecclestone

*Pictures, Words, Printed Music Joint Copyright Organization (BONUS)
Box 27095
S–10251 Stockholm
Sweden
Phone: +46 8 667 88 85
Fax: +46 8 665 33 23
Key representative: Elisabeth Lind-Petri

*Pro Litteris
Universitätsstrasse 96
CH—8033 Zurich
Switzerland
Phone: +41 1 36 31 350
Fax: +41 1 36 31 463
Key representative: Ernst Hefti

Publishers Association (PA)
19 Bedford Square
London   WC1B 3HJ
United Kingdom
Phone: +44 171 580 6321
Fax: +44 171 636 5375
Key representatives: Clive Bradley, John Davies (PLS/CLA) and Nicolas Thompson (PLS/CLA)

Publishers Licensing Society Ltd (PLS)
90 Tottenham Court Road
London   W1P 9HE
United Kingdom
Phone: +44 171 436 5931
Fax: +44 171 436 3986
Key representative: Nicolas Thompson

*REPROBEL scrl
29 avenue Jeanne
B-1050 Brussels
Belgium
Phone: +32 2 627 52 00
Fax: +32 2 627 52 52
Key representative: Frédéric Young

Société Belge des Auteurs, Compositeurs et Editeurs (SABAM)
Rue d'Arlon 75–77
B—1040 Brussels
Belgium
Phone: +32 2 286 82 11
Fax: +32 2 231 18 00
+32 2 230 05 89
Key representative: Jacques Folon

Société des Editeurs de Musique (SEM) (Music Publishers' Society)
175, rue Saint-Honore
F-75040 Paris Cédex 01
France
Phone: +33 1 4296 8911
Fax: +33 1 4286 0283
Key representative: François Leduc

*Stichting Beeldrecht
Kerkstraat 310
NL–1017 HC Amsterdam
The Netherlands
Phone: +31 20 627 7147
Fax: +31 20 624 7953
Key representative: C. G. M. Berendsen

*Stichting LIRA
Prof. E. M. Meijerslaan 3
NL–1183 AV Amstelveen
The Netherlands
Phone: +31 20 5407 317
Fax: +31 20 5407 453
Key representative: Marja Kok

*Stichting Reprorecht (SR)
Prof. E. M. Meijerslaan 3
NL—1183 Av Amstelveen
The Netherlands
Phone: +31 20 54 07 310
Fax: +31 20 54 07 453
Key representative: André F. Beemsterboer

Stichting tot bescherming en handhaving van fotoauteursrechten 'Burafo'
Singel 146
Postbus 17192
NL–1001 JD Amsterdam
The Netherlands
Phone: +31 20 620 8692
Fax: +31 20 638 0968
Key representative: Erik M. Terheggen

Svenska Bokförläggare Föreningen (SBF)
Drottninggatan 97
S-11360 Stockholm
Sweden
Phone: +46 8 736 19 40
Fax: +46 8 736 19 44
Key representative: Kenth Muldin

Syndicat National de L'Edition (SNE)
35 rue Grégoire de Tours
F-75006 Paris
France
Phone: +33 1 4441 2890
Fax: +33 1 4325 3501
Key representative: Jean Sarzana

Text and Academic Authors Association Inc (TAA)
Box 535
Orange Springs, FL 32182–0535
USA
Phone: +1 904 546–5419
Dr Gerald C. Stone—President
Phone: +1 701 777–3831
Fax: +1 701 777–5099
Key representative: Dr Ronald E. Pynn

NATIONAL COPYRIGHT AGENCIES

*Union des écrivaines et écrivains québécois (UneQ)
3492, rue Laval
Montréal, Québec H2X 3C8
Canada
Phone: +1 514 849–8540
Fax: +1 514 849–6239
Key representative: Rose-Marie Lafrance

*VEGAP
(Visual Entidad de Gestión de Artistas Plásticos)
Museo Nacional de Antropologia (MNA)
E-28040 Madrid
Spain
Phone: +34 1 549 71 50
+34 1 549 27 97
Fax: +34 1 544 45 49
Key representative: Javier Gutiérrez Vicén

*Verwertungsgesellschaft Bild-Kunst (VG Bild-Kunst)
Poppelsdorfer Allee 43
D–53115 Bonn
Germany
Phone: +49 228 91 53 416
Fax: +49 228 91 53 438
Key representative: Gerhard Pfennig

*Verwertungsgesellschaft WORT (VG WORT)
Vereinigt mit der V. G. Wissenschaft
Goethestrasse 49
D-80336 München
Germany
Phone: +49 89 51 41 20
Fax: +49 89 51 41 258
Key representatives: Ferdinand Melichar and Frank Thoms

*VG MUSIKEDITION
Verwertungsgesellschaft zur Wahrnehmung von
Nutzungrechten an Editionen (Ausgaben) von Musikwerken
Königstor 1
D–34117 Kassel
Germany
Phone: +49 561 15616
Fax: +49 561 77 38

Key representatives: Prof Dr Christoph-Hellmut Mahling and Woolfgang Matthei (General Secretary)

Appendix 9
UK ORGANISATIONS INVOLVED IN THE ADMINISTRATION OF COPYRIGHT AND RIGHTS IN PERFORMANCES

ORGANISATIONS THAT ISSUE LICENCES

Christian Copyright Licensing
PO Box 1339
Eastbourne
BN21 4YF
Tel: 01323 41771
Fax: 01323 417722

Copyright Licensing Agency
90 Tottenham Court Road
London   W1P 0LP
Tel: 0171–436 5931
Fax: 0171–436 3986

Design and Artists Copyright Agency
Parchment House
13 Northburgh Street
London   EC1V 0AH
Tel: 0171–336 8811
Fax: 0171–336 8822

Educational Recording Agency
74 New Oxford Street
London   WC1A 1ES
Tel: 0171–436 4883
Fax: 0171–636 2402

International Federation of the Phonographic Industries
54 Regent Street
London   W1R 5PJ
Tel: 0171–434 3521
Fax: 0171–439 9166

Mechanical Copyright Protection Society
Elgar House
41 Streatham High Road
London   SW16 1ER
Tel: 0181–664 4400
Fax: 0181–769 8792

Ordnance Survey
Copyright and Legal Affairs
Romsey Road
Maybush
Southampton
SO16 4GU
Tel: 01703 792795
Fax: 01703 792535

Performing Rights Society
29/33 Berners Street
London   W1P 4AA
Tel: 0171–580 5544
Fax: 0171–631 4138

Phonographic Performance Ltd
Ganton House
14–22 Ganton Street
London   W1V 1LB
Tel: 0171–437 0311
Fax: 0171–734 2986

APPENDIX 9

Video Performance Ltd
Ganton House
14–22 Ganton Street
London   W1V 1LB
Tel: 0171–437 0311
Fax: 0171–734 9797

ORGANISATIONS CONCERNED WITH BUT NOT GENERALLY ENGAGED IN COLLECTIVE LICENSING

Association of Authors' Agents
37 Goldhawk Road
London W12 8QQ
Tel: 0181–749 0315
Fax: 0181–749 0318

Association of Illustrators
29 Bedford Square
London   WC1B 3EG
Tel: 0171–636 4100
Fax: 0171–580 2338

Association of Learned and Professional Society Publishers
48 Kelsey Lane
Beckenham
Kent BR3 3NR
Tel: 0181–658 0459
Fax: 0181–663 3583

Association of Photographers
9/10 Domingo Street
London EC1Y 0TA
Tel: 0171–608 1441/5
Fax: 0171–253 3007

Asssociation of Professional Composers
34 Hanway Street
London   W1P 9DE
Tel: 0171–436 0919
Fax: 0171–436 1913

Authors' Licensing and Collecting Society
74 New Oxford Street
London   WC1A 1ES
Tel: 0171–255 2034
Fax: 0171–323 0486

Benesh Institute of Choreology
12 Lisson Grove
London   NW1 6TS
Tel: 0171–258 3041
Fax: 0171–724 6434

British Academy of Songwriters, Composers and Authors
34 Hanway Street
London   W1P 9DE
Tel: 0171–436 2261
Fax: 0171–436 1913

British Actors' Equity Association
Guild House
Upper St Martin's Lane
London   WC2B 9EG
Tel: 0171–379 6000
Fax: 0171–379 7001

British Computer Society
1 Sanford Street
Swindon
Wiltshire
SN1 1HJ
Tel: 01793 417417
Fax: 01793 480270

British Institute of Professional Photography
Fox-Talbot House
Amwell End
Ware
Herts
SG1 9HN
Tel: 01920 464011
Fax: 01920 487056

British Phonographic Industry Ltd
25 Savile Row
London W1X 1AA
Tel: 0171–287 4422
Fax: 0171–287 2252

OTHER UK ORGANISATIONS INVOLVED IN COPYRIGHT

Broadcasting, Entertainments, Cinematograph and Theatre Union
111 Wardour Street
London   W1V 4AY
Tel: 0171–437 8506
Fax: 0171–437 8268

Business Software Alliance
First Floor
Leconfield House
Curzon Street
London   W1Y 8AS
Tel: 0171–491 1974
Fax: 0171–495 3101

Chartered Institute of Journalists
2 Dock Offices
Surrey Quays Road
London   SE16 2XU
Tel: 0171–252 1187
Fax: 0171–232 2302

Chartered Society of Designers
29 Bedford Street
London   WC1B 3EG
Tel: 0171–631 1510
Fax: 0171–580 2338

Composers' Guild of Great Britain
34 Hanway Street
London   W1P 9DE
Tel: 0171–436 0007
Fax: 0171–436 1913

Federation Against Copyright Theft
7 Victory Business Centre
Worton Road
Isleworth
Middlesex TW7 6ER
Tel: 0181–568 6646
Fax: 0181–560 6364

Federation Against Software Theft
2 Lake End Court
Taplow
Maidenhead
Berks
SL6 0JQ

Tel: 01628 660377
Fax: 01628 660348

International Pen (English Centre)
7 Dilke Street
Chelsea
London   SW3 4JE
Tel: 0171–352 6303
Fax: 0171–351 0220

Motion Picture Association
European Office
270–272 Avenue de Tervueren
B-1150 Brussels
Belgium
Tel: +32–2 778 2711

Music Publishers' Association
3rd Floor
Strandgate
18–20 York Buildings
London   WC2N 6JU
Tel: 0171–839 7779
Fax: 0171–837 7776

Musicians' Union
60/62 Clapham Road
London   SW9 0JJ
Tel: 0171–582 5566
Fax: 0171–582 9805

National Union of Journalists
Acorn House
314 Gray's Inn Road
London   WC1X 8DP
Tel: 0171–278 7916
Fax: 0171–837 8143

Patent Office
Concept House
Cardiff Road
Newport
Gwent
NP9 1RH
Tel: 01645 500505
Fax: 01645 813600

APPENDIX 9

Periodical Publishers Association
Imperial House
15–19 Kingsway
London   WC2B 6UN
Tel: 0171–379 6268
Fax: 0171–379 5661

Poetry Society
22 Betterton Street
London   EC2 9BU
Tel: 0171–240 2810
Fax: 0171–240 4818

Producers Alliance for Cinema and Television
Gordon House
10 Greycoat Place
London   SW1 1PH
Tel: 0171–233 6800
Fax: 0171–233 8935

Publishers Association
19 Bedford Square
London   WC1B 3HJ
Tel: 0171–580 6321
Fax: 0171–636 5375

Publishers Licensing Society
90 Tottenham Court Road
London   W1P 9HE
Tel: 0171–436 5931
Fax: 0171–436 3986

Registry of Copyright at Stationers' Hall
The Registrar
Stationers' Hall
Ave Maria Lane
London   EC4M 7DD

Tel: 0171–248 2934
Fax: 0171–489 1975

Royal Academy of Arts
Burlington House
Piccadilly
London   W1V 0DS
Tel: 0171–439 7438
Fax: 0171–434 0837

Royal Photographic Society
The RPS National Centre of Photography
The Octagon
Milsom Street
Bath
BA1 1DN
Tel: 01225 462841
Fax: 01225 448688

Society of Authors
84 Drayton Gardens
London SW10 9SB
Tel: 0171–373 6642
Fax: 0171–373 5768

Training Film & Video Association
Bolsover House
5–6 Clipstone Street
London   W1P 7EB
Tel: 0171–580 0962
Fax: 0171–436 2606

Writers' Guild of Great Britain
430 Edgware Road
London   W2 1EH
Tel: 0171–723 8074/6
Fax: 0171–706 2413

Appendix 10

SIGNATORIES TO INTERNATIONAL COPYRIGHT CONVENTIONS

COUNTRY	Berne Convention (as at 16/11/95)	UCC (as at 16/11/95)	Rome Convention (as at 01/09/95)
Afghanistan			
Albania	✓		
Algeria		✓	
Andorra		✓	
Angola			
Antigua and Barbuda			
Argentina	✓	✓	✓
Armenia			
Aruba			
Australia	✓	✓	✓
Austria	✓	✓	✓
Bahamas	✓	✓	
Bahrain			
Bangladesh		✓	
Barbados	✓	✓	✓
Belarus		✓	
Belgium	✓	✓	
Belize		✓	
Benin	✓		
Bhutan			
Bolivia	✓	✓	✓
Bosnia & Herzegovina	✓	✓	
Botswana			
Brazil	✓	✓	✓
British Virgin Islands			
Brunei			
Bulgaria	✓	✓	✓
Burma			
Burundi			
Cambodia		✓	
Cameroon	✓	✓	
Canada	✓	✓	
Cape Verde			

APPENDIX 10

COUNTRY	Berne Convention (as at 16/11/95)	UCC (as at 16/11/95)	Rome Convention (as at 01/09/95)
Central African Republic	✓		
Chad	✓		
Chile	✓	✓	✓
China	✓	✓	
Colombia	✓	✓	✓
Comoros			
Congo	✓		✓
Costa Rica	✓	✓	✓
Croatia	✓	✓	
Cuba		✓	
Cyprus	✓	✓	
Czech Republic	✓	✓	✓
Denmark	✓	✓	✓
Djibouti			
Dominica			
Dominican Republic		✓	✓
Ecuador	✓	✓	✓
Egypt	✓		
El Salvador	✓	✓	✓
Equatorial Guinea			
Estonia	✓		
Ethiopia			
Fiji	✓	✓	✓
Finland	✓	✓	✓
France	✓	✓	✓
Gabon	✓		
Gambia	✓		
Georgia	✓		
Germany	✓	✓	✓
Ghana	✓	✓	
Greece	✓	✓	✓
Grenada			
Guatemala		✓	✓
Guinea	✓	✓	
Guinea-Bissau	✓		
Guyana	✓		
Haiti	✓*	✓	
Holy See	✓	✓	
Honduras	✓		✓
Hungary	✓	✓	✓
Iceland	✓	✓	✓
India	✓	✓	
Indonesia			
Iran			
Iraq			
Ireland	✓	✓	✓

SIGNATORIES TO INTERNATIONAL COPYRIGHT CONVENTIONS

COUNTRY	Berne Convention (as at 16/11/95)	UCC (as at 16/11/95)	Rome Convention (as at 01/09/95)
Israel	✓	✓	
Italy	✓	✓	✓
Ivory Coast	✓		
Jamaica	✓		✓
Japan	✓	✓	✓
Jordan			
Kazakhstan		✓	
Kenya	✓	✓	
Korea (North)			
Korea (South)		✓	
Kuwait			
Kyrgyztan			
Laos		✓	
Latvia	✓		
Lebanon	✓	✓	
Lesotho	✓		✓
Liberia	✓	✓	
Libya	✓		
Liechtenstein	✓	✓	
Lithuania	✓		
Luxembourg	✓	✓	✓
Macedonia—the former Yugoslav Republic of	✓		
Madagascar	✓		
Malawi	✓	✓	
Malaysia	✓		
Maldives			
Mali	✓		
Malta	✓	✓	
Mauritania	✓		
Mauritius	✓	✓	
Mexico	✓	✓	✓
Moldava—the Republic of	✓		
Monaco	✓	✓	✓
Mongolia			
Morocco	✓	✓	
Mozambique			
Namibia	✓		
Nepal			
Netherlands	✓	✓	✓
New Zealand	✓	✓	
Nicaragua		✓	
Niger	✓	✓	✓
Nigeria	✓	✓	✓
Norway	✓	✓	✓
Oman			

COUNTRY	Berne Convention (as at 16/11/95)	UCC (as at 16/11/95)	Rome Convention (as at 01/09/95)
Pakistan	✓	✓	
Panama		✓	✓
Papua New Guinea			
Paraguay	✓	✓	✓
Peru	✓	✓	✓
Philippines	✓	✓	✓
Poland	✓	✓	
Portugal	✓	✓	
Qatar			
Romania	✓		
Russian Federation	✓	✓	
Rwanda	✓	✓	
St Kitts & Nevis	✓		
St Lucia	✓		
St Vincent & the Grenadines	✓	✓	
Samoa			
San Marino			
Saudi Arabia		✓	
Senegal	✓	✓	
Seychelles			
Sierra Leone			
Singapore			
Slovakia	✓	✓	✓
Slovenia	✓	✓	
Solomon Islands			
Somalia			
South Africa	✓		
Spain	✓	✓	✓
Sri Lanka	✓	✓	
Sudan			
Surinam	✓		
Swaziland			
Sweden	✓	✓	✓
Switzerland	✓	✓	✓
Syria			
Tadjikstan		✓	
Taiwan			
Tanzania	✓		
Thailand	✓		
Togo	✓		
Tonga			
Trinidad & Tobago	✓	✓	
Tunisia	✓	✓	
Turkey	✓		
Uganda			
Ukraine	✓	✓	

SIGNATORIES TO INTERNATIONAL COPYRIGHT CONVENTIONS

COUNTRY	Berne Convention (as at 16/11/95)	UCC (as at 16/11/95)	Rome Convention (as at 01/09/95)
United Arab Emirates			
United Kingdom	✓	✓	✓
United States of America	✓	✓	
Uruguay	✓	✓	✓
Uzbekistan			
Venezuela	✓	✓	
Vietnam			
Yemen			
Yugoslavia	✓	✓	
Zaire	✓		
Zambia	✓	✓	
Zimbabwe	✓		
Total	**117**	**95**	**48**

*From 11 January 1996

Appendix 11

EUROPEAN COMMISSION GREEN PAPER ON COPYRIGHTS AND RELATED RIGHTS IN THE INFORMATION SOCIETY

The Green Paper highlights the following issues which are, or are becoming, significant:

(1) The convergence between technologies (such as telecommunications and television), with digitisation as the common denominator, leading to the development of multimedia products, as well as the provision of services at long distance (such as teleworking and telebanking).

(2) Recognition of the necessity to provide legal certainty to investors in the new technology, particularly bearing in mind its ability to cross borders. Traditional notions of copyright and related rights, which historically have been limited in their territorial application, will have to be reviewed to take account of new technological developments. For example, the concepts of 'author', 'originality' and 'first publication' need to be reappraised, as does the status of rights holders' rights. The concepts of 'private' or 'fair' use also need to be reviewed, in the context of which the distinction between 'communication to the public' and 'private communication' will be crucial.

(3) Digital technology also means that multimedia works may be created out of works and data which are currently covered by different legal provisions. A separate legal status for such works may therefore be required.

The EC has also identified nine key areas which it considers vital in assessing the impact of digital technology on IP rights. These are briefly summarised below.

(1) **Applicable law** While copyright and neighbouring rights have traditionally been applied on a national basis, reciprocated by third countries on the principle of national treatment, data are now able to flow freely across borders. In addressing the problems this poses, the Commission looks to the Cable and Satellite Directive, 93/83/EEC for guidance. It therefore suggests that the applicable law ought to be the law of the Member State from which a provider transmits, rather than the territory where the transmission is received. It is also possible that such a principle could apply internationally, though the Commission recognises that harmonisation at this level is more problematic.

(2) **Exhaustion of rights and parallel imports** The Commission emphasises the distinction between copyright in relation to products and services. Although the general rule in the EU is that the first marketing of a product is by or with the

consent of the rights holder and this means that he cannot prevent its subsequent resale throughout the Community, the provision of a service does not exhaust a rights holder's ability to authorise or prohibit the subsequent provision of that service. (*See* eg the Computer Programme Directive, 91/250/EEC, the Software Directive and the Rental and Lending Rights Directive, 92/100/EEC.) Hence, once a rights holder has marketed a video or record within the Community, he will be unable to prevent its subsequent resale throughout the Community; his right has been exhausted. In contrast, the provision of a service, such as the screening of a film, does not exhaust the rights holder's ability to authorise or prohibit subsequent screenings.

The Commission considers that the principle of non-exhaustion of rights in relation to services may be applied to the provision of services in the information society, albeit the concept of exhaustion of rights (in relation to products) should not apply outside the Community.

(3) **Reproduction right** Digital technology facilitates copying or reproduction of protected works to the detriment of rights holders; but it also provides the scope for better controls on copying and reproduction than analogue technology. The Commission considers the Software Directive a useful precedent in leading to possible harmonisation of protection in this area. The Commission also draws attention to the ability of technology itself to control unauthorised reproduction when considering possible exceptions to the reproduction right.

(4) **Communication to the public** In the light of the ability of digital technology to facilitate large-scale private use, the concept of 'communication to the public' needs to be defined if communication over networks such as the Internet are not to become a free for all. The Commission looks to interested parties for guidance in assessing the scope of this concept.

(5) **Digital dissemination or transmission right** The ability of digital technology to exchange the content of protected works on electronic databases has prompted certain rights holders to seek the introduction of a new exclusive right of digital dissemination or transmission. The Commission appears keen to create such a right on the basis of a narrow definition, primarily to avoid overlapping with regulation in the broadcasting sector. The Commission considers the principles of the Rental Rights Directive could be extended to create such a right, which would apply to point-to-point transmissions used for commercial activities, such as video on demand.

(6) **Digital broadcasting right** The development of digital broadcasting threatens neighbouring rights holders, particularly in the context of the CD market. This is a problem because they are not holders of exclusive rights, and the Commission suggests their right to equitable remuneration could be extended on a harmonised basis, although it seeks suggestions as to how this may be achieved.

(7) **Moral rights** Digital technology means that an author's work may be easily modified or reprocessed. While the Berne Convention ensures the existence of an author's moral right even after his economic rights have been assigned, EU law generally leaves the issue of moral rights to individual Member States. With the ability of digital technology to modify works, the Commission believes the time has come to examine the lack of harmonisation in this area, particularly in view of the division of interest between authors and performers (who would prefer the moral right to be strengthened) and publishers, producers and broadcasters (who believe

moral rights create uncertainty in the exploitation of works and therefore discourage investment).

(8) **Acquisition and management of rights** The advent of multimedia products means it is becoming increasingly difficult to identify the different rights holders involved in their creation, and to obtain the necessary licences at a reasonable price. The Commission suggests the way ahead may be to establish a centralised system of administration. This would involve regrouping collecting societies, which are currently organised by sector. It suggests establishing such a system on a voluntary basis, without prejudicing the ability of individual rightholders to provide individual conditions of licence. It also stresses the need to ensure the legal framework is sufficiently strong to avoid fracturing the market and creating dominant positions which could be abused.

(9) **Technical systems of protection and identification** In order to protect rights holders, the Commission considers it essential to establish a system to identify works and performances, as well as the installation of compatible systems on equipment to enable those works or performances to be identified. Although legislation exists prohibiting the unauthorised circumvention of technical systems of protection (the Software Directive), no legislation exists which actually requires the installation of such technical systems. The Commission suggests compulsory standards may therefore have to be imposed.

INDEX

Acquisition of rights—
  agreements—
    contents of, 13.4
    drafting, 13.3
    formal, requirement of, 13.1
    key issues, 13.3.1
    negotiating, 13.3
  checklist, 12.2.1
  clip art and multimedia tools, in, 12.1.7
  Copyright Tribunal, 12.5
  existing rights framework, 13.2.1
  fallbacks, 12.6
  fees and royalties, 12.2.1
  films, in, 12.1.5
  fine art works, in, 12.1.3
  full grant, 12.6.1
  graphics and illustration, in, 12.1.6
  identification of rights and rights holders, 11.1
  licensing. *See* Licensing
  literary works, in, 12.1.1
  matching rights, 12.6.4
  music, in, 12.1.8
  new approaches to, 13.2.2
  open rights, 12.6.5
  origin of rights, 11.4
  performance, in, 12.1.4
  photographs, in, 12.1.2
  recordings, in, 12.1.4
  reservation of rights—
    first refusal, right of, 12.6.3
    options, 12.6.2
  reversion, 13.2.2
  software, in, 12.1.10
  sound recordings, in, 12.1.8
  source materials, 11.3
  tasks, identification of, 11.1
  television broadcasts, in, 12.1.5
  title searches, 12.1.10
Advertising—
  Advertising Standards Authority, 10.1.4
  restrictions on, 10.4
Agents—
  Commercial Agents Directive, 15.2.4
Analogue representations—
  characteristics of, 1.1
Artistic works—
  copyright, 3.2.1
Audio-visual technologies—
  analogue, 1.1

Brand name—
  strong, building, 7.4.3
British Board of Film Classification—
  role of, 10.1.5
  videos, classification of, 10.3.4
Broadcast—
  acquisition of rights in, 12.1.5
  blanket licences, 12.1.8
  copyright, 3.2.3
Broadcasting Complaints Commission—
  role of, 10.1.3
Broadcasting Standards Council—
  role of, 10.1.3
Broadcasting—
  regulatory bodies—
    Advertising Standards Authority, 10.1.4
    Broadcasting Complaints Commission, 10.1.3
    Broadcasting Standards Council, 10.1.3
    Independent Television Commission, 10.1.2

Cable programmes—
  copyright, 3.2.4
Cable television—
  asynchronous transfer mode, 1.2.2
  on-line services, 1.2.2
CD TV—
  development of, 1.2.1
CD-ROM—
  physical distribution systems, 1.2.1
  rights, origin of, 11.4
Clip art—
  acquisition of rights in, 12.1.7
Communications—
  Bangemann Report, 2.2.1
  European regulation, 2.2.1
  standards, 2.2.1
  UK Government policy, 2.1.1
  UK Labour Party policy, 2.1.2
Compact Disc-Interactive—
  development of, 1.2.1
Company—
  infringement of copyright, liability for, 7.2.2
Competition—
  anti-competitive practices, investigation of, 16.3.4
  copyright, and, 4.7
  distribution licence, terms of, 15.2.1
  EC law—
    abuse of dominant position, 16.4.4
    agreements affecting trade, 16.4.3

INDEX

Competition—*contd*
  EC law—*contd*
    Article 85, 16.4.3
    Article 86, 16.4.4
    authorities, 16.4.1
    exercise of intellectual property rights, controlling, 16.4.2
    exhaustion of rights, 16.4.2
    national law, prevailing over,, 16.4
    Treaty provisions, 16.2, 16.4.2
  Monopolies and Mergers Commission, reference to, 16.3.3
  multimedia products, and, 2.2.1
  resale prices, in, 16.3.6
  restraint of trade doctrine, 16.3.2
  restrictive trade practices, 16.3.5
  UK law—
    authorities, 16.3.1
    statutes, 16.2
Computer programs—
  acquisition of rights in, 12.1.10
  back-up copies, making, 3.9.1
  case law, 6.1.2
  copying or adaptation, 4.2.2
  decompiling, 4.2.2
  different levels, existing at, 6.1
  EC Software Directive—
    all elements of program, protection of, 4.2.1
    implementation in UK, 4.2
    lawful user rights, 4.2.2
    relevance of, 4.2
    scope of protection, 6.1.1
  European Leisure Software Producers Association, 10.1.6
  hardware distinguished, 6.1.1
  ideas behind—
    case law, 6.1.2
    statutory framework, 6.1.1
  moral rights, exclusion of, 8.7
  multimedia products, key role in, 14.5
  non-literal copying, 6.1.2
  ownership and licensing, warranties on, 7.4.1
  patenting, exclusion from, 7.3.1
  statutory framework for protection, 6.1.1
  studying, 4.2.2
Computers—
  magnetic storage media, 1.2.1
  optical storage media, 1.2.1
  PC-based systems, 1.2.1
  software. *See* Computer programs
Confidentiality—
  breach of, 7.3.5, 10.5.1
  information, protection of, 7.3.5
  licence agreement, term in, 15.2.1
Consumer protection—
  on-line services, and, 15.3.8
Convergence—
  barriers to, 1.1.4
  trend towards, 1.1.4
Copyright—
  access denial, 7.4.4
  administration, UK organisations, App 9
  assignment, 3.5.1

Copyright—*contd*
  authorship—
    joint, 3.4.2
    meaning, 3.4
    moral rights. *See* Moral rights
    multimedia work, of, 3.4.1
    owner distinguished, 3.4
  Berne Convention, 5.3.1
    signatories, App 10
  broadcast, in, 3.2.3
  cable programmes, in, 3.2.4
  categories of work, 3.2
  civil and common law approaches, 5.2
  collecting societies, 12.4, App 1
  compilation, in, 6.2
  compulsory licensing, 12.3
  computer program, making back-up copy of, 3.9.1
  Conventions, 5.3
  copy protection, 7.4.4
  criticism or review, use for, 3.9.1
  current events, reporting, 3.9.1
  duration of—
    EC law, 4.3
    extended or revived copyright, 4.3.2
    harmonisation upwards, 4.3.1
    UK law, 3.6
  education and library uses, 3.9.1
  electronic form, works in, 3.9.1
  European law—
    competition law, and, 4.7
    draft Database Directive, 4.5. *See also* Database
    Duration of Copyright Directive, 4.3
    Green Paper, 4.6, App 12
    harmonisation, 4.1
    Rental and Lending Rights Directive, 4.4
    Software Directive, 4.2. *See also* Computer programs
  existence, formalities for, 12.1.10
  fair dealing, 3.9.1
  film, in, 3.2.2
  GATT/TRIPS Accord—
    enforcement, 5.4.1
    free trade agreement, as, 5.4
    moral rights, exclusion of, 5.4
    principles of protection, 5.4
  Green Paper, 3.1.1
  identification schemes, 7.4.4
  incidental inclusion, 3.9.1
  infringement—
    adaptation, 3.8.1
    checklist, 7.1
    civil remedies, 7.2.1
    companies and directors, liability of, 7.2.2
    copying, 3.8.1
    criminal remedies, 7.2.2
    Customs and Excise, powers of, 7.2.2
    enforcement, 7.2
    infringing copies, 3.8.2
    international protection, 7.2.2
    liability for, 7.1.3
    person suing for, 7.2.1
    primary, 3.8.1, 7.1.1
    publication of photograph without consent as, 10.5.2

INDEX

Copyright—*contd*
  infringement—*contd*
    publishing, 3.8.1
    secondary, 3.8.2, 7.1.2
    substantial part of work, copying, 7.1
  licensing, societies for, 12.1.8
  literary, dramatic, musical and artistic works, in, 3.2.1
  management initiatives for electronic rights, App 2
  multimedia works, in—
    diffusion rights, 6.3.2
    elements, protection of, 6.3.1
    films, 6.3.1
    infringement. *See* infringement, above
    on-line issues, 6.3.2
    piracy, responding to, 7.4.5
  national agencies, App 8
  national right, as, 3.1.1, 5.1
  on-line service, licensing works for, 15.3.4
  originality, 3.3
  owner—
    author distinguished, 3.4
    employment contract, clause in, 3.5.1
    first, 3.5.1
    multimedia work, in, 3.5.2
  performance, rights in. *See* Performer's rights
  permitted acts, 3.9.1
  piracy—
    fighting, 7.4.4
    responding to, 7.4.5
  published edition, in, 3.2.5
  publisher's right of protection, 3.2.7
  recording, rights in. *See* Recording rights
  research or private study, copying for, 3.9.1
  restricted acts—
    adaptation, 3.8.1
    copying, 3.8.1
    primary, 3.1.1
    primary infringements, 3.8.1
    publishing, 3.8.1
    secondary infringements, 3.8.2
  Rome Convention, 5.3.3
    signatories, App 10
  software, in, 6.1. *See also* Computer programs
  sound recording, in, 3.2.2
  title searches, 12.1.10
  tracking products, 7.4.4
  transfer of, 3.10
  Tribunal, 12.5
  UK legislation, 3.1
  Universal Copyright Convention, 5.3.2
    signatories, App 10
  warning wording, 3.7
  work, multimedia as, 3.2.6

Damages—
  infringement of copyright, for, 7.2.1
Data protection—
  EC Directive, 10.6.2
  legislation, 10.6.1
  multimedia works, in relation to, 2.2.1, 10.6
  principles, 10.6.1
  Registrar, 10.1.8

Databases—
  compilation, protection as, 6.2
  Directive—
    definition, 4.5
    foreign companies, protection of, 4.5.1
    harmonisation of law, 4.5
    makers under, 4.5
    materials, rights in, 4.5.2
    restricted acts, 4.5
    recommendations for, 4.5.2
    UK law, 4.5
    user's rights, 15.4.2
Defamation—
  defamatory statements, 10.1
  digital media, by, 10.1
  justification, 10.5.3
  on-line—
    defences, 10.2.4
    draft legislation, 10.2.3
    measures against, 10.1
    out-of-court settlements, 10.2.3
    US case law, 10.2.2
  service providers, liability of, 10.2.1
Design right—
  registered designs, 7.3.6
  semiconductor topographies, 7.3.6
  unregistered designs, 7.3.6
Development—
  contract terms, 14.3.1
  feasibility study, 14.3
  keys to, 14.1
Diffusion rights—
  sample clause, 6.3.2
Digitisation—
  advantages of, 1.1.1
  concept of, 1.1
  convergence, leading to, 1.1.4
  disadvantages of, 1.1.2
  limitations, 1.1.2
  recording and reproducing information by, 1.1
  standards, 1.1.3
Director—
  infringement of copyright, liability for, 7.2.2
Distance selling—
  Directive, 15.3.8
Distribution—
  agreement, heads of, 15.1.4
  checklist, 15.2.4
  Commercial Agents Directive, 15.2.4
  distributor—
    options not involving, 15.1.5
    selecting, 15.1.5
  goals, 15.1
  licence—
    commercial clauses, 15.2.2
    competition law restrictions, 15.2.1
    confidentiality, 15.2.1
    definitions, 15.2.1
    financial provisions, 15.2.1
    form of, 15.1.3
    government approvals, 15.2.2
    improvements, 15.2.2
    information, 15.2.2
    infringement of rights, 15.2.1

251

INDEX

Distribution—*contd*
  licence—*contd*
    law and jurisdiction, 15.2.2
    marketing, 15.2.2
    ownership, validity of, 15.2.1
    parties, 15.2.1
    production and quality control, 15.2.2
    recitals, 15.2.1
    sample clauses, 15.2.1
    sub-contract, 15.2.1
    sub-licence, 15.2.1
    supply of goods, 15.2.2
    technical knowledge, transfer of, 15.2.2
    term, 15.2.1
    termination, 15.2.2
    terms of, 15.2.1
    warranties, 15.2.2
  licensees—
    approaches to, 15.1.2
    negotiations, considerations before entering into, 15.1.1
    restrictions on, 15.2.1
  on-line—
    avenues for, 15.3.1
    commercial services, 15.3.3
    consumer protection, 15.3.8
    controls, 15.3.5
    encryption, 15.3.5
    home shopping, 15.3.8
    liability for, 15.3.6
    licensing works for, 15.3.4
    local area networks, 15.3.2
    regulation, 15.3.7
    security, 15.3.5
Dramatic works—
  copyright, 3.2.1

Electrocopying—
  definition, 3.1.2
Electronic books—
  development of, 1.2.1
Electronic rights—
  classification of, App 3
  copyright management initiative, App 2
Entertainment services—
  licences, 15.3.7
Entertainment systems—
  UK Government policy, 2.1.1
European Leisure Software Producers Association—
  role of, 10.1.6
  video games, rating, 10.3.4
European Union—
  competition law. *See* Competition
  copyright law. *See* Copyright
  Information Superhighway within ambit of, 2.2
Exploitation—
  choice of method, factors influencing, 14.2.4
  co-production, 14.2.2
  direct sale, 14.2.1
  in-house production, 14.2.1
  joint ventures, 14.2.2
  sample clause, 15.2.1
  sub-licensing, 14.2.3

Fibre optics—
  use of, 1.2.2
Films—
  acquisition of rights in, 12.1.5
  British Board of Film Classification, 10.1.5
  copyright, 3.2.2, 6.3.1
  definition, 3.2.2
  multimedia works, as part of, 6.3.1
  privacy, right to, 8.4
  rental and lending rights, 4.4
Fine art—
  acquisition of rights in, 12.1.3

General Agreement on Tariffs and Trade—
  Trade Related Aspects of Intellectual Property Rights (TRIPS) Accord—
    enforcement, 5.4.1
    free trade agreement, as, 5.4
    moral rights, exclusion of, 5.4
    principles of protection, 5.4
Graphics—
  acquisition of rights in, 12.1.6
G7 nations—
  information society, aim for, 2.3

Home shopping—
  on-line services, 15.3.8
Illustrations—
  acquisition of rights in, 12.1.6
Independent Committee for the Supervision of Standards for Telephone Information Services (ICSTIS)—
  establishment of, 10.1.1
Independent Television Commission—
  regulation by, 10.1.2
Information—
  confidentiality, 7.3.5
  digitisation. *See* Digitisation
  recording and storing, 1.1
Information society—
  Bangemann Report, 2.2.1
  EC Green Paper, App 12
  G7 Nations, in, 2.3
  UK Government policy, 2.1.1
  UK Labour Party policy, 2.1.2
Information Superhighway—
  Bangemann Report, 2.2.1
  European Union, in, 2.2
  on-line platforms, 1.2.2
  standards, 2.2.1
Insurance—
  production, of, 14.4.2
Integrated Services Digital Network—
  digital information, sending, 1.2.2
Intellectual property rights. *See also* Copyright, etc.
  competition law provisions, 16.4.2
  exploitation. *See* Exploitation
  multimedia products, for, 2.2.1
  piracy—
    fighting, 7.4.4
    responding to, 7.4.5
  registering, 7.4.2
Internet—
  address names, 7.3.4

INDEX

Internet—*contd*
  advertising on, 10.4
  defamation on—
    defences, 10.2.4
    draft legislation, 10.2.3
    measures against, 10.1
    out-of-court settlements, 10.2.3
    service providers, liability of, 10.2.1
  distribution on, 15.3.1
  elements of, 1.2.2
  netiquette, 10.1
  obscenity on, 10.3.3

Joint ventures—
  types of, 14.2.2

Laser Disc—
  development of, 1.2.1
Licensing—
  agreements—
    contents of, 13.4
    drafting, 13.3
    key issues, 13.3.1
    negotiating, 13.3
  benchmarks, creation of, 11.1 11.1
  collecting societies, 12.4, App 1
  compulsory, 12.3
  distribution. *See* Distribution
  existing rights framework, 13.2.1
  fees and royalties, 12.2.1
  on-line service, for, 15.3.4
  societies for, 12.1.8
  strategies for, 13.2
  sub-licensing, 13.3.1, 14.2.3
  user—
    copying, control of, 15.4.1
    database protection, 15.4.2
    issues, 15.4
    limitation of liability, 15.4.4
    shrinkwrap, 15.4.3
Literary works—
  acquisition of rights in, 12.1.1
  copyright, 3.2.1
Local area networks—
  distribution on, 15.3.2

Mechanical rights licences—
  grant of, 12.1.8
Media content—
  regulatory control over, 10.1, App 4
Mergers—
  reference to MMC, 16.3.3
Monopolies—
  reference to MMC, 16.3.3
Moral rights—
  Berne Convention signatories, App 7
  computer programs, exclusion of, 8.7
  consent to infringement, 8.6
  droit de repentir, 8.7.1
  droit de suite, 8.7.2
  duration, 8.5
  false attribution, 8.3
  France, in, 8.9
  integrity, right of, 8.2

Moral rights—*contd*
  multimedia products, in, 8.9
  paternity, right of, 8.1
  photographs and films, right to privacy of, 8.4
  transitional provisions, 8.10
  TRIPS, exclusion from, 5.4
  United States, in, 8.8
  waiver—
    clauses, 8.6.1
    France, not permitted in, 8.7
    power of, 8.6
Multimedia platforms—
  competing, 1.2
  development of, 1.2
  physical distribution systems, 1.2.1
Multimedia tools—
  acquisition of rights in, 12.1.7
Multimedia works—
  acquisition of rights in. *See* Acquisition of rights
  copyright. *See* Copyright
  development. *See* Development
  distribution. *See* Distribution
  exploitation. *See* Exploitation
  production. *See* Production
  software, 14.5
Musical works—
  acquisition of rights in, 12.1.8
  copyright, 3.2.1

Networks—
  local area, distribution on, 15.3.2
Nuisance—
  privacy, protection of, 10.5.4

Obscenity—
  children, images of, 10.3.3
  legal framework, 10.3
  on-line services, on, 10.3.4
  publication, definition, 10.3.3
  statutory definition, 10.3.1
Office of Telecommunications—
  establishment of, 10.1.1
On-line platforms—
  services, 1.2.2
  types of, 1.2.2
On-line services—
  commercial, 15.3.3
  distribution by. *See* Distribution
Optical storage media—
  types of, 1.2.1

Passing off—
  concept of, 7.3.3
  reputation, protection of, 10.5.5
Patents—
  computer programs, exclusion of, 7.3.1
  Conventions, 7.3.1
  protection of, 7.3.1
Performer's rights—
  acquisition of, 12.1.4
  administration, UK organisations, App 9
  assignable, not, 9.8
  consent, obtaining, 9.9
  copyright legislation, within scope of, 9.1

INDEX

Performer's rights—*contd*
  duration, 9.7
  estate, accruing to, 9.8
  exceptions, 9.6
  grant of, 12.1.8
  infringing acts, 9.4.1
  performance, meaning, 9.2
  reciprocal protection, App 6
  remedies for breach, 9.10
Photo CD—
  development of, 1.2.1
Photographs—
  acquisition of rights in, 12.1.2
  privacy, right to, 8.4
  publication without consent, 10.5.2
Physical distribution systems—
  magnetic storage media, 1.2.1
  on-line, 1.2.2
  optical storage media, 1.2.1
  PC-based, 1.2.1
  TV-based, 1.2.1
  types of, 1.2.1
Pornography—
  on-line services, on, 10.3
Privacy—
  confidentiality, breach of, 10.5.1
  defamation, action in, 10.5.3
  infringement of copyright, as, 10.5.2
  multimedia products, and, 2.2.1
  nuisance, 10.5.4
  photographs and films, in, 8.4
  physical intrusion, protection against, 10.5.4
  reform, proposals for, 10.5.7
  regulatory controls, 10.5.6
  rights of, 10.5
  trespass, 10.5.4
Production—
  agreement, 14.4
  agreement checklist, 14.4.3
  insurance, 14.4.2
  keys to, 14.1
  project management, 14.4.1
  reporting structures, 14.4.1
  source materials, 14.4.3
Publicity—
  regulatory controls, 10.5.6
  reputation, protection of, 10.5.5
  right of, 10.5.5
Published edition—
  copyright, 3.2.5

Recording rights—
  acquisition of, 12.1.4
  consent, obtaining, 9.9
  defences to infringement, 9.5
  duration, 9.7
  infringing acts, 9.4.1
  qualifying countries, 9.3
  remedies for breach, 9.10
  scope of, 9.3
Restraint of trade—
  common law doctrine, 16.3.2
Rights—
  acquisition of. *See* Acquisition of rights

Rights—*contd*
  multimedia, sample clause, 12.1.1
Royalties—
  key issues, 12.2.1
  licensing agreement, in, 13.3.1

Semiconductor topographies—
  design, protection of, 7.3.6
Sound recordings—
  acquisition of rights in, 12.1.8
  copyright, 3.2.2
  rental and lending rights, 4.4
Sponsorship—
  restrictions on, 10.4
Stamp duty—
  charge of, 15.5.4
Standards—
  evolution of, 1.1.3
  incompatible, 1.1.3
  Information Superhighway, for, 2.2.1

Tandy VIS—
  development of, 1.2.1
Taxation—
  PAYE, 15.5.2
  performers, payments to, 15.5.2
  stamp duty, 15.5.4
  value added tax, 15.5.3
  withholding tax, 15.5.1
Telecommunications—
  Bangemann Report, 2.2.1
  DTI Command Paper, 2.1.1
  grossly offensive or indecent, obscene or menacing character, transmission of, 10.3.2
  ICSTIS, 10.1.1
  licences, 15.3.7
  OFTEL, 10.1.1
  UK Government policy, 2.1.1
  UK Labour Party policy, 2.1.2
Telephone networks—
  asymmetric digital subscriber loop, 1.2.2
  Integrated Services Digital Network, 1.2.2
  on-line services, 1.2.2
Trade marks—
  common law, at, 7.3.3
  Internet address names, 7.3.4
  likeness or name as, 10.5.5
  registered, protection of, 7.3.2
  right to use, acquisition of, 13.3.1
  unregistered, 7.3.3
Trade unions—
  list of, App 5
Trespass—
  privacy, protection of, 10.5.4
TV-based systems—
  types of, 1.2.1

Unfair contract terms—
  consumer contracts, in, 15.2.3

Value Added Tax—
  charge of, 15.5.3
Video CD—
  storage on, 1.2.1

INDEX

Video games—
   age-rating, 10.3.4
   systems, 1.2.1
   Video Standards Council, 10.1.7
Video works—
   acquisition of rights in, 12.1.8
   BBFC classification, 10.3.4

Warranties—
   licensing agreement, in, 13.3.1, 15.2.2
   obtaining, 7.4.1
Withholding tax—
   scope of, 15.5.1

3DO—
   development of, 1.2.1